Worldwide Praise for *The Synergistic Church*

Synergy happens when there is interaction and cooperation of two or more organizations, producing results greater than any one of them will produce separately or standing alone. Synergistic networking is happening more and more in the Body of Christ and as a result, the Church is closer to fulfilling the Great Commission than ever before. In his new book, *The Synergistic Church*, Dr. James O. Davis has defined what the synergistic church is, describes precisely what it looks like and how it functions. Dr. Davis has devoted his life to bringing leaders and denominations together for Gospel expansion and this new book is a major landmark in that lifelong journey.
—**Dr. Timothy Hill**, General Overseer,
Church of God, Cleveland, TN

Dr. James O. Davis, in his landmark book, *The Synergistic Church*, takes the roof off so the Church can experience revival and tears the walls down so the Church can evangelize the world. When you read this book, you will experience a massive paradigm shift in your missional ministry for years to come!
—**Dr. James Morocco**, Founder,
Kings Cathedral & Chapels, Kahului, Maui, HI

The Synergistic Church is a powerful tool for an extraordinary vision destined to equip the greatest army of pastors and leaders in Church history. This will be essential to completing the Great Commission in our generation.
—**Dr. Dick Eastman**, International President Emeritus,
Every Home for Christ

The Synergistic Church is a must read for any pastor or leader at this time in history. This wonderful book explains that in order to lead people during times of trouble and rapid change, the church has to remove the roof and knock down the walls between it and society, to be reached. Dr. Davis so aptly points out: "The church known more for its steeple than its people is a church known more for its past than its present." The heart cry of this book for a "synergistic" church is, I believe, the heart cry of God. God is looking for churches that are relevant, dynamic, living bodies of believers. This great book will help many achieve the great goal that Christ lays before them of reaching the lost, enabling them to minister beyond the limitations that come against them.

—**Rev. Tommy Barnett**,
Assembly of God Phoenix, AZ

Te stunning movemental expansion of the first-century church, emboldened by the persecution they faced, gave them a profound level of synergy. A level of synergy that was somehow lost over the centuries in our institutions and denominations. Like the prophets of old, Dr. James O. Davis has been calling the church to reclaim that first-century synergy so we can at last finish the Great Commission. This book is a road map for how we can reclaim the synergy needed to complete our high calling. Maranatha!"

—**Mr. David Reeves**, President,
Unfolding Word, Orlando, FL

Dr. James O. Davis' book, *The Synergistic Church*, ignites a flaming passion for reaching people with the life-changing message of Jesus. Ministry leaders in any organization will be affirmed to press onward with clarity and zest. This is a manual of hope that dispels the "ought' to reach people to "want" to reach people.

—**Dr. Larry Lamb**,
Cielo Vista Church, El Paso, TX

Relationships are the most valuable thing God has given us, and I have never met anyone who is more passionate, and purpose driven to develop authentic relationships with other ministers for the purpose of fulfilling the great commission than Dr. James O. Davis. His new book *The Synergistic Church: The Answer To Fulfilling The Great Commission* is a must read for any man or woman who genuinely wants to reach people for Jesus. It will change your world!

—**Rev. Gary Brothers,** Lead Pastor,
Cape First, Cape Gaudreau, MO

Get ready to be inspired by this book from Dr. James O. Davis—an evangelist who truly understands the times and seasons of the Church. His calling is to equip, encourage, and bring synergistic participation among the body of Christ to fulfill the Great Commission. Fresh insights from the Holy Spirit will be gained as you explore the profound truths of his latest work. *The Synergistic Church* offers the key to fulfilling the Great Commission.

—**Rev. Dave Allman**,
New Life Church, Poland, OH

If there is one man that has a heart to bring churches together to synergize for the Great Commission, it is Dr. James O. Davis. Having known him for over two decades, he is one of the most connected people in the Body of Christ. His passion for souls, for the Church, has not diminished with the passing of time, but only increased. The keys, the principles, and the values in his latest book, *The Synergistic Church: The Answer To Fulfilling The Great Commission*, will be a blessing and inspiration to whoever reads it. I heartily recommend this book for all those wanting to be a part of what God is doing on the earth today!

—**Rev. Peter Mortlock**. Founding Pastor,
City Impact Church, Auckland, New Zealand

At the end of the 19th century the urging slogan was "During this generation" for the completion of the Great Commission. The Gospel must reach every ethnic group and every language. After more than 100 years of announcing the "During this generation" the Church still struggles with finalizing the task. The Church has enough resources, enough churches, enough people, enough education, enough money, even much prayer. Yet the most important task in the world is not finished.

To this situation of evaluation of the effectiveness and determination of our mission mindness of the churches and Believers, Dr. James O. Davis' book *The Synergistic Church: The Answer To Fulfilling The Great Commission* is most timely. We need not to take another delay of 100 years. It is time to fulfill the task given by Jesus! For this action, *The Synergistic Church* is a book which comes for an urgent need: Hundreds of millions of Believers need to synergize their efforts through the power of the Holy Spirit.

Dr. Davis sees the role of the pastors decisive in motivating everyone to take their responsibility in the final lap. The synergy of this collaboration is similar as the expand of Christianity in the first century. He leads his readers to these original resources that have enabled the expansion of the global church in the past centuries and especially also in the last 100 years in the Pentecostal-Charismatic revival and renewal. This book is a handbook in keeping in mind which really matters in divine movements.

—**Dr. Arto Hämäläinen**,
Chairman of the African Pentecostal Mission (APM),
Chairman of the Pentecostal Commission
on Religious Liberty (PCRL),
Founding chairman of the World Missions Commission of the
Pentecostal World Fellowship (WMC/PWF),
Pentecostal European Mission (PEM),
and the Pentecostal Asia Mission (PAM).

"How wonderful and pleasant it is when brothers live together in harmony! ... And there the Lord has commanded his blessing, even life everlasting" (Psalm 133:1, 3). These ancient words of the psalmist have been read, announced, and preached by thousands but no one has sought to live this truth more than Dr. James O. Davis. His life and ministry passion is to bring into glorious synergy all who call Jesus *Lord* and thus experience the commanded blessing of the ONE who gave us the Great Commission. Dr. Davis in *The Synergistic Church* has given us a gift that will help the Church to grow together in love, deepen the bond of peace, and enjoy the blessing and anointing of the Lord. I commend to you this crucial and powerful word that comes to us at a pivotal time and from a visionary, tireless leader, and friend whose heartbeat is to see *The Synergistic Church* in its glorious revelation.

—**Dr. Kevin J. Holt**, Lead Pastor,
Glad Tidings Church, Muncie, IN

Dr. James O. Davis is passionate about the Great Commission. This is observable by glancing at his many years as an evangelist and ambassador to reach across denominational barriers to collaborate and mobilize the body of Christ to finish the Great Commission. *The Synergistic Church* provides followers of Christ and leaders for Christ a cooperative blueprint for fulfilling the Great Commission locally and globally. This book is a necessary read to be missionally effective in the twenty-first century!

—**Dr. Donald J. Immel,**
PennDel Ministry Network Superintendent

Dr. James O. Davis carries an inspiration that provokes grace to excel in your call to lead. *The Synergistic Church* will illuminate your leadership command for impact and change.

—**Dr. Emmanuel Ziga**, President,
Emmanuel Ziga Ministries, Seattle Area, WA

Dr. James O Davis continues to be a vision caster, vision inspirer, and vision achiever! As you read *The Synergistic Church*, allow God to cascade a vision in your life that will propel you to action. As we multiply our efforts to fulfill the Great Commission, we will see a wave of life change that is desperately needed in our world today.

—**Dr. Greg Lyons**, Founder/President, Global Surge, Manila, Philippines, and President, Louisiana Baptist University, Shreveport, LA

"The former account I made, O Theophilus, of all that Jesus began both to do and teach" (Acts 1:1). In the former account in Luke 1:3, Luke addresses a man named Theophilus, as most noble. His name means God lover. There's something about a God lover. God lovers love God first, their families second, the church third. Since I've met Dr. James O. Davis, he has always been a God lover. His worldview, as far as the Gospel is concerned, is synergistic. The whole Gospel to the whole world until everyone is reached, and he maintains it must happen in the only lifetime we have. He knows the importance of people in all of this. Since the inception of the Global Church Network, his mission has been to synergize. As you read, *The Synergistic Church*, may the Holy Spirit empower you to become synergistic in your Love God, His Son, and His Church.

—**Rev. Randall Van Nelson**, South Africa Leader, International Pentecostal Holiness Church

If anyone understands synergistic leadership, it is Dr. James O. Davis. In his latest book, *The Synergistic Church: The Answer To Fulfilling The Great Commission,* he explains, from the decades of life experiences what it takes to tie the relational knots necessary for global impact. When you read it, your life and ministry will never be the same!

—**Rev. Patrick Paul**, Bahamas Assemblies of God General Superintendent

Jesus Christ promises that He will be with those who set out to fulfill the Great Commission, and the New Testament is about all those who went out of their ways to do just that. Dr. James O. Davis is a model example of someone who goes out of his way to fulfill the Great Commission in our time, and someone who inspires our churches to do the same. I encourage everyone to pick up *The Synergistic Church* that will help us to get back on track on what we should have been doing from the beginning: go and make disciples of all peoples.

—**Dr. Byoungho Zoh**,
Tongdok Bible Church, Tongdok Bible App, Seoul, Korea

I am honored to have worked alongside Dr. James O. Davis, an exceptional leader in the worldwide Great Commission movement. His steadfast commitment to bringing the church together for this mission is truly remarkable. I highly recommend reading and sharing his book, *The Synergistic Church*.

—**Dr. Ronnie W. Floyd**,
Speaker, Author, Ministry Strategist, and Pastor Emeritus of Cross Church, Former President, Southern Baptist Convention

Dr. James O. Davis is a gift to the whole body of Christ. *The Synergistic Church* will teach and encourage every believer that you can't do it alone. We need one another and we can learn some of the secrets that are shared in the book that can help us all to become effective in evangelizing more people in the years to come.

—**Dr. Suliasi Kurulo**, Founder,
World Harvest Center, Oceania CoChair,
Global Church Network, Suva, Fiji

Dr. James O. Davis in his latest book *The Synergistic Church* has given us an urgent reminder of what Jesus meant by the word Church and what this Church would be like. He answers the question of what Jesus meant by "other sheep I have who are not of this fold," and His prayer in John 17 "that they all maybe One as we are One." The Church like our human bodies has many parts but still its one body. *The Synergistic Church* is a must read for all believers!

—**Dr. John O. Smith**, CCH,
General Superintendent, Assemblies of God,
CoChair/Global Church Network, Georgetown, Guyana

In today's rapidly changing and hyperconnected world, the Church of Jesus Christ faces significant challenges, but it has also been entrusted with an unprecedented opportunity to proclaim the gospel throughout the world! To seize this opportunity, the Church will need leaders who—in total reliance on the Holy Spirit—are ready, willing, and able to transcend traditional boundaries, employ effective ministry strategies, and partner with like-minded brothers and sisters in Christ to yield greater results for the Kingdom of God than they ever could alone. Dr. James O. Davis is such a leader, and *The Synergistic Church* is the playbook we need today as we carry out the great work Jesus Christ has entrusted to us!

—**Dr. Ben Lovvorn**, Executive Pastor,
First Baptist Church of Dallas

The Synergistic Church is not just a phenomenal book, it should be essential reading for those in ministry. I don't know of any person who is more committed and driven to seeing the Great Commission fulfilled then Dr. James O. Davis. And in spite of this massive load on his shoulders, he is able to carry it with grace and tenderness. So honoured to be able to recommend this book!

—**Rev. Yang Tuck Yoong**, Chairman,
The Alliance of Pentecostal & Charismatic Churches in Singapore

Jesus prayed, "Father let them be one as We are one." Jesus wouldn't have prayed that if it couldn't come true. Dr. James O. Davis' heart doesn't just beat for the harmony of the Church, but in *The Synergistic Church* gives the blueprint for it. For Dr. Davis, it isn't just words, it's his life. I pray we will put into action his invaluable insights and the wisdom gained from decades of living out Jesus' prayer.

—**Mr. Ken Harrison**, President/CEO,
Promise Keepers, Colorado Springs, CO

THE SYNERGISTIC CHURCH

THE ANSWER TO FULFILLING THE GREAT COMMISSION

JAMES O. DAVIS

FOREWORD BY ROBERT JEFFRESS

Orlando, Florida

The Synergistic Church
Copyright © 2023 James O. Davis

James O. Davis
P. O. Box 411605
Melbourne, FL 32941-1605 www.JamesODavis.com

Contents and/or cover may not be reproduced in whole or part in any form without written consent of the author.

Unless otherwise indicated, Scripture quotations are from the New American Standard Bible, © 1960, 1962, 1963, 1968, 1971, 1972, 1973, 1975, 1977 by the Lockman Foundation, La Habra, California.

Scripture quotations designated NIV are from the New International Version, © 1973, 1978, 1984 by the International Bible Society. Published by Zondervan Bible Publishers, Grand Rapids, Michigan.

Scripture quotations designated TLB are from The Living Bible, © 1971 by Tyndale House Publishers, Wheaton, Illinois.

Scripture quotations designated KJV are from the King James Version, Public Domain.

ISBN: 979-8-9855197-1-6

Billion Soul Publishing
Orlando, Florida
www.billionsoulpub.com

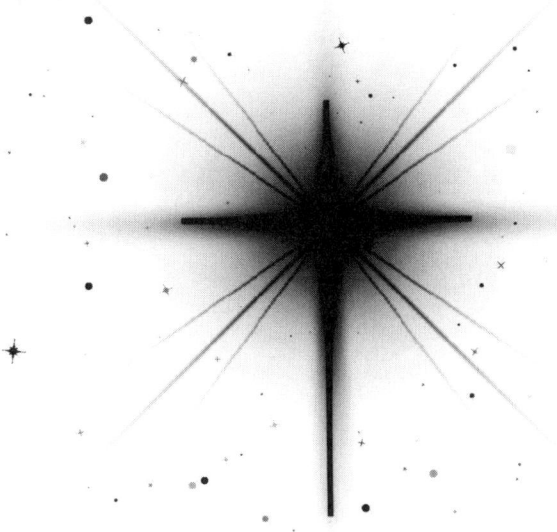

In Dedication To

Dr. Craig Keener
who has surrendered his will,
suffered in his walk, served his world,
and scholastically taught God's Word
to synergistically fulfill the Great Commission
in colleges, cultures and countries.

Table of Contents

Acknowledgements xvii
Foreword xix
Introduction xxvii

PART ONE: THE CHURCH WITH NO LIMITS

1. A World of Hyperchange 5
2. Plandemic Leadership 17
3. A Church with No Roofs and No Walls 25
4. The Synergistic Church Blueprint 45

PART TWO: THE CHURCH WITH NO ROOFS

5. Our Confidence in God 59
6. Our Calling By God 91
7. Our Character Before God 115
8. Our Committed to God 135

PART THREE: THE CHURCH WITH NO WALLS

9. Our Interdependent Cooperation 159
10. Our Impactful Communication 181
11. Our Ingenious Compassion 203
12. Our Innovative Creativity 221

Conclusion 241

Appendix 1
   Why and How the Great Commission
   Will Be Finished 251

Appendix 2
   Synergistic Global Missions 269

Appendix 3
   Synergizing Across the Lines 281

Appendix 4
   The Global Church Network 287

Recommended Reading 297
About The Author 305
Books and Resources 309
Endnotes 311

Acknowledgments

This book is the product of synergy among family members, dynamic leaders, and fellow laborers of Christ from around the globe. A special heartfelt thanks to Sheri Davis and Jackie Chrisner, who provided outstanding editing and revising. I am most grateful to Sheri Depuy for her creative art design for the book cover and internal images. Kathy Curtis always provides stellar book layouts. Truly, we can do more together than we can by ourselves.

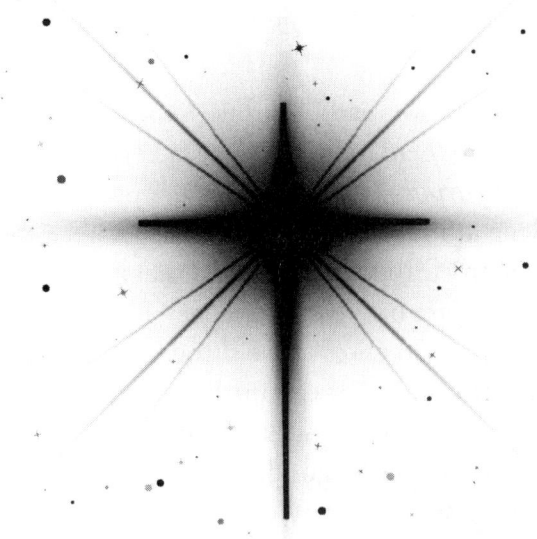

Foreword

In Jesus' high priestly prayed, He said, I do not ask on behalf of these alone, but for those also who believe in Me through their word; that they may all be one even as you, Father, are in Me and I in you, that they also may be in Us, so that the world may believe that You sent me (John 17:20-21).

When Jesus prayed this prayer, he was not just praying for his current disciples but for those who would hear the Word of God over the last 2,000 years. He prayed that the Believers become one like the Trinity is one. There is synergy in the Trinity. There are three distinct persons in the Godhead and the sum of the whole is greater that the Father, Son and Holy Spirit just being separate identities.

In First Corinthians 3:9, we learn through the Apostle Paul, "We are fellow-workers with God." Fellow-workers is derived from, "syergoi," and denotes a synergy between each other and with God. When we synergize our talents and skills together under the divine direction of God, mighty power is the result.

In Romans 8:28 we read, *"And we know that all things work together for good to them that love God, to them who are the called according to his purpose"* (Romans 8:28). This one verse will help us to go to sleep at night when nothing else will.

There are many things in this world that are not good. In and of themselves they are bad, even terrible. However, by the chemistry of the cross—God takes these things that in themselves are bad and God compounds them in the crucible of his omnipotence. He synergizes them with the hand of his love, and they become to us that which is good. They become to us flavors of life and they nourish us.

"Work together" comes from *synergia,* from which we have the term, *synergy or synergize.* This term is the genius of this magnificent promise. In His God-ness and goodness, God weaves all things together, for those who love Him, into a one-word conclusion: GOOD. Nothing can frustrate this, because no one and no thing has power beyond the One who created all things. They are under His feet. God synergizes all things together to accomplish His divine purpose in our lives. The sum of the whole is greater than its individual parts.

First, we learn **the certainty of this divine synergy**. Paul says, *"And we know that all things work together."* This is not conjecture. This is not surmising. He says, "We know that it is true." The promises of God are yea and amen in Jesus Christ.

Dr. F. B. Meyer said, "On an occasion, if any promise of God should fail, the Heaven would clothe themselves with sackcloth. The sun, the moon, and the stars would reel from their courses. The universe would rock. And, a hollow wind would moan through a ruined creation the awful message that God can lie. But, thank God, while many may lie, God cannot lie. He abides faithful."

We should take our eyes off the waves of life and place our eyes on God's mighty tide. The same God that programmed the planets to draw that tide back and forth is the God that controls our lives. He is the same God that controls this universe.

Foreword

Next, we understand **the completeness of this divine synergy**. Paul writes, *"And we know that all things work together for good"* (Romans 8:28). Not some things, not a few things, and not most things. There is nothing that is outside the realm of this promise. He says all things work together for good.

We know that the *sweet things* work together for good. Thank God for the kiss of a baby, for the love of a wife, for friendship, for health, for happiness, for the local church, for joy and for music. God takes these things and God uses them for good even when we're not good. The Bible says, *"...the goodness of God leadeth thee to repentance?"* (Romans 2:4).

What about the *sorrowful things*? They work together for good also. In Jeremiah 24:5, we can see how God dealt with his ancient people, Judah. We read, *"Thus saith the LORD, the God of Israel; Like these good figs, so will I acknowledge them that are carried away captive of Judah, whom I have sent out of this place into the land of the Chaldeans for their good."*

What about the *sinister things* in life? In Genesis 50, Joseph is front and center of God's divine plan. A person would find it difficult to find anything bad said about Joseph. I know he was a sinner like the rest of us, but how he was mistreated. If you would read the story of Joseph, you would find that he was betrayed by his brethren. He was put into a pit and left for dead. And, then brought out of that pit and sold into slavery. After he was sold into slavery, he was cast into prison. He was maligned and ridiculed. But, in Genesis 5:20, he said, *"But as for you, ye thought evil against me; but God meant it unto good."*

Even the *satanic things* God works together for our good. God allowed the devil to buffet Job in the Old Testament. Yet, Job said, "My faith became like pure gold" (Job 23:10).

Furthermore, our God takes the *simple things* in life and synergizes them together for our good. Did you know that the very hairs of your head are numbered? Did you know not a blade of grass moves without God's permission?

Third, we know **the cause of this divine synergy.** Why does it happen this way? Paul says, "and we know that God works all things together for good." Things in themselves don't work together. Where God does not rule, God overrules. God is the one who brings order out of confusion and harmony out of discord. It is not that things that work together for good. The good is the result of God synergizing them together it.

What is this divine synergy? God takes the evil that assaults us and combines it with His working, His weaving, His divinely manipulating hand, joining them together in such ways that the end result is good.

Fourth, there is a **condition for this divine** synergy. It's not just automatic. The Bible says. *"And we know that all things work together for good to them that love God..."* (Romans 8:28).

So, for those who are loving God and are called according to His purpose, He synergizes multiple forces—good and evil, light and dark—and brings them to a beneficial result for us. He does NOT say that all things are good in the believer's life. He does not say that He is the cause of all things. He cannot be, because He is not the author of evil, and He should never be accused of such. However, we can rest of the biblical reality, for those who love God, He miraculously synergizes together all things for our good.

Last, we know the **consequences of this divine synergy.** How do all things work together for good? For us to be wealthy? No. For us to be healthy? Not necessarily. That we will be happy. Perhaps, but not necessarily. What are the consequences? We read, *"And we know that all things work together for good to them that love God, to them who are the called according to his purpose"* (Romans 8:28).

What is His purpose? We read, *"For whom he did foreknow, he also did predestinate to be conformed to the image of his Son, that he might be the firstborn among many brethren..."* (Romans 8:29). What is the ultimate outcome of this supernatural synergy? The consequence of it, is that we will be like Jesus.

Foreword

A lot of people have the wrong idea regarding why God works together all things for our good. They think, everything is working together for good. Imagine a man driving down the road. While he is driving down the road, one of his tires blow out and he says, "Oh well, praise God, all things work together for the good, there is a sale on tires somewhere." Yet, this is not what Romans 8:28 means.

God may arrange a sale on tires out of mercy and I think frequently He does. Yet, God's plan for you is not necessarily that you have new tires on your tires. God's plan for you is that you are like Jesus and that you will be conformed to the image of His Son.

For those whom He foreknew, He also predestined to become conformed to the image of His Son, so that He would be the firstborn among many brethren; and these whom He predestined, He also called; and these whom He called, He also justified; and these whom He justified, He also glorified. What then shall we say to these things? If God is for us, who is against us? (Romans 8:29-31).

God is leading somewhere for those who follow Him. He has called them out on purpose, and nothing will thwart His ultimate agenda. He is making us like His Son and chipping away everything that does not look like Him. This world is the oven where this baking occurs … the melting pot where the dross is sloughed off and the sanctifying happens. And God causes all things to accomplish this glorious result.

Even death does not interrupt this process, but rather, completes it! It is the ultimate fear of most people, but the ultimate good for the Believer. He sheds the sin-weakened earth-suit and takes on the glories of heaven, soon to get a completely glorified body, impervious to sin and decay and death.

Nothing can overcome us; nothing can stop us. Why? God is with us, and His divine synergy is at work in all things for our good.

Christians around the world are being tortured and killed for their faith in Christ. More are being martyred for Christ today than ever before. If seen only from the world's viewpoint, we see that this divine synergy does not seem to work for good in their lives. Nevertheless, God's sovereign synergy is at work in their lives. It is beyond our mental comprehension, but God takes the worst evil we can imagine, and weaves it with His promise and reality of eternal life and rewards.

What is the end result? What men meant for evil, God joined with His goodness. These faithful martyrs enter instantly into the presence of God and receive the highest rewards for all of eternity in heaven. The devil's supposed outward victory becomes the believers' assured and glorious victory. Oh grave where is your victory? Oh death where is your sting?

For more than thirty years, Dr. James O. Davis has been synergizing Christian relationships throughout the Body of Christ. In *The Synergistic Church: The Answer to Fulfilling the Great Commission*, Dr. Davis shows us the synergistic paradigm to experiencing a church without limits, a Church without roofs and a church without walls. When divine synergy is released in the Church, the Church will be without limits, and go further together than we have ever gone before; will have no roofs, and will have divine connection with God like never before; and will have no walls, and will reach more people for Christ than ever before.

As you read this powerful book, it will become clear that you are learning from a synergistic leader, who by the grace of God has built the largest pastors' network in the world. He teaches out from firsthand knowledge how to synergize and mobilize in order to finalize the Great Commission. Dr. Davis not only knows why the Great Commission will be completed but knows how to accomplish it in this generation. He knows that the main thing that the leader must do is to keep the main thing the main thing.

Foreword

As you read The Synergistic Church, your mind will be enlarged, your soul will be enriched, and your life will be empowered by the principles and practices of the synergized lifestyle.

—Dr. Robert Jeffress
First Baptist Dallas
May, 2023

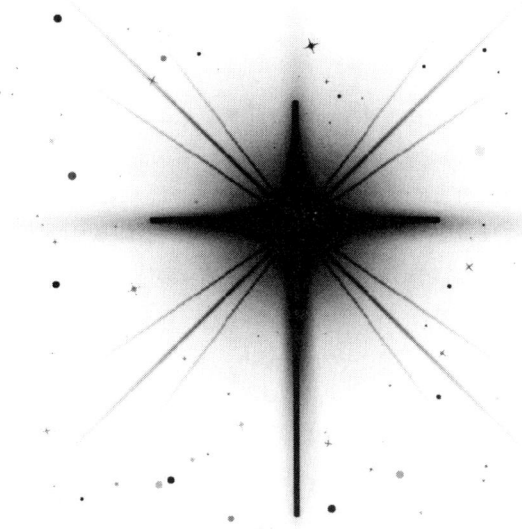

Introduction

If our movement is not moving, it is not a movement. If our movement is not moving, it could be a monument. There is a countless number of Christians and Christian organizations, that have not moved in years. Even though they talk about "their movement," they have not moved in their mentality, methods, models, and ministry in years, if not decades.

The most important person in every community on earth is not the governor, the congressman, the senator, or even the President. The most important person in every community is the local, Spirit-filled pastor. As goes the pastor, so goes the community. We must move from steeples to peoples; from fame to faith; from money to the Master; from spending to investing; from net worth to network; from philosophers to practitioners; from about only the reached to the unreached; from ivory towers to grassroots. We are not about doing old business as usual that did not finish the job. We are about embracing the new face of Christianity that works together to complete the Great Commission.

In a previous generation, the Western Church sowed, and a great harvest returned. Today, old maps will not work in new lands. The Synergistic Church is not about the Western Church telling pastors worldwide how to complete the Great Commission. We are not about telling others what to do, but asking how we can add value to do it better. We are not about the West headed to the Rest, but about the Best going to the Rest. We believe that every church, regardless of its size, and every Christian, whether known or unknown, can add value to the entire Body of Christ.

The Great Commission was given to finish. Everything the Lord has started, he has finished. When He created the heavens and the earth, he finished it. When Jesus died on the cross, He said, "It is finished." When eternity begins, the old world will be finished. We are commanded and commissioned to finish the Great Commission. What is the solution? The Synergistic Church. If we are to finish the Great Commission, we cannot care who gets the credit, as long as God gets the glory. We must move from "Me" to "We" if "They" will ever hear about "Him." The Global Church Network (GCNW.tv) is not about egos and logos, but about souls, souls, and souls.

The late Adrian Rogers said, "James, it is not whether you know the devil but does the devil know you." The Synergistic Church is about placing the global vision in the hot halls of hell and announcing to every demonic force: WE WILL SYNERGIZE, MOBILIZE AND FINALIZE THE GREAT COMMISSION IN OUR GENERATION! It is about emptying hell to fill up heaven.

The Synergistic Church is not about adding but multiplying; not about taking longer but about finishing the Great Commission even sooner. Should we answer our global challenge, in the next ten to fifteen years, we will plant churches and equip pastors/leaders both in the easiest and hardest places on earth.

Introduction

For the first time in history, it is possible for today's preschool children – our children and grandchildren – to live long enough to witness the Gospel being preached to every person.

The Synergistic Church is about everyone. Everyone is a somebody in the Body of Christ. We don't need elbows jostling for position. We need hands, hearts, and heads serving the greater good. It is not just about leadership, but relationship.

The words of past generations on whose shoulders we stand still echo in the heavenlies, "BRING BACK THE KING!" The world itself is calling, "Give us Truth!" We cannot bring back those who would bring back the king. We alone are the stewards of those to whom we are called, our own generation.

Completing the Great Commission is not about money; it's about motivation. We have enough money, enough members enough minutes, enough methods, enough models in the Kingdom of God. The reason we have not finished the Great Commission is that we have not motivated enough. Some would rather turn inward to fight one another than turn outward to fight alongside each other. The problem is not a "how to," but a "want to."

A century ago, if a missionary missed a ship, it was a missed opportunity by years. Through perilous travel, intermittent communication, and meager resources, they forged ahead with a rallying cry, "BRING BACK THE KING!" Where is the passion with which they cried bitter tears for those dying without Christ? Where is the heart tug that pulled them to brave any voyage, skirt no jungle and fight harder with each mounting difficulty?

The words of past generations on whose shoulders we stand still echo in the heavenlies, "BRING BACK THE KING!" The world itself is calling, "Give us Truth!" We cannot bring back those who would bring back the king. We alone are the stewards of those to whom we are called, our own generation.

A small group of executives works together each year to make "Mickey Mouse" the most recognized name on earth. We have 2.4 billion Christians and growing on earth. If we want to, we can finish spreading the Name above all Names, "JESUS CHRIST!" More than two billion people do not know the meaning of Christmas or why we celebrate Easter. We are getting ready for the Second Coming and they have not heard of the First Coming. A church that is not winning the lost is lost itself.

This Lord is challenging us to become a part of something bigger than ourselves. We need to put on the whole armor of God, not to watch it shine in the polished mirrors of fellowship halls but to watch it work in the battle to share with this world the eternal Gospel of Christ.

One day, the King of the Universe will descend through eternity into time, walking on clouds, the diadem of glory on His head and a rainbow of victory wrapped around His shoulders. From the celestial shores of heaven, we will look back across our lives and realize that the Lord did not promise smooth sailing but a safe landing. In heaven, we can no longer win souls. We will be unable to accomplish the very goal for which Jesus died.

All of heaven is cheering us on. We need to be motivated about what motivates heaven. Will you invest your time to build bridges or fences? We can achieve more together than we ever could alone by synergizing our efforts to bring back the King.

Since the birth of Christ between 4BC and 6BC, there have been approximately 75 to 80 generations. Generations have come and gone and yet the Great Commission has not been completed. Over time, normally movements become the opposite of what they were when they were stated. The first generation generates; the second generation motivates; the third generation speculates; the fourth generation dissipates. This is the cycle of movements. The only way out of a decline is an upward vision to

Introduction

stimulate the next generation. The Synergistic Church provides the needed upward vision for this generation.

You hold in your hands a ministry roadmap to help you to navigate your life in new, exciting uncharted leadership lands. I believe The Synergistic Church provides a success path, whether you serve in the local church, in a national or international ministry, denomination or fellowship, or on the mission field.

THE SYNERGISTIC CHURCH

**NO LIMITS
NO ROOFS
+ NO WALLS**

THE SYNERGISTIC CHURCH

PULPIT

Hyperchange
Leadership
No Roofs No Walls
Church Blueprint

Confidence
Calling
Character
Commitment

Cooperation
Communication
Compassion
Creativity

PART ONE

A CHURCH WITH NO LIMITS

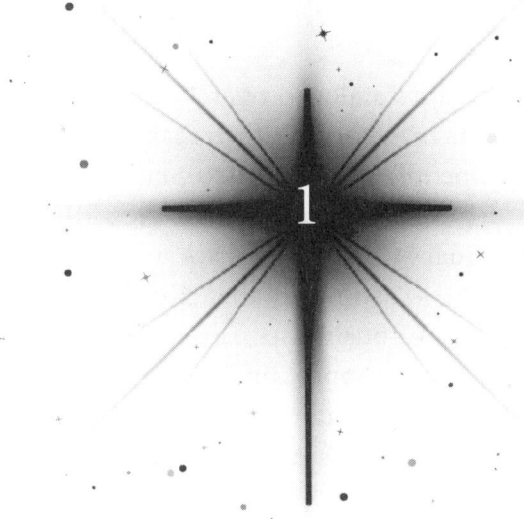

A World of Hyperchange

We live in a world that is rapidly changing. The explosion of technology and information has created an environment of change and innovation that is unprecedented. According to sociologists, the cultural shifts that used to take decades are now occurring every few months. This whirlwind of change is overwhelming. It is impossible for anyone to keep pace with all the developments that are taking place in the world.

Through technology, we are becoming a faster-paced and more connected culture than ever before. Communication now happens in real-time: live streaming, instant messaging. We can keep track of responses and comments down to the second. New ways of gathering and utilizing information have revolutionized the institutions of society. The distribution of knowledge and information is now as important as the creation of new knowledge and the discovery of new information.

In 1969, there were only four primitive websites on the World Wide Web. By 1990, over 333,000 existed. By the end of 1997, there were over 20 million. In 2001, the popular search engine,

Google.com, claimed it cataloged over 1.6 billion websites and added more each day. According to researcher George Barna, almost 50 million people in the United States alone may soon use the Internet for religious experiences. According to Forbes Advisor, as of January, 2023, there are 1.13 billion websites and every minute it is estimated that 200 websites will have been built. Over 71% of businesses have a website that plays a crucial role in operations. Approximately 6.8 billion people own cell phones, and around 23 billion text messages are sent daily. That is approximately 270,000 texts a second. Social media has climbed upon the shoulders of technology with approximately 4.8 billion utilizing Facebook, YouTube, WhatsApp, Instagram, and TikTok, according to Data Reportal. Businesses, News outlets, and factions of local government now have specific divisions devoted to social media presence, engagement, branding strategy, and influence. From Twitter to Pinterest, millions upon millions of people are meeting on digital platforms to share content, build and grow businesses, spread awareness, and constantly strive to educate, entertain, and most importantly, influence.

Society is greatly impacted by Moore's Law which states that the power of computer processing doubles every 18 to 24 months. As a result, the world is moving faster and faster; it is involved in a hyperchange. This is the new world in which our Lord Jesus Christ is building His Church.

As Christ builds His Church, it is our responsibility as His leaders to prepare ourselves so we can have effective ministries even in these challenging times. But how can we lead effectively in ministry when everything is changing so fast that we feel like it is impossible to keep up? With every passing year, it is becoming more difficult to remain relevant, yet Christ has called us to help build His Church in the midst of this hectic matrix.

Through the enabling power of the Holy Spirit, we can catapult beyond our cultural challenges. We must become a church that creatively reaches beyond the current barriers to ministry—a church that is a vibrant, holy influence on the new frontier of the twenty-first century—a church of believers who reflect Christ's glory and effectively minister to the spiritually needy imprisoned within the chaotic world system. Our message is timeless, but it must be presented to people in ways they can understand and will accept.

As Christ builds His Church, it is our responsibility as His leaders to prepare ourselves so we can have effective ministries even in these challenging times.

God wants to grow churches that are relevant without compromising biblical truth—churches that know how to connect with the culture around them without forsaking timeless biblical principles. God's Word is as relevant today as it was when God first presented it to humanity; however, we must become effective communicators of that message by staying in touch with our times.

As ministers in this new era, we must constantly reevaluate our ideas and assumptions and their implementation. Unless we do, it will be impossible to be relevant and connect with unbelievers in today's world. We cannot become so comfortable that we ignore the changes that are occurring all around us. We must do this while maintaining the critical balance between innovative thinking and scriptural directives. This is especially important if ministry is to effectively reach a digital generation.

MAPPING THE NEW WORLD

Many years ago, William Edward Perry, the famous English explorer, mapped out most of the Southern Polar Cap. Those who travel to that desolate, subzero continent arb e still using his maps today. On one particular expedition, he and his crew, having completed mapping an uncharted region, were preparing to hike to another unfamiliar location. On the eve of their departure, they studied the stars and determined their exact coordinates. As the sun rose, they began a hard, lengthy journey north to this unmapped region. They marched through the ice and snow all day long with the freezing air burning their lungs. As the sun set, they made camp, totally exhausted from their trip. After their evening meal, Perry studied the stars again to determine their exact coordinates. He was stunned to learn that even though he and his crew had journeyed north all day, they were now farther south than when they began that morning. After struggling to solve this problem, they discovered that although they had traveled north, they were on a giant ice sheet that was floating south faster than they were walking north. Although they were going in the right direction, they were sliding away and did not even know it.

In which direction are you headed? Many people are marching north with ideas and plans; but sadly, the undercurrent of our shifting culture is pulling them farther away from the realization of their goals.

Just like Perry's men, they struggle and press ahead only to find themselves farther and farther away from achieving their ministry objectives. These are pivotal times in history. The Church is being assailed on all sides by forces strong and dangerous. Eastern religions are sweeping the globe; blatant satanism, witchcraft, pluralism, and moral relativity infect all aspects of society, including the church. Like Paul, we understand that we wrestle not against flesh and blood but against supernatural forces (Ephesians 6:12). In these last days, it will take supernatural leadership to pilot the church through these dangerous waters.

It is impossible for the church not to be affected by this powerful shift taking place because it exists in the culture that is going through the great shift. Many struggle to understand the church's response to this changing world. Should the church embrace this hyperchange and abandon all we are currently doing, or should we remain steadfast in our approaches and structure and prevent change from taking place? Or is the answer somewhere in between? How do we maneuver amid this hyperchange knowing what to keep and what to let go?

***Like Paul, we understand that we wrestle
not against flesh and blood but against supernatural forces
(Ephesians 6:12).***

In the struggle to remain culturally relevant as well as maintain the true distinctive of the Christian church, two approaches are dominant. Some have reacted to the change by preferring to preserve who they are more than connecting with the world around them and have become self-absorbed.

This is often done with a sincere desire to "keep the faith" and not compromise. The byproduct of this isolation is often a lack of relevance in the form and function of the local church. In the attempt to adhere to the essentials of faith, we may mistakenly perpetuate nonessentials of the faith or, worse, become unaware of the needs of the culture. When we disconnect with the world around us or disconnect with other believers, our isolation prevents us from healthy fellowship and evangelism. Isolating themselves from the changes that are taking place, they build walls that keep the change from affecting them.

Another approach to the rapidly changing world is to weave the elements of culture into the church activities without adequate discernment. Viewing any change or advancement as a powerful new way to revitalize the church, the emphasis is less on God's direction and more on our own ability to work the cultural shifts to our favor. This methodology can often prevent the church from following God's desires for it because the church trusts in its own ability and power to advance.

Churches that follow these paths begin with good intentions but are often unwillingly separated from God and the mission they originally set out to accomplish. The answer is for both sides to find new ways of relating to our shifting culture through new breakthroughs in methodology while remaining grounded in and supported by God's timeless foundational principles.

In addition to the polarizing effect of churches either isolating themselves from culture or caving into it, many pastors are not applying the basic truths for supernatural living that are outlined in God's Word. These pastors are committed to pursuing God's purposes, but all too often forget to rely on His infinite power and resources. They pray to know God's will; but then when He reveals what He wants them to do, they launch out in their own strength to accomplish the goal. God does not intend us to work independently of Him. He wants us to hold His hand and work together like Father and child in accomplishing His task. It is when we let go of His hand and try to do the impossible on our own that frustration sets in and over time can lead to more serious problems.

MANDATING: CHANGE OR DIE

It has been said that most people will not change until the price of not changing becomes greater than the cost of the change itself. We must change. If we do not, it will cost us everything. There is no longer any option. Those who cling to outdated methods and practices are becoming obsolete. These groups continue to do the same things they have always done, not because of religious faith or devotion but because they always have done it that way. They lack the real power they claim to possess, and the world sees them as archaic. They refuse to change and eventually will die.

There are those who have abandoned biblical principles in their zeal to be accepted by the culture around them. Consequently, they may achieve increased attendance and popularity, but they are not producing many fruitful disciples for Christ. If we are not willing to change to meet the needs of those whom God wants to bring to us, we too will die.

It has been said that most people will not change until the price of not changing becomes greater than the cost of the change itself. We must change. If we do not, it will cost us everything.

For example, imagine an I-beam in your front yard. (An I-beam looks like a capital "I" and is used in construction.) Suppose we lay this I-beam in your front yard, and it stretches to the house across the street. Your neighbors come outside to look in wonder at this 120-foot beam in your street. Imagine that we are standing at the opposite end of the I-beam, 120 feet away, holding a $100 bill. All you must do is walk across the I-beam in front of your friends, and we will give you the money. Would you come? Of course, you would; it is relatively easy.

Now suppose we move the I-beam to Kuala Lumpur, Malaysia. In Kuala Lumpur, there are two buildings side by side called the Petronas Towers. They are tallest buildings in the world, standing 1,483 feet tall. This time the I-beam barely bridges the gap between the two buildings. You are on the roof of one building, and we are on the other. "Listen, if you will walk—not crawl—across this I-beam in five minutes, we will give you another hundred dollars." Would you do it this time? Probably not. "But it is the same I-beam you crossed yesterday in your front yard! What if I increased the prize to a thousand dollars? What about a million dollars?" Are you still unwilling to take such a risk? Most people value their lives more than the money offered to do such a daring feat.

Let us change the circumstances again. This time, standing on the other rooftop are two kidnappers holding your two-year-old daughter. If you do not cross the beam immediately, they will drop your daughter. Now you must decide how important it is to cross the beam. What is more valuable to you? Most people to whom we have presented this scenario say they are willing to attempt the walk. They would not do it for any amount of money, but their love for their child means more and causes them to step out. When the challenge becomes personal, it is amazing how willing people are to take a risk.[4] They are more willing to change when the price of not changing becomes greater than the change itself. How high does the price of changelessness have to become before we will begin to rethink our evangelism strategies and embrace solid, Spirit-filled change today?

We are on the brink of a new world. The I-beam has been laid before us, and the world is dangling in the hands of the enemy. The leadership of the Church is standing on the edge of a great divide. The dangers are incredible; but we remember that though the conditions are different, the I-beam is the same one we traversed yesterday in our front yard.

Unlike in our story, we do not have to cross the beam alone; the Holy Spirit accompanies us as we traverse the narrow rail to the other side. It will be windy and slippery on the journey, but we must work our way across the divide and help save the world from the hands of the enemy.

MAKING THE CHANGE

The first-century church also existed in a world of rapid change. In addition to a radical religious shift from Judaism and paganism to Christianity, the world at that time was going through a massive political upheaval with the advancement of the Roman Empire. Following the establishment of the church on the Day of Pentecost, we see that the first-century church, even during its own rapid changes, worked to keep their connection with each other and the world as well as with God. These early believers did not withdraw from the world—they moved into it. Immediately after Pentecost, believers were proclaiming the good news of Jesus Christ to the world (Acts 2:14-36; 3:11-26; 4:1-11). They did not isolate themselves from the world; they sought to evangelize it. Where nonbelievers were found in the Temple, Christians were there. When Jews went to the synagogue, believers were there.

Immediately after Pentecost, believers were proclaiming the good news of Jesus Christ to the world (Acts 2:14-36; 3:11-26; 4:1-11).

In addition, early believers did not isolate themselves from each other but devoted themselves to fellowship (Acts 2:42) and continued in one mind in the temple day by day (Acts 2:46). They worked together in harmony. The walls of separation and isolation were down. Just like the early believers, we are one body, unified in the Spirit. However, all too often we refuse to work together to accomplish God's purposes.

The first-century church was also centered on God. Acts 2:42 records that Christ's followers devoted themselves to the apostles' teaching. They were devoted to the gospel of Jesus Christ, not wavering in their commitments. The early church is full of examples of the importance of prayer and guidance from God. Amid adversity, the church prayed to God for guidance and protection (Acts 4:24-31). When the church was faced with controversy, they sought the direction of God for the answer (Acts 6; 15). They worked in harmony with God for His direction and guidance. Nothing stood as a barrier between them and their creator.

We pursue God's goals but ignore or even reject the principle that we are all different parts of the same body and must work together in harmony for maximum ministry impact.

There has never been a more important time for the Church to follow the pattern of the first-century church and lead a lost world in the right direction. Moral relativism has allowed a sense of irresponsibility to pervade our culture. The ship of culture is adrift in a sea of turmoil and discord. More than ever, leaders are needed to pilot this ship into the peaceful harbor of God's grace.

As indicated earlier, this turmoil has affected many church leaders. Consequently, many pastors have not been able to confront the rising tide of depravity, and God's Church is suffering. George Barna, the Christian statistician, revealed startling trends regarding church members in America in one of his annual studies of American faith and religious beliefs. While 82 percent of church members pray, only 37 percent read their Bible outside of church; 41 percent of people who attend church do not consider themselves born again! Other studies indicate that 90 percent of church members misunderstand the person and ministry of the Holy Spirit.

Clearly, leaders must help the Christian church right its course. The only way to combat this rising flood of apathy is through the power of the Holy Spirit. We must have confidence and faith in the power of the Holy Spirit to lead us beyond these limitations. Society and the church have been gripped with fears about the future. Our rapidly changing world leaves people wondering where we are headed. Too often, these limitations are holding back God's people from being the powerful, fruitful church He has called us to be.

While many in the church shrink back from the hyperchanging culture and are oblivious to the assault of the advancing attack of the enemy, it is obvious from Barna's report as well as similar studies that we are in a pivotal time in church history. We must be alert to the change taking place around us and work diligently to turn back the rising tide of evil in the world. Just as leaders like Martin Luther preserved the true gospel during turbulent times, it is necessary for us to rise to the occasion and lead the church in this age of hyperchange.

But we must be clear. It is not enough simply to lead a church; we must lead a church that shines the light of the gospel in a way that balances biblical standards with innovation and theological principle with modernization. Let us draw a clearer picture of such a church—a church without limits, with no roof and with no walls.

Plandemic Leadership

One such recent massive problem where we have needed the guiding hand of God holding onto ours is the COVID Pandemic that shut down churches and businesses around the world. There are many theories surrounding this event: spiritual, political, and scientific, but regardless of any or all of them, it has changed our landscape.

I have been seriously pondering this global shift that overtook the earth in a few short months of time. We became very familiar and even comfortable with hearing the word "pandemic." At the beginning, it was more of a shock and unrealistic. I've been thinking about the leadership differences between pandemic leadership and plandemic leadership. I believe that really, in a nutshell, plandemic leadership summarizes how we're going to move through these uncharted lands with life, ministry, and the fulfillment of the Great Commission. I want to lay some thoughts upon your heart to stir you to action. I pray that the Holy Spirit deposits these thoughts down deep into your soul, into your congregation, into your staff or your friends. I believe there are some distinct differences between pandemic leadership and plandemic leadership. I realize that the pandemic has come and gone. However, we are living in a season earth where more global problems will be coming our way. This teaching will help prepare us to be able to surf over future tidal waves of chaos and keep moving toward our missional goals.

First, when it comes to pandemic leadership, he or she panics and prays. But the plandemic leader pauses, prays and plans.

First, when it comes to pandemic leadership, he or she **panics and prays**. But the plandemic leader **pauses, prays and plans**. At the beginning, this may seem like a subtle difference, but it's a huge difference because this leader chooses to move with a plan The other leader is more reactionary, anxious, and fearful. Usually, the person who runs away because of fear does not necessarily think of the path on which he/she is choosing to run. Before long, he or she has gone days or months in the wrong direction.

Second, the pandemic leader is **moved by fear**. The plandemic leader is **motivated by faith**. When we think of fear, oftentimes, we think of the person who measures a glass of water by being half empty rather than half full. He or she throws a summary over the whole problem and says, one shoe fits all, rather than being more pragmatic in his or her approach. During this timeframe, we have watched governors in America apply this approach to their people. It has been unbiblical, impractical, and unbalanced. Their leadership is measured by fear. They take short little steps instead of believing God can help us to take huge steps.

When it comes to the plandemic leader, they are motivated by faith. I don't mean wishful thinking. I don't mean hopeful thinking. I don't mean just positive thinking. I'm not putting faith in faith or hope in hope. I'm saying that by faith, God will do something in your life.

When I think of Noah, for example, Scripture says that he was moved by the coming flood; there was fear in his heart. Yet, he didn't sit there and wait for the flood to engulf him. God gave him a plan to take him and his family through the flood until they arrived at other side. Instead of being moved by fear, we're to be motivated by faith.

Third, the pandemic leader **worries and waits** whereas the plandemic later **worships and walks**. In other words, when a person is "scared to death," he or she does not move. They are like a deer in headlights. They don't make any changes; they just hope that tomorrow is a little better. They check the news all the time wondering if it's just a little better than it was yesterday. However, the plandemic leader, worships and walks. In other words, he views the opportunity as a worship opportunity and asks God for a path to walk on. When the Lord shows the path, he or she gets on with walking!

About fifteen years ago, I went through a terrible time. During that period in my life, I paused, pondered, and prayed. I asked the Lord to give me a list of winning steps I needed to have in order to walk through what was surrounding my life. I made a list of ten steps to victory. Once I knew the path to take, no matter what was going on that day, I stayed on the winning path. No matter if I got good news or bad news, I stayed true to the list that God gave me. Whether somebody did something good or something ugly to me during that timeframe, I stayed on the list. I challenge you to worship and walk; make a list of the steps you need to take to come out on the other side. Please do not get stuck in the "worry and wait mode," but worship and walk.

Fourth, the pandemic leader **wishes to go back**, but the plandemic leader **works to move forward**. I thank God for history. I thank God for your history and my history. Without our history, we would not have authenticity. There are a lot of things in my life you can have. But there's one thing you can't have and that is my history. Without it, I don't have authenticity and neither do you.

We thank God for what He's done in the past. We thank God for all he has accomplished in our history. One person said many years ago, history just stands for His Story. I like that. We thank God for His Story. But we don't wish to go back. We work to go forward. I submit to you there's not much left back there.

I thank God for the history we can read. I thank God that we can talk to men and women about what has happened in different generations. Yet, I submit to you, we need fresh vigor, vitality, and victory today. We need what God has done yesterday, again today. So, we don't just wish to go back. We work to go forward. We believe that there is victory in the valley and miracles on the mountain. Dr. Kenneth C. Ulmer, Founder of Faithful Central Bible Church says, "The worst place to be is where God was. God did a lot in 'the was' but He is not there today."

The next quality is that the pandemic leader **complains about the problem**, while the plandemic leader will **create a solution**. I like what Dr. Dennis Whatley said so many years ago in Psychology of Winning. If you've never listened to this series, I encourage you to get your copy soon. He said, "You can always spot the losers in life, because they spend all their time making others look bad, so they look good. In other words, he doesn't have to be mature, if he can make someone else look immature. He doesn't have to clean his car, if he can take the keys and scratch up his neighbor's car. He doesn't have to cut his grass if he can toilet paper his neighbor's yard." This is not who we are. We're not going to spend every day in the midst of this pandemic and complain about the problem. We're going to create solutions.

Sixth, the pandemic leader **defines normal in the past**, but a plandemic leader **defends that normal is in the future**. Now, I hope you pay attention to what I am about to say, because Christ is our normal, not the circumstances, not the crowds and not the chaos. Our normal is not found in yesterday, last year, last month, or last decade. Our life in Christ is our normal. I love what Dr. Leonard Sweets said to me earlier this year. He said, "It's not that Christ is behind us pushing us to go forward. Christ is in front of us, pulling us to where He is." Let that statement sink in.

In Psalm 23: 4, David said "I walk through the valley of the shadow of death."

We are not moving into a "new normal." In other words, we are not going to live a compromising life. Watchman Nee used to say, "Many Christians have lived the abnormal Christian life so long, that they think it is normal." I submit to you that we don't need to get back to normal. We need to go forward, not to find a new normal, but the normal that's in Christ Jesus and Him alone. We don't have to compromise. We don't have to water it down. Christ has given us the victory and in Him we walk day by day believing that victory is for us. The pandemic leader thinks about the past and what was normal back then. The plandemic leader moves forward and believes that God has something powerful for him or her today.

Seventh, the pandemic leader **seeks to eliminate**, but the plandemic leader **serves to navigate**. There is a world of difference between elimination and navigation. There are some things you can't change. You can't determine what the laws may be in your area for the pandemic, but you can navigate victoriously for the future. You may not be able to determine what others may say or do, but you can navigate through the critics and cynics to what God has for you.

In Psalm 23: 4, David said "I walk through the valley of the shadow of death." Not stopping or setting up camp but walking through. We can't determine where the sun is, but we can determine where our heart is. We can't determine how deep the valley is, but we know that God is under us and above us and all around us. In addition, David said, "I shall fear no evil." Instead of us seeking to eliminate, let's serve to navigate. Let's navigate our people through this. Let's navigate our churches through this pandemic. Let's navigate our families through this chaotic time. God has a compass for you and me.

The eighth quality is the pandemic leader **allows society to describe them**, but the plandemic leader **allows Scripture to direct them**. There came a time during this pandemic when governments around the world determined what is essential and non-essential. What was so frustrating to me and no doubt to you, was that the Church was listed in the nonessential category. I realize that government leaders should know better than this. Yet, sinners are blinded to the Gospel. For the most part, they don't see the value of the local church. Whether they know it or not, it is Christ and His Church, that keeps a nation or community together!

The Church is in the healing business, in the teaching business, in the holistic value-adding business, in the marriage business and so much more! This is our finest moment if we choose to get a hold of it and not to allow society to describe or define us. Our value and definition are found in Christ. We're going to be defined by Christ and be directed by Scripture.

Ninth, the pandemic leader, **turns inward and holds on**, but the plandemic leader **turns outward and reaches out**. This pandemic gives us the opportunity to evangelize, winning souls and multiply disciples like never before. We're not going to turn inward and hold on hoping that it is going to get better. We're going to reach out like never before.

I'm so thrilled to see the online capacities of churches being developed during this digital age. I submit to you that we need to win the lost at any cost. We must evangelize or we will cease to be essential anywhere. If your church is not interested in winning the lost, making disciples and transforming societies, then probably your church is non-essential. Reinhard Bonnke said, "A church that is not interested in winning the lost, is lost itself."

Lastly, a pandemic leader **mimics the majority**, but the plandemic leader **masters the moment**. This is our finest hour; we are to seize it! God has trusted us with this pandemic. Let's not mess it up!

Let's believe that God will enlarge our life and that He is in the midst of doing something greater and grander than ever before.

Instead of being pandemic led, we're going lead in the pandemic, in pain and problems. We're not going to mimic the majority and walk around with fear and dread and hopelessness. We're going to master the moment, live by faith and walk it out, believing that God orders our steps and our stops. Thus, I challenge you to believe that God's best for you is in the days to come.

I challenge you to motivate your members, measure your momentum and master your moment. Let's believe that God will enlarge our life and that He is in the midst of doing something greater and grander than ever before.

The twenty-first century church must have leaders who are equipped and filled with the Holy Spirit to lead others through these rapidly changing times. As we survey the new territory before us, we realize it is remarkably different from the land through which we have previously journeyed. Old maps will not work in new lands. We need new maps to guide us. If we are dependent on outdated plans and methods for ministry, we will be ineffective. Future ministry requires leaders who are grounded in the Scriptures and understand the culture around them but, most of all, leaders who are responsive to the guidance of the Holy Spirit. Whether you are a pastor or lay leader, you must be empowered with supernatural ability to have an effective ministry in this new millennium.

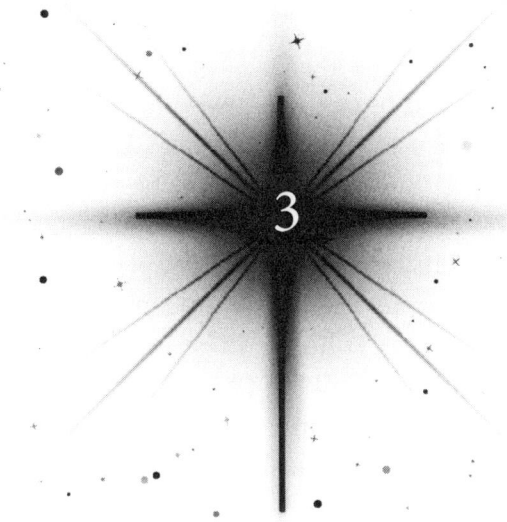

A Church with No Roofs and No Walls

From the 1930s through the 1960s, East Africa experienced a great spiritual revival. Thousands of people committed their lives to Jesus Christ during this period of history. Many different mission organizations and national church leaders joined together to be a part of this mighty move of God. The Africans wanted their church to be "a church with no roof and a church with no walls." A church with no roof has no obstructions to separate it from God's free flow of love, forgiveness, power, and blessings. A church with no walls has no barriers to isolate it from fellow believers in other churches and from those who are without Christ.

The synergistic church is "a church with no roof and no walls." A church with no roof and no walls is one that reaches a postmodern culture without breaking its commitment to orthodox biblical standards. We believe no other theme can better match our desires for discipleship and evangelism. This is really what the Lord Jesus Christ would have His Church look like. In the early days of Christianity before magnificent cathedrals and massive church structures, the body of Christ was not defined by its buildings but by its people. In fact, a church that is known more for its steeple than its people is a church known more for its past than its present. We need to move beyond the limitations of our church culture and become more like the apostolic Church of the first century (Acts 2:42). We must remove the things of this world that prevent us from understanding and connecting with God. We also must put aside the differences and divisive issues that keep us from appreciating and joining others in harmonized ministry. The more we understand how to be united with God and His awesome power, the more we will be able to be unified with each other.

We must remove the things of this world that prevent us from understanding and connecting with God. We also must put aside the differences and divisive issues that keep us from appreciating and joining others in harmonized ministry.

The African revival revealed something many of us have forgotten as we have tried to advance Christ's gospel. We are to work in harmony with God and each other so we can fulfill the will of our heavenly Father. We are to be centers of Christ's love and beacons of God's presence to those around us. We must spiritually strive to be a church with no roof and no walls, to minister beyond the limits that have prevented the church from working in unity and harmony with God and man.

SYNERGY IN MINISTRY

The church of the twenty-first century, the church that ministers beyond limits, is a church that is synergistic. What do we mean by synergistic? Synergy is a business term that is popular in management and leadership circles. The Oxford English Dictionary defines synergy as "joint working, cooperation…that results in increased effectiveness, achievement, etc., produced as a result of combined action or cooperation."[1]

The church of the twenty-first century, the church that ministers beyond limits, is a church that is synergistic. Synergy is a business term that is popular in management and leadership circles. The Oxford English Dictionary defines synergy as "joint working, cooperation…that results in increased effectiveness, achievement, etc., produced as a result of combined action or cooperation."

Synergy is also a scientific term used in biochemistry, pharmacology, and physiology as "the interaction of elements that when combined produce a total effect that is greater than the sum of the individual elements or contributions." The principles of synergy have been in existence from early in history. For centuries, people have worked together to accomplish great tasks that they could not do on their own. The pyramids and the Great Wall of China were not built by one individual but by many people working together. It took the combined effort of everyone involved to achieve the goal. It took synergy.

In the New Testament, the Apostle Paul used *synergeo* in many different contexts to demonstrate that the sum of the whole is greater than its individual parts. In essence, *synergeo* means "to work together, help in work, be partner in labor, to put forth power together with and thereby to assist" (1 Cor. 16:16; 2 Cor. 6:1; Mark 16:20; Rom 8:28).

In Romans 8:28, Paul teaches that God synergizes all things together for His purpose and for our benefit. Think about this for a moment. God shows us how the universe in general and things on earth in particular "work together" to create a greater value than its individual elements.

In Seven Habits of Highly Effective People, Stephen Covey defines his sixth habit, synergy, as "the sum is greater than the whole."[2] However, this only begins to explain the nuances of "synergy," especially as it relates to the church. God created us to live and work in harmony with Him and others in the body of Christ. As we do, He multiplies the results of our combined efforts. He takes the loaves and fish we bring Him and uses them to accomplish the impossible (Matthew 14:13-21).

Every person has been entrusted with gifts and resources that are vital to the well-being of Christ's Church (Romans 12:6-21). As a result, we are all equal and important members of a team. Synergy is developed as each person contributes to the whole. In Covey's words, "The sum product from the team is much greater than the sum total of all the individual achievements."[3]

Synergistic churches are dynamic, living bodies of believers. They work cohesively together to achieve the goals that Christ lays before them just like the various parts of the human body work together to carry out daily activities.

Every person in the church—from top to bottom—works together to fulfill the Great Commission. People must first work in synergy with God, their creator, and then with each other. God provides the direction and guidance while the team of believers serves as the resources and manpower God uses. He uses us as we make ourselves available to Him.

Synergy provides an important energy that helps to propel the ministry of the local church.

Jesus prayed in John 17:21 "that they all may be one; as thou, Father, art in me, and I in thee" (KJV). Unity is not something believers work to attain; rather, unity is the nature of the Church. It is a spiritual benefit of a believer's relationship to Christ, the Head. This is why Paul encourages us to "preserve" the unity of the Church, not to create or manufacture it (Ephesians 4:3).

Synergy is closely related to unity. Christ's desire for His disciples was not only that they would be one in the Holy Spirit but also that they would achieve more together than they could accomplish alone. Synergy is this dynamic that occurs among a local body of believers who are dedicated to walking together in the unity of Christ. A synergistic church is one that is committed to the practical implementation of Christ's prayer in John 17:21 and, because of that commitment, enjoys the fruit of multiplied effectiveness.

The synergistic church advances the kingdom of God with greater effectiveness because it utilizes every member and all its resources to the maximum potential. It is a church focused on bringing people together with Christ and with each other. Synergy is formed and strengthened through relationships. The priority of synergistic churches is to disciple believers and help them develop a committed, growing relationship with Jesus Christ and then to form strong relationships with other believers. This exemplifies the community of faith Jesus Christ desires. When we are part of a community that values one another, the lost are attracted to Christ's kingdom. Everybody is a somebody in the body of Christ.

PEOPLE-CENTERED, NOT PROGRAM-DRIVEN

People are not looking for a program to follow, but a powerful vision to embrace. Relationships require one key ingredient—people. The church of the twenty-first century is not only made up of people, but it is also focused on people. Synergy requires the cultivation of relationships that produce trust and accountability. This involves more than small group meetings or clever programs. It requires a continual emphasis on encouraging people to connect with God and each other. A synergistic church is people-centered because it is Christ-centered. Jesus came to save people and build strong relationships while He was on earth.

We must develop our programs based upon the needs of people. The church exists for the purpose of ministering to people. In the past, churches have been tempted to emphasize events and programs more than people. A successful church may have a strong bus ministry, Vacation Bible School, day care, youth activities, or whatever the popular program of the day might be. This is not to devalue the importance of quality programs and events for they are necessary parts of the local church. If we are not careful, however, the program becomes more important than the people coming to the program. Programs are justifiable only as long as they meet the needs of the people who attend them. As members of the body of Christ, we must make the people of the church one of our top priorities.

Christ cared enough for people that He died on the cross for their sins. We should care enough about people to introduce them to our Savior and help them grow in Him. The generation of Gen Xers, Millennials Gen Z-ers, do not appreciate a program-centered church. They are looking for authentic, experiential faith that meets them where they are and allows them to be a part of a greater spiritual picture. They need a place to connect and belong so they can receive from God and others. This is where the synergistic church can meet the needs of a new generation.

Synergistic churches do not just have events or programs for the program's sake. They structure what they are doing to meet people's needs and fulfill their God-given mission. They understand that people are important to God; therefore, they must be important to the church.

INTERDEPENDENCE VS. INDEPENDENCE

Synergy is achieved through the Holy Spirit who enables us to work interdependently with each other. To truly achieve synergy, the leadership and members of the church must live their lives under the principle of interdependence. It is important to understand the impact of this concept on the local church. To achieve interdependent synergy, openness, and authenticity are required. Unbiblical power structures and struggles must be left behind, and biblical paradigms of teamwork and trust must be embraced. Leadership and authority are shared with the team thereby empowering every part of the church to be active in the mission of the church. The synergistic church emphasizes interdependence, not religious hierarchy.

To truly achieve synergy, the leadership and members of the church must live their lives under the principle of interdependence.

This synergistic approach utilizes the God-given gifts of each member of the church. This is true within the local church as well as in the Church, universally. Synergistic churches carry the interdependence from their own church to the community. The spirit of competition gives way to the spirit of cooperation as the body of Christ works together to reach its community, providing vital assistance to the needy and leadership to the city.

The days of territorialism and "sheep stealing" must be long gone. The synergistic church, the church of the future, will be a church "where the logos and egos are left at the door." It will not be concerned with personal advancement and prestige. What is most important is that people are being transformed by Christ. The independent spirit of Christian mavericks creates Christian hermits in a world where networking has become vitally important. At the other extreme, if we do not pay heed to this, our churches will become mere community centers full of much activity but not much accomplishment, busyness, not business.

VISIONARY LEADERS FOR A NEW TIME

The greatest asset for building the synergistic church is strong leadership. Paul writes, "And He gave some as apostles, and some as prophets, and some as evangelists, and some as pastors and teachers, for the equipping of the saints for the work of service, to the building up of the body of Christ" (Ephesians 4:11-12). One of the most important people in any community is a Spirit-filled pastor. One of the greatest assets to any city is the presence of a pastor who hears from God and is not afraid to act in obedience. The greatest asset to any church is believers who are filled with the Holy Spirit and are committed to working together for the cause of Jesus Christ. The synergistic church is filled with laity, pastors, church leaders, evangelists, missionaries, and counselors who are working in harmony with God's direction and in cooperation with each other.

This key component of the church and the community is often overlooked. Church leaders are typically underpaid and underappreciated. They face spiritual battles in addition to the normal challenges of everyday life. We value each of these pastors highly and pray earnestly that God would bless and anoint them for a ministry that is even more effective than before. God did not intend for them to wander powerless and alone in the harvest field to which He called them. The future of the church is in the hands of its present leaders. They must determine now what kind of leader they will be—independent mavericks or synergistic leaders. They need to know who they are in Christ and why God has called them into ministry.

The church of the future will need leaders who are constantly being changed into the image of Christ. They must live in humility before God and submit themselves to the Holy Spirit's direction. The synergistic church will need leaders who live interdependently in their communities. In fact, Jesus taught that the one who seeks to be a leader must be a servant of all.

THE IMPORTANCE OF LEADERSHIP

John Maxwell has said, "Everything rises and falls on leadership."[4] Barriers will be encountered by every church leader. Leaders must break through these barriers and limitations that have handcuffed the growth of their churches. These barriers will become the stepping stones to greatness when overcome through faith and determination. Great leaders focus on the value and purpose of trials, not the pain.

A God-inspired vision is worth living for, but a God-given cause is worth dying for.

Despite the seemingly insurmountable barriers, we believe the greatest days of the church are ahead. Statisticians report that there are more people coming to Christ every day than ever before. The future of the church rests in the strength of its leaders. If the leadership is inadequate, the church will not prosper. If the leadership simply maintains, then the church will never progress. However, if the leadership of the church is determined to move forward, then the church will also grow.

We must know the difference between having a "cause" and having a vision for our lives and ministries. A God-inspired vision is worth living for, but a God-given cause is worth dying for.

Jesus said, "If anyone wishes to come after Me, he must deny himself, and take up his cross and follow Me" (Mark 8:34b). We must be committed to a cause worth getting up for every day, something worth dying for.

Many books are available on leadership and management, and The Synergistic Church joins a growing list of books for Christian leaders. However, this is not a book on how to do leadership. This book is about being, not doing. After over forty years of ministry, it has become clear that one must be something before one can do something. We have also discovered that one must be something before one can say something. This book will not give quick-fix steps to implement in your church to experience church growth. The distinctive of the synergistic church is what we must become in Christ if we are to accomplish our mission and goal. This is even more important as the Information Age engulfs us.

> **Becoming an effective leader is a lifelong journey, not a singular event. It is a process spiritual transformation that takes place every day in the life of a follower of Jesus Christ.**

In *The Telecosm*, George Gilder, has been a textbook for my course on Visionary Leadership, states that information and the speed with which that information is reaching us double every six months.[5] Bombarded by competing voices, people are not looking for information givers; they are looking for someone to help them use that information to take them where they long to be. They are looking for a leader. Becoming an effective leader is a lifelong journey, not a singular event. It is a process spiritual transformation that takes place every day in the life of a follower of Jesus Christ. That transformation is begun in us by Christ and continues every day of our lives through the power of the Holy Spirit (Philippians 1:6).

The Apostle Paul lived the life of a synergistic leader. Paul had been to all the right schools, was an expert in the Law and the Prophets, was a friend of the disciples, and even saw a vision of Christ; yet he submitted himself to the process of daily transformation. This apostle who had seen the risen Christ on the Damascus Road realized the necessity of dying daily (Galatians 2:2). He was dependent upon the Spirit of God to transform him into whom he needed to become in Christ. While his physical body was experiencing the aging process, his inner man was being renewed every day (2 Corinthians 4:16). Reliance on Jesus Christ and a willingness to be led by the Holy Spirit made Paul a powerful servant leader.

In Galatians 5:16-26, Paul revealed the fruit of the Spirit which are also the fruit of successful ministry: love, joy, peace, patience, kindness, goodness, faithfulness, gentleness, and self-control. A present-day leader's ministry depends upon the Spirit's guidance just like Paul's did. Even Paul, who wrote a significant portion of the New Testament, needed the daily guidance of the Spirit. Paul's ministry effectiveness was directly proportionate to the health of his relationship with God.

THE SYNERGISTIC LEADER

The distinctiveness of the synergistic church must also be embraced by the leadership of that church. Too many times, those in church leadership do not differentiate between their own spiritual walk with God and their church work. If the church is going well, then their spiritual life is going well. If the church is struggling, then they are struggling. It is obvious that these two areas of the minister's life may be related, but they are not equal. All who are called upon to lead God's people must be wholly committed to Jesus Christ. They must be something before they do something.

When we assume that our hard work and effort are the equivalent of devotion and humility before God, we make a grave mistake. It is then that we focus more on doing than being. It is a faith that is lived with our hands but not found in our hearts. There is no synergy with God as we minister. We work for Him rather than with Him. We work independently rather than inviting Him to live in us and through us.

Others are so task-oriented they do not have time to relate to the people to whom they are ministering. New converts are just another "notch on their spiritual gun." These people constantly compare the number of people in attendance or the size of their latest event with other churches and pastors. Conversations with these people always revolve around the three B's: buildings, budgets, and bodies. It almost seems that a larger sanctuary, a bigger budget, and more bodies have greater importance than relationships or life change in their congregations. Sadly, these kinds of leaders seek to achieve a celebrity status because of pride and arrogance. They view themselves as apart from the common believer, thinking they are in a different "class" because of the ministry they have built. They lack the relationships that result from synergy, and soon the kingdom they have built will crumble away. These leaders bring shame to the Church of Jesus Christ. They will not be able to continue this prima donna attitude on the new frontier of ministry.

Synergistic leaders are not consumed with "territories" and denominationalism but with reaching the lost for Christ.

People today desire leaders to whom they can relate—those who are real and who serve in humility before Christ; those who are not afraid to reveal their weaknesses, knowing that others will work with them to compensate for their deficiencies. They know that in return they will help others to utilize the many talents and gifts God has given them. These leaders are necessary for the growth and health of the church. It is these kinds of leaders who have the confidence to work together with other leaders to reach their communities for Christ.

Synergistic leaders are not consumed with "territories" and denominationalism but with reaching the lost for Christ. They trust God to guide them as they build the synergistic church on the new frontier. It is a frontier that takes them far beyond anything they can ask or even imagine. It is a ministry that is truly beyond all limits.

SILO LEADER VS SYNERGISTIC LEADER

Over the last twenty years, I have been asked a lot of questions regarding synergizing pastors and leaders toward the fulfillment of the Great Commission. I encourage you to read, my book entitled, *How To Make Your Net Work*, if you are serious about networking to accomplish a goal bigger than yourself. The question I have been asked the most is, "What is the greatest challenge you have faced in the building of the Global Church Network (GCNW.tv). The greatest challenge by far is the changing of mindsets of pastors, Christian leaders, and business leaders. How we view our world at large and the Body of Christ in this world, will determine how we set our missional goals in our community, country, and continents. We see the Church through the lens of who we truly are in life. With this before us, note carefully the differences between silo thinking and synergistic thinking.

First, silo leaders **set unrealistic missional goals**. Even though they believe the missional goal is realistic, over time it will become apparent that the goals are not realistic. Of course, if the goals are small, like growing the local by 50 people over the previous year or increasing the organization/denomination by 10% in the next twelve months, then, the silo leader can most likely figure out a plan to achieve it. However, when it comes to fulfilling the Great Commission, it is not impractical, but impossible for one person or one organization to accomplish it.

Why is the silo approach unrealistic? First, because it is the commission, not the mission. Second, with the growth of population, now at eight billion, headed to nine billion in the next ten years; it is not remotely possible for a silo person or organization to complete the Great Commission.

Synergistic leaders **set realistic goals**. They know from the beginning that it is not possible to accomplish the Great Commission by themselves or by their organization/denomination alone. These leaders take the long look instead of the short look in ministry. They believe it is possible to grow their local churches and/or their organizations/denominations, while at the same time synergizing with others toward finishing the Great Commission.

We must never forget, if we are going to finalize the Great Commission, it is the wind of the Spirit, that moves the leaves, that moves the limbs, and the tree.

Second, silo leaders **possess a** spirit of superiority. These leaders believe that their doctrine and distinctives are superior to everyone else's. I know of one major denomination that used to sing a song with these words, "The _____ is right, hallelujah to the Lamb."

Additionally, silo leaders have become "tree huggers." They used to believe that it is the wind that moves the leaves, that moves the limbs, that moves the tree. Yet, today, they believe they can shake the tree to move the limbs and the leaves. We must never forget, if we are going to finalize the Great Commission, it is the wind of the Spirit, that moves the leaves, that moves the limbs, and the tree. We could never do this alone, no matter how big we have become.

I learned this leadership lesson more than 20 years ago. On one occasion, I was visiting with a Pentecostal leader friend at his office. While we were talking, he began to share condescending words about a close non-Pentecostal leader friend of mine. The essence of the words being shared with me was if this leader was like him, then he could have accomplished more in his life. While he was sharing this, I thought to myself, he does not even know my friend or know the prayer life of him.

When our meeting was over, when I got into my car to drive home, I prayed, "Lord, please teach an important networking lesson from this encounter." The Lord whispered to me, "It is always easier to network with a person who knows there is more of the Lord and hungry to experience it, than it is to work with a person who believes he/she has it all and is no longer hungry."

Synergistic leaders **practice a spirit of humility**. They realize upfront that they are not the "gospel sheriff." They choose the onramp of relationships throughout their city or throughout the Body of Christ. Synergistic leaders do not push down what God has raised up. They take the time to get to know fellow Brothers and Sisters in Christ.

The late Dr. Bill Bright, the Founder of Campus Crusade for Christ (Today, Cru), used to say to me, "The main issue is not how long we can live, but how long we can love. A lot of leaders have stopped loving a long time before they stopped living." Repeatedly, the Apostle Paul said, "love all the saints" and to "pray for all the saints." Do you love all the saints? Do you pray for all the saints?

When it comes to achieving a local, national, or global missional goal of evangelism and discipleship, humble synergistic leaders reach out to tie relational knots to build a net that works. No knot, no net. They keep the main thing the main thing. And the main thing for a synergistic leader is to keep the main the main thing. The main thing is finalizing the Great Commission.

Third, silo leaders mainly **focus on egos and logos**. They view their church name or denomination name as the brand. I remember receiving an invitation to go and speak to a significant organization about networking. The leader shared with me, "We really desire to learn how to network, but we are concerned about losing our brand."

Please do not misunderstand. When the Lord calls us to begin a church or an organization, it is important that we represent and steward our ministry. I fully subscribe to this responsibility and mentality. Yet, there are those individuals who come only to pick fruitful relationships for their cause and not the greater cause, the Great Commission. Some years ago, I watched a well-known author have the unethical audacity to meet with leaders in our green room at the biennial Synergize Conference (Synergize.tv) to raise money for his organization. He was so siloed that he was willing to not only pick the fruit that he did not grow but receive an offering from where he did not sow.

Synergistic leaders **focus on we go** instead of egos and logos. An old African proverb is: If you wish to go fast, go alone; if you wish to go far, bring others with you. Just think about this truth for a moment. In every glorious endeavor, in every grand business, in every great athlete, there is a "we go." I challenge you to research history and you will conclude, that if I am going to move from success to significance, I am going to need a lot of amazing friends in my life. While the silo leader is willing to die for doctrinal distinctives, the synergistic leader believes it is possible to respect all the different distinctives in the Body of Christ and complete the Great Commission at the same time.

As it relates to synergizing, mobilizing and finalizing the Great Commission, the "we go" philosophy is a must in order to cross the finish line. For too long, the Church has been in the wishing circle instead of the winning circle. The wishing circle is filled with egos and logos, but the winning circle is filled with the "we go".

Synergistic leaders realize that the brand is Jesus and not their local church, parachurch or denomination. Jesus is the greatest magnetic force of all. Yet, over the last 25 years, particularly in the Western world, local churches have adopted the attraction model instead of the missional model. In other words, if we can make our local church appealing enough people will come. I believe we should vacuum the church, clean our bathroom, have excellent music, incredible preaching and a phenomenal website. I believe all of this and more.

Nevertheless, the greatest and grandest magnetic force of all time is Jesus Christ. We will not find anywhere in the New Testament, where the lost are commanded to attend the local church. However, we will find commandments where we are told to go out and compel them to come to the house of God. If we would make "Jesus the brand," and lift Him as high as possible, our churches will grow, and our denominations and fellowships will glow!

> *Synergistic leaders know that the Church does not have a shortage of fish, but a shortage of laborers.*

Silo leaders are **selfish regarding the harvest**. They find it difficult to share the harvest, because they are convinced that their doctrinal view is more accurate than others. As a result of this, not only will they fail at finalizing the Great Commission, but they do also not have as many friends as they possibly could. This approach to ministry is one of a small pie mentality instead of an unlimited pie ministry.

Synergistic leaders **share regarding the harvest**. I am sure you are familiar with the story of Peter fishing all night and not catching any fish. Then, in the morning, though exhausted, Peter meets Jesus. Jesus commands him to cast his nets on the other side of the boat. There is a miraculous catch of fish, and the nets are breaking. Peter has a huge decision to make and does not have much time to make it. If he decides to keep all the fish and try to get them in the boat, he will lose the entire catch and have an empty net. What does Peter do? He calls for the other boats nearby. There was enough fish to fill Peter's boat and the other boats.

Synergistic leaders know that the Church does not have a shortage of fish, but a shortage of laborers. Jesus said, "the harvest is plentiful, but the laborers are few." We give praise to the Lord for the growth of the Church worldwide and for the great number of laborers. Yet, we do not have enough laborers to finish the Great Commission.

Are you willing to share the fish and trust the Lord with His harvest? The harvest is not ours. We do not save the lost; but only present the Gospel to them. Jesus does the saving, and we do the discipling. The saving work is the easiest work. Jesus can save anyone. Discipling is the hardest work the local church or the Church does each year.

The silo leader tries to bring the breaking net into his/her boat. The synergistic leader invites the other boats to join him/her in gathering the harvest. He or she knows it is far better to share the harvest and have multiple boats filled, rather than lose the harvest altogether. Are you willing to share the harvest, even if it means that newly saved people end up in a different church or denomination or fellowship?

Last, but not least, silo leaders and synergistic leaders **measure success differently**. Silo pastors celebrates that his/her local church is growing while his/her city remains lost year after year. I am sure that this is not intention. Synergistic pastors rejoice with the growth of their churches but at the same time allocates 10% to 15% of their time to building relational bridges into their community and city.

Several years ago, I was fortunate to minister in a local church for nearly two weeks in revival services. The Lord was saving the lost, ministering to the sick and empowering believers. While I was there, on one afternoon, I was fortunate to teach the lead team of the church. After our teaching session, I mentioned to the pastor, that when I depart for the hotel, I was thinking about driving across the street to try to meet the pastor of a different church of a different denomination. When I mentioned this, the pastor said, "Please do not do this."

I responded, "Why not?"

He said, "I have never walked or driven across the street to meet him."

My response was, "Do you believe he is on our team? Do you realize that you will never win, much less reach this large city without him?"

The silo leader can grow his or her church, but will not reach his or her city, nation or world. The synergistic leader will grow and go and not dry and die.

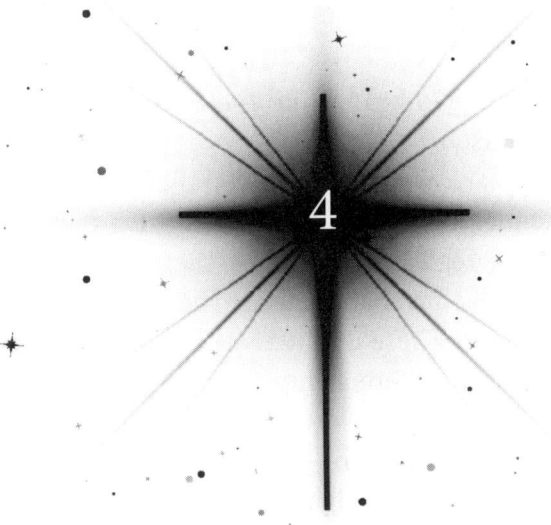

The Synergistic Church Blueprint

In Chapter 1, we surveyed the new world that is in transition around us. We discussed the necessity of changing how we see the world and the importance of understanding the Information Age in which we live. We believe the church God is building for the future is a church that is built upon the principle of synergy. While each church is unique, all must work together to meet the needs of ministry in a changing world. It may be a challenge for some to abandon old forms and ingrained traditions. Unlike many strategies for ministry, we will not highlight the six steps to building a church or the three necessary programs that will make a church grow. These kinds of "secret steps of church growth" will not help in the twenty-first century.

The principles and plans that have made one church grow may not work in another church. The diversity that has resulted from the digital world and globalization creates new challenges for churches. The needs of a church in Collegeville, Arkansas, will be different from Los Angeles, California. That is why this book is not a quick fix to church growth. There are no shortcuts to true growth. Only God can build the Church and draw men and women to Himself.

Through the years, we have observed that the churches that apply the principles of synergy see the most growth. Though their needs and strategies are different, these churches all have common distinctives that enable them to be effective lighthouses in their communities. These distinctives are not exhaustive nor the answer for every problem a church will face.

They are by no means the be-all and end-all of planting and growing a church, but they are vitally important to the fulfillment of Christ's mandate to advance the gospel.

The crusade in East Africa provided us a slogan that illustrates the genius of the synergistic church. The synergistic church is a church with no roofs and no walls. Just as on the Day of Pentecost, the fire of heaven can fall upon us because there is no roof to block its descent and the wind of the Spirit can blow across us because there are no walls to hinder its flow. It is our prayer that God will spark the flames of revival in every church and spread it by the wind of the Holy Spirit.

A CHURCH WITH NO ROOFS

The East African church understood that the most important aspect of any church is its vital connection with God. When the roof is off, nothing blocks the Spirit of God from moving in and among His people. It experienced a massive revival that swept much of Africa for many years because of its connection with God. There are four characteristics or distinctives of an unhindered, synergistic relationship with God: confidence, calling, character, and commitment. Each is an answer to the limits a church must move beyond. Synergy moves us beyond what we can become or achieve by ourselves.

Beyond Fear and Self-Reliance

The church without a proper understanding of who God is and how He works in our lives is limited in its impact in this world. Without the assurance of the sovereign work of God, we are left to take the ministry of Christ into our own hands and rely on our own power to accomplish the will of God. Worse yet, we can become so afraid of the results of our actions that we never do anything. World events such as the destruction of the World Trade Center, the rise of terrorism, war, identity theft, and much more can cause fear to grip the world and even the church when we do not trust in God. Some are prevented from moving forward because of fear of the unknown. Both limitations—self-reliance and fear—stem from a misunderstanding of who God is and where we place our confidence. When we do not place our faith and trust in an all-powerful God who desires to bless us because of His unfailing love, we are forced to step out in our own strength or not step out at all.

Paul writes in 2 Timothy 1:7: "God has not given us a spirit of timidity, but of power and love and discipline." We know we have nothing to fear because when the roof is off, we place our confidence in God. We can see Him at work on our behalf, and we respond to Him in faith. We know He is working in us to do the work He has called us to do. Scripture tells us to "trust in the Lord with all your heart and do not lean on your own understanding. In all your ways acknowledge Him, and He will make your paths straight" (Proverbs 3:5-6). By having a clearer understanding of God's magnificent attributes, we do not rely on our own strength but trust in Him to provide for us. We reflect His glory to the world as we learn more and more about who God is. As a result, we trust in God's character, rely on His Word for guidance, and depend on His Spirit to empower us to live holy lives.

Beyond Doubt and Uncertainty

Laurie Beth Jones in her book, The Path, states that the number one fear of people is having lived a meaningless life.[1] In the midst of change, a sense of uncertainty plagues the church and the world. This uncertainty has caused many to doubt the work they are doing or doubt the things they thought were true. James 1:6 tells us that "the one who doubts is like the surf of the sea, driven and tossed by the wind." When we doubt our calling, we cannot persevere in the ministry because we lack the assurance of knowing that we are really called to do what we are doing.

In saving His harshest words for religious leaders whose character did not match their words, Jesus taught that one of the greatest mistakes of ministry is to misrepresent the gospel through an unfaithful, hypocritical lifestyle.

Researchers tell us that the average length of stay for pastors is continually decreasing. Church leaders are leaving the ministry every day because they question their calling. As the world changes rapidly around us, it is important that ministers of the gospel do not let uncertainty and doubt influence them. Those who minister for Christ must know they are called to preach the gospel. When the roof is off, we trust in the calling of God. Unfortunately, there are too many people attempting to lead the church who have never been called to do so. The call of God upon the lives of ministers is the anchor that gives them stability as the rest of the world crumbles. Because of their calling, Jeremiah, Isaiah, and Ezekiel could each trust in the message they were delivering despite the attacks of their enemies and the lack of response from their hearers (Jeremiah 1; Isaiah 6; Ezekiel 3). Jesus did not begin His earthly ministry until after He had fasted and sought His Father's face for forty days. There is no better way to determine God's call. If you are in doubt of your calling, follow the Lord's example. It is imperative that all leaders understand the nature and power of their ministerial calling. We can trust in this calling when trials and setbacks occur for, we know we have a divine commission.

Beyond Hypocrisy and Unfaithfulness

The world is looking for people who live consistent, godly lives. Most individuals are aware of their own shortcomings. They look to others who can model as well as preach holy living. Sadly, the church world has often neglected modeling faith as well as preaching faith. Hypocrisy has long been a deserved accusation against the church. We cannot allow our effectiveness to be limited by an inability to live like Jesus wants us to live. Synergistic churches minister beyond the limits of hypocrisy and unfaithfulness. When the roof is off, our character is constantly being molded into the image of Christ. Christ works in us to develop this character. Romans 12:1-2 admonishes us to be transformed by God. In Romans 12:9, we are commanded to love without hypocrisy, living consistent lives. As His vessels, we open to God, and He shapes us into what we need to be and whom we need to become through Him. He transforms us as the potter transforms lumps of clay into works of art. He helps us to overcome sin in our lives and gives us the strength to fulfill the ministry He calls us to do. In saving His harshest words for religious leaders whose character did not match their words, Jesus taught that one of the greatest mistakes of ministry is to misrepresent the gospel through an unfaithful, hypocritical lifestyle. The synergistic leader is a leader whose character is in harmony with Christ.

Beyond Self-Centeredness and Idolatry

The life of faith is a life that is devoted to God. When we acknowledge Jesus Christ as our Lord and Savior, we are committed to following Him as His disciple. Discipleship requires us to obey Christ's commands. Disobedience reveals our self-centeredness and lack of devotion. By placing our own needs or desires before Christ's commands, we fall victim to a form of idolatry. Titus 1:15-16 says: "To the pure, all things are pure; but to those who are defiled and unbelieving, nothing is pure, but both their mind and their conscience are defiled. They profess to know God, but by their deeds they deny Him, being detestable and disobedient and worthless for any good deed."

When the roof is off, synergistic churches demonstrate wholehearted surrender to God.

We demonstrate our commitment to God by communicating with Him through prayer and fasting (Acts 13:3; 14:23). We also demonstrate our commitment to God by focusing our lives and thoughts on Him through praise and worship (Luke 24:53; Acts 2:47) as well as aggressively pursuing the fulfillment of the Great Commission (Matthew 28:19-20).

A lack of devotion will limit the connection we have with God because we value ourselves and other things as being more important than God (1 Samuel 15:1-23). This violates the very foundations of our faith. When we live a life of commitment, we move beyond the limits of our own shortcomings. In order to pastor a synergistic church, we must be willing to allow the wind of the Holy Spirit to blow the roof off.

A CHURCH WITH NO WALLS

The African church experienced revival because its walls were down. The synergistic church does not keep God's presence inside. It is not enough simply to receive God's presence; we must share Him with the world around us. We are a church that has no walls. We biblically and practically approach the community around us to create a center of refreshing and power.

We are open to the eyes of the world, modeling before them the Spirit-filled life that results from the roof being off. We are acting as salt and light to the world. The walls that once held us in have fallen and now serve as bridges to the world around us. We represent real, authentic faith and invite the world to come and join in our worship of the creator. The synergistic church is in the middle of the marketplace, working and growing as a beacon of hope to those who need it. The openness of the synergistic church is seen and felt in four distinctives: cooperation, communication, compassion, and creativity. Each distinctive helps the church move beyond the limitations it faces.

Beyond Jealousy and Isolationism

It is sad that for too long the church has been known for isolationism and jealousy rather than cooperation. Many churches and pastors view themselves as small kingdoms that compete with other rival churches for people and profits. When God moves in one church, other churches often do not rejoice in God's outpouring of blessing but ridicule them and become jealous. These limitations have prevented churches from efficiently reaching their communities and modeling the love for each other that Christ commanded.

Synergistic churches are not afraid to partner with other churches and groups because they live beyond the limits of isolation and jealousy. We must not be concerned with "who gets the converts" or whether "my church is bigger than your church." We must work together in love and humility as we preach the gospel. This kind of unity in spirit was what Paul prayed would happen in the Philippian church:

Therefore, if there is any encouragement in Christ, if there is any consolation of love, if there is any fellowship of the Spirit, if any affection and compassion, make my joy complete by being of the same mind, maintaining the same love, united in spirit, intent on one purpose. Do nothing from selfishness or empty conceit, but with humility of mind regard one another as more important than yourselves; do not merely look out for your own personal interests, but also for the interests of others (Philippians 2:1-4).

Those who need a helping hand should not have to turn to the government for assistance but should find the church to be a place where they can receive physical and spiritual healing.

When the walls are down, the church cooperates with those around them. The principles of synergy and interdependence should mark every avenue of church life. We serve each other in humility knowing that when we do, we model the attitude of Christ (Philippians 2:5-8). Synergistic churches find ways to model cooperation across racial, economic, denominational, and social lines. The walls have come down and the bricks that have fallen are used to build bridges to unite us. While it is easier to build fences than bridges, we must be willing to exchange our personal, manmade fences for God-given bridges to a world without hope or truth.

Beyond Ambiguity and Irrelevance

Communication is vital to the life of the twenty-first-century church. Never before have we experienced such an explosion of information. Technology has increased the number of people in the world communicating with one another. Direct broadcast and streaming services have brought an unimaginable number of entertainment and information channels into every home, and nearly everyone has access to mobile devices and technology.

The number of "voices" the average person hears has increased exponentially. The church's voice and message must be clear and relevant as we make our way in the new century, speaking to the world around us.

Paul reminds us: "For if the bugle produces an indistinct sound, who will prepare himself for battle?" (1 Corinthians 14:8). Our message must be understandable to everyone. When the walls are down, the church demonstrates effective communication. The synergistic leader and the synergistic church give a clear message. The greatest truths die in the minds of those who cannot articulate them. If we do not preach the message to the lost, they will never hear the message of the gospel. If they do not hear, they will not be able to believe (Romans 10:14). While the world is awash with many piercing, opposing, seductive messages and sounds demanding attention, the church must sound a clear call of repentance that speaks to the heart of the culture around it.

Beyond Apathy and Insensitivity

Those who need a helping hand should not have to turn to the government for assistance but should find the church to be a place where they can receive physical and spiritual healing. The church should also be active in love. The Church of Jesus Christ is the recipient of the greatest gift of compassion and love the world has ever seen. It was because God loved us that He gave His Son to die for us (John 3:16). As recipients of God's love and compassion, we must reflect that love to the world as well. An apathetic church does not care what is going on around it, forgetting that it was love that first brought its members to Christ. It is more concerned about its own needs than the needs of others. We must pray that God will remove our insensitivity to the hurts of others and make us aware of community needs. "If a brother or sister is without clothing and in need of daily food, and one of you says to them, 'Go in peace, be warmed and be filled,' and yet you do not give them what is necessary for their body, what use is that?" (James 2:15-16).

We must minister the love of Christ beyond the limitations of apathy and insensitivity. When the walls are down, the church is filled with heartfelt compassion. In fact, it is this compassion for a hurting world that contributed to the fall of these walls. Compassion motivates us to carry the good news of the gospel to those who are lost. It forces us to value the families who make up our churches and plan ways to strengthen them. It is through "compassion ministries" that we make a significant impact on today's society. As believers, we are to be devoted to each other in love while at the same time not forgetting those who are in need around us (Romans 12:10-16).

Beyond Closed Mindedness and Inflexibility

For the church to continue to be a powerful voice in its community, it must stay on the cutting edge of creativity. While the message of the gospel is sharp and powerful, we must not present it in outdated, ineffective forms (Hebrews 4:12). We cannot expect the methods of yesterday to hold fast today when the world around us has changed so rapidly. We must use the latest in technology to make our message relevant and timely. We are not bound by old paradigms but must constantly strive to be on the cutting edge. Those who choose to be close-minded and inflexible have not heeded the words of Jesus: "no one puts new wine into old wineskins; otherwise the new wine will burst the skins and it will be spilled out, and the skins will be ruined" (Luke 5:37).

The synergistic church ministers beyond the limitations of inflexibility and close-mindedness. When the walls are down, the church is on the cutting edge of creativity. The church that is ineffective in communicating the gospel must adapt its methods to the changing culture. Inflexibility prevents the church from moving forward with statements like, "We have never done it that way before." Through creativity, synergistic leaders must focus their minds to achieve innovation and spur imagination.

A CHURCH THAT MODELS INTERDEPENDENCE

The synergistic church and its leadership create greater value by working together rather than by working independently. Their interdependence enables them to accomplish the tasks Christ entrusted to them. Through their confidence, calling, character, and commitment, they are able to move beyond the limitations of fear, self-reliance, doubt, uncertainty, hypocrisy, unfaithfulness, self-centeredness, and idolatry because the roof is off their church. Through cooperation, communication, compassion, and creativity, they can move beyond the limitations of apathy, insensitivity, ambiguity, irrelevance, jealousy, isolationism, inflexibility, and close-mindedness because the walls are down in their church.

The eight distinctives mentioned above work together to creative an effective pulpit ministry as depicted in the illustration on the following page. These distinctives of the synergistic church are not new or unique. In fact, many of these characteristics are seen in action in your ministry and church. However, we all must focus our lives and energies on the task of helping to fulfill the Great Commission in the twenty-first century. It is the Holy Spirit who has enabled us to be a part of so many different ministries and still maintain the essentials of biblical faith.

These distinctives become the bedrock for building a synergistic church. They are discussed in detail in the following chapters. As you read, write down ideas and thoughts that challenge you. Capitalize on the concepts the Holy Spirit births in you by making them a part of your own spiritual journey as well as your church's. We pray your life will be lived in synergistic harmony as the Spirit of God allows you to live your life in a church that has "no roof and no walls."

PART TWO

A CHURCH WITH NO ROOFS

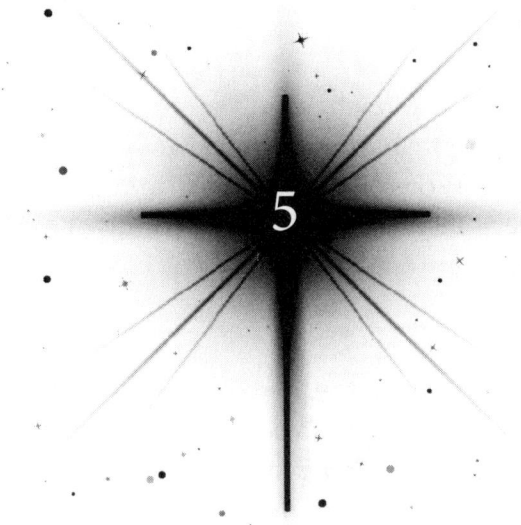

Our Confidence in God

Jesus Christ gave the most effective strategy for church growth over two thousand years ago. While teaching His disciples, He told them, "I will build my church and the gates of Hell will not prevail against it" (Matthew 16:18). True church growth is when Jesus Christ builds His Church by drawing people to Himself. Speaking of His death, He said, "If I be lifted up from the earth, I will draw all men unto me" (John 12:32 KJV). Despite the problems the world is facing today and the enormous challenges and struggles the evangelical church must overcome, God is still building His church.

The essential element of the synergistic church is the realization that God is in control of all that we do and all that we are. We are centered on God as a church, as a body, and as individuals.

While others may doubt the future and run from the many adversities that come our way, we have confidence—faith—that we can continue in the mission we have been called to accomplish because of our relationship under our sovereign, all-powerful, loving God and Savior.

We can live and grow beyond the limits of fear and disappointment because we have faith in the God whom we serve. We have faith in His Word to guide us through the new territories into which He is leading us. We have faith that His Spirit will enable us to move into new depths of His love.

Despite the problems the world is facing today and the enormous challenges and struggles the evangelical church must overcome, God is still building His church.

This confidence in God enables us to fulfill our calling in life. It enables us to know that God, the grand architect of the Church, is working today to build His Church through us. If we will be diligent to hear His voice and lift Him up before all of humanity, He will continue to draw them to Himself. This synergistic approach—God working through us—is the only way the church will ever be truly built on a solid foundation beyond the limits that now restrict the church's impact. The synergistic church and its leadership rely upon God to guide them by His Spirit and His Word. We work in harmony with Him as we travel the course He has charted before us.

THE PERSONHOOD OF GOD BIRTHS CONFIDENCE

Many years ago, Dr. James Montgomery Boice of the Bible Hour radio program interviewed Dr. Bill Bright for his radio show. One of the first questions asked was, "What is the most important truth to teach any follower of Christ?" Dr. Bright said he felt the Holy Spirit answer through him saying, "The attributes of God." This launched a journey of discovery and learning about God that resulted in his highly recommended book, GOD: Discover His Character.

Everything about our lives—our attitudes, motives, dreams, actions, words, perceptions, literature, music, and interaction with others—is influenced by our view of God.

We react to the situations of life based upon our beliefs about God. If we have a wrong view, it leads to problems in every other part of our life. It also affects the lives of everyone we influence. Leaders define their ministry through understanding who God is, what God does, and where God leads them. It gives faith and confidence for the race ahead. When we start with the creator of the universe, our magnificent God who is worthy of all glory and worship, how can we fail?

How big is your God? If you had to explain Him to an unbeliever, what words would you use to describe Him? No one can completely understand the full complexity or impact of God's nature and essence. If humanity could understand God, He would not be God; however, we are convinced that the defining reality of any person's life is their knowledge and personal relationship with the God of the Bible.

THE PICTURE OF GOD BRIGHTENS CONFIDENCE

Our picture of God dictates how we understand and relate to God. In his best-selling book, Knowing God, J. I. Packer states, "The ignorance of God—ignorance both of His ways and of the practice of communion with Him—lies at the root of much of the church's weakness."1 As leaders, we must know God not only for ourselves but also to be able to teach others about Him. The Christian life is a walk of faith, and that which is not of faith is sin. "Without faith it is impossible to please [God]" (Hebrews 11:6), but our faith must have an object. The size of our faith will be determined by our understanding of the one in whom we choose to place our faith for our faith is no greater than its object. If we choose to place our faith in ourselves, our faith will be restricted by our limitations; therefore, we must learn to place our faith in the God of the Bible.

As we meditate on His greatness, God's attributes will inspire us to trust Him for greater things for "as [a man] thinks within himself, so he is" (Proverbs 23:7). The more we meditate on the love and the wonder of our great God and Savior, the more our own self-centered thoughts are replaced. The right perception of God forces us to evaluate our lives and reach out to the world with the message of Jesus Christ. Ignorance of who God is and how we commune with Him weakens the walk of faith. Leaders must not be ignorant of these vital truths.

The picture of God that we have in our hearts and minds establishes the way we live our lives.

We can only gain a correct view of God by studying His attributes and His character. The study of God is an adventure that lasts a lifetime. No one book, much less one chapter in a book, can fully represent all the aspects of the God of the universe. We suggest you begin the journey with the book, GOD: Discover His Character. Let it be the beginning of a lifelong passion to know God. Study what the Bible says about Him, meditate on His attributes, and see His sovereign hand at work in your life. Become like Paul who wanted only to "know Him and the power of His resurrection" (Philippians 3:10). God is real. He is present everywhere and full of unlimited power and majesty; therefore, we must study and meditate on His marvelous nature.

Have you ever wondered what God looks like? When Michelangelo painted the Sistine Chapel, he struggled with painting the face of God. Throughout history, artists have rendered God in a variety of ways, but all lack the true awareness of the real God of the universe.

Those who view God as a mean disciplinarian who meddles in the affairs of helpless humanity are often judgmental and have problems with authority. If we view God as a happy Santa Claus figure who only loves and forgives His children, we assume He will not hold us responsible and accountable for our sinful actions because He is so loving. If we view God as a heavenly bellman running to and from throughout the universe to meet our needs, we will most likely abuse His goodness and grace. None of these common perceptions of God are true. The picture of God that we have in our hearts and minds establishes the way we live our lives.

In the study of God, we must realize that the human mind is incapable of fully grasping the totality of God. Our finiteness limits our understanding of the infinite. We must be careful not to have a human-centered view of God lest we limit the ability of God to work in our lives. Everything in this world, even the universe, is finite. Only God is infinite. The prophet Isaiah wrote, "Who has measured the waters in the hollow of His hand, And marked off the heavens by the span, And calculated the dust of the earth by the measure, And weighed the mountains in a balance And the hills in a pair of scales? Who has directed the Spirit of the Lord, Or as His counselor has informed Him?" (40:12-13). His infinite nature means He has no limits or boundaries. Each of His attributes—love, holiness, mercy, justice, goodness, etc.—are also infinite. They are unlimited in their scope and expression.

We also see that God is self-existent. God was not "created." He exists outside the created plan and order of this world. When we "create" something, we rework existing materials to "create" something new. He created the universe out of nothing, and He exists apart from it; therefore, He is wholly different and independent of His creation.

God is also eternal. Time for humanity has a beginning and an end. We use time to mark periods of history, special occasions, and even future events. They all have a beginning and an end. We use time to mark periods of history, special occasions, and even future events. They all have a beginning and an end. God, however, is not bound to a "space-time" continuum. He exists eternally. God experiences all the events of history simultaneously—past, present, and future. This means that what God does in history is also impacting history. When Jesus Christ of Nazareth, God in human form, died on the cross over two thousand years ago, He died for all of humanity—past, present, and future.

Not only is God infinite, but He is also self-sufficient. Without food, water, and oxygen, all living things on Earth die. God is a living being, but He is not dependent upon outside assistance for sufficiency. God is not vulnerable, nor does He need help in any way. At times, His planning and sovereignty allow individuals to participate in His activities, but He is not dependent upon them. We can approach God in faith, knowing that nothing is impossible for the One who can do all things.

In the study of the nature of God, it is important to understand that all His attributes, qualities, and characteristics are interrelated. We cannot understand them separately from each other and fully appreciate them. For the sake of study, it is necessary to isolate these concepts; but in God's economy, they are all working together in cohesion, allowing them to be fully expressed to humanity.

THE POWER OF GOD BRINGS CONFIDENCE

God is the creator of all things. He spoke the unfathomable vastness of our universe into existence and laid the foundations of the world. We see His power and divine nature through His creation. This creative power alone is enough for people not to have any excuse for not knowing and worshipping their creator.

Synergistic Leaders know that the God they serve is the originator of all things, and this provides assurance regarding the planning and execution of the leadership to which God has called us. Because God has created everything, we trust His ability to work in our lives. His ability to create assures us of His ability to sustain.

We do not serve a weak God! We serve the God who spoke, and the sun and more than 100 billion galaxies came into existence. He waved His hand across an empty sky, and an array of stars filled the night. Each star is the representative of a solar system light-years from Earth, full of unknown planets and moons. His power in creation is evidenced every night we look up and see the billions of stars that cover the heavens.

Because God is a creating God, the synergistic church understands that its work and ministry are birthed in the heart of God.

Because God is a creating God, the synergistic church understands that its work and ministry are birthed in the heart of God. It is God who begins the work and builds His Church. As stewards of the work God creates, we do not own the church. It is God's responsibility to grow the church as we follow in obedience to His direction. We respond to His creative power in worship and trust. We know that the same hand of God that separated the dry land from the waters and molded the first man from clay created us.

The God of creation knows everything that takes place in the lives of His creation and works on our behalf. We can trust that God will not fail us just as He did not fail in creating the world. Any problem we face as leaders is insignificant compared to the challenge of creating and maintaining the universe.

Not only did God create the world, but He also remains in control of the world. His power is revealed not only in His Son, Jesus Christ (1 Corinthians 1:24) but also in the order of the universe. Everything has its purpose and its place, and He upholds and maintains it by the power of His Word (Hebrews 1:3). Without God's unique control in the world, all would be chaos. This sovereign control must be understood in the balance of all of His attributes, and all of the attributes of God must be viewed together in order to have an accurate picture of God. His sovereignty must be viewed in light of His justice, compassion, love, and mercy. For example, God is not a tyrant who reigns over the world with an iron fist. His love and compassion prevent Him from such unholy uses of power and control.

Because of the sovereignty of God, we understand He is the omniscient ruler of the universe who rules in holiness and goodness. God is the source of all truth and knows everything that can ever be known. He never learns anything. He is not shocked at the course of human events or surprised at the actions of mankind. Only He knows everything about humanity and history.

"The eyes of the Lord are in every place, Watching the evil and the good" (Proverbs 15:3). "The Lord looks from heaven; He sees all the sons of men; From His dwelling place He looks out on all the inhabitants of the earth, He who fashions the hearts of them all, He who understands all their works" (Psalm 33:13-15).

When we go to God in prayer, we are not informing God of our needs for He already knows them, but we show our dependence upon Him by taking our needs to the God who knows all the answers.

God is omnipotent. Daniel tells us that "it is He who changes the times and the epochs; He removes kings and establishes kings; He gives wisdom to wise men and knowledge to men of understanding" (2:21). Because He is the creator, He stays in control. Jeremiah uses the image of a potter's wheel to describe the control God has over creation. The hands of the potter (God) shape His creation. If the creation does not develop into what the potter desires, he is free to reshape it. As ruler of the universe, God can reshape His creation by overseeing its administration.

He rules in holiness and goodness. God sits on the throne of righteousness because He is holy. We never need to fear that He will act out of cruel motivation. He is a gracious sovereign who encourages us to "draw near with confidence to the throne of grace" (Hebrews 4:16). His holiness separates Him from His creation, allowing Him divine rule over creation. He oversees and controls history, hoping to reveal Himself and show His compassion to the world. We lead Christ's Church knowing that we may be piloting the ship, but it is God who is moving the ship forward. God is in control; we only communicate His vision and truths to His people.

THE PASSION OF GOD BLOSSOMS CONFIDENCE

The God revealed to us in Scripture is a God of compassion. He loves the Church He has created, and that same love should be its distinguishing characteristic. "Let us love one another, for love is from God; and everyone who loves is born of God and knows God. The one who does not love does not know God, for God is love. By this the love of God was manifested in us, that God has sent His only begotten Son into the world so that we might live through Him" (1 John 4:7-9). He calls us His followers—His children; and in the greatest act of love, He sent His own Son to die for our sins. God loves us and wants that same love to be a part of our lives. "A new commandment I give to you, that you love one another, even as I have loved you, that you also love one another" (John 13:34).

In His essential nature and in all His actions, God loves. In a world that has distorted real love through hedonism and greed, we must turn to God to see real love.

His love affects all the expressions of His character and attributes. The psalmist proclaims, "The Lord is good; His lovingkindness is everlasting" (Psalm 100:5). We were created as objects of God's love. Love becomes the doorway to knowing God in an intimate way. His love is unchanging and free. In fact, we can do nothing to prevent God from loving us, and we can do nothing to deserve His love. He is the source of all love.

Our view of God determines how we will relate to God. Our perception of God determines our entire life and ministry. It affects who we are and how we live every aspect of our lives. Our understanding of who God is and how we relate to Him determines our friends, our thoughts, our feelings, and our actions.

How big is our God? What does He look like? The Lord has given us a list of His many attributes and below are 13 of God's attributes with an appropriate response to each of them.

OUR PROACTIVE RESPONSES TO GOD BUILDS CONFIDENCE

In the holy light of who God is, we can embrace personal responses to Him. Each of these humble responses build confidence in who our God is, His love for us, and His abiding presence in our lives. Be sure to learn the 13 attributes of God and live them out each day.

1. Because God is a personal Spirit, I will seek intimate fellowship with Him.
2. Because God is all-powerful, He can help me with anything.
3. Because God is ever-present, He is always with me.
4. Because God knows everything, I will go to Him with all my questions and concerns.
5. Because God is sovereign, I will joyfully submit to His will.
6. Because God is holy, I will devote myself to Him in purity, worship, and service.
7. Because God is absolute truth, I will believe what He says and live accordingly.
8. Because God is righteous, I will live by His standards.
9. Because God is just, He will always treat me fairly.
10. Because God is love, He is unconditionally committed to my well-being.
11. Because God is merciful, He forgives my sins when I sincerely confess them.

12. Because God is faithful, I will trust Him to always keep His promises.
13. Because God never changes, my future is secure and eternal.

Throughout the previous pages, I have attempted to talk about God. An adequate discussion would fill this book and a hundred more just like it. The longer we serve Him, the more we know of Him. He reveals Himself in new ways every day. We continue to learn more, and our picture of who God is grows and another color is added to the stained-glass window. Our prayer is that as leaders, we will continue to grow in the knowledge of our great God and Savior.

THE PRECEPTS OF GOD'S WORD BROADENS CONFIDENCE

God speaks to His people through His Word. Throughout this book, biblical stories are used not only as illustration but also as the basis for principles and strategy we must take to live beyond the limits. This is because the Bible is God's revelation of Himself to mankind in which He reveals the plan of salvation. God's inspired, inerrant, holy Word serves as the roadmap, compass, clock, and guide on the journey of faith. Through God's Word, we receive an explanation of history, hope for the future, peace in the midst of trials, and direction when we are lost. When we obey His Word, we can trust in Him and confidently live the life of faith.

It is sad how many of God's people never consult the Word of God.

Synergistic leaders must be "people of the Book," delighting in reading and studying the revelation of God. They must meditate on God's words. They have hidden the Bible in their hearts in order that they might not cause offense to God (Psalm 119:11). You cannot love someone whom you do not know, and you cannot know someone with whom you do not spend time. To know Him is to love Him. To love Him is to trust Him. To trust Him is to obey Him. To obey Him is to be blessed. To know Him, we must make the reading, studying, memorizing, and meditating on His Word a priority in our daily lives.

Developing a quiet time with God can be one of the most rewarding and challenging parts of the Christian leader's walk.

As we lead the church in this new world, we must be in God's Word today. This time with the Savior is the pivotal moment during the day where we connect with the source of life and power. During these moments alone with God, He provides us with fuel for the day and speaks and prepares us for the road they must travel together. It is important to remember that Daniel could face the lions with confidence because He talked with God daily.

Developing a quiet time with God can be one of the most rewarding and challenging parts of the Christian leader's walk. Many struggle with setting aside an hour or even thirty minutes a day with the Lord. There are many voices competing for the time of the Christian leader, and it is easy to become sidetracked and not allow this important aspect of the life of faith to be developed. It is possible to create a time to meet God alone. However, it is more than possible; it is necessary for we cannot minister to others unless we have spent time with God.

THE PRIORITY OF GOD'S WORD BEGETS CONFIDENCE

How seriously do we take Matthew 6:33 when it says: "Seek ye *first* the kingdom of God" (KJV Emphasis added)? Do you have your quiet time in the morning, the first motion and intent to begin a new day? Or do we grab our phone, browse social media, the news, catch up on what we missed during the night, then begin to open our email, type out a few responses, and then rush to make coffee, breakfast, get the kids ready, get ourselves ready? Before you know it, the morning has been eaten up and the Bible on your bedside table or in your office hasn't been touched. I encourage you to actively and purposefully set aside a time to study and meditate upon the Word of God and protect that time. Treat that time as the sacred moment it is. God is the source of power and life.

THE PREPAREDNESS OF OUR TIME BEFORE GOD BESTOWS CONFIDENCE

Do not approach your time with God haphazardly. Many leaders plan and prepare meetings with executives, deacons, or church staffs but never prepare for their meeting with God. Leaders do not just "wake up" and "meet God." They prepare themselves for the maximum benefit of receiving and communicating with God.

We must physically prepare for this time by being alert and undistracted. Determine the best time for you. Some people need to get dressed and have breakfast before beginning a quiet time. Others cannot become distracted by anything and immediately go to the Word of God. It may be necessary to accomplish light chores around the house because of family schedules and then meet with the Lord.

However, as much as possible, give God your first thoughts, and first moments. We are commanded to give God our first fruits, the first day of the week, and our first thoughts when making a decision. Distractions build upon other distractions, needs, priorities, work, obligations, etc. Putting God first must become a conscious habit. I have sought to "seek God first" by reading and praying before I do anything else in the morning, including eating breakfast.

We must also be mentally alert. Our quiet time with God is not an extension of physical rest. Prayer and the study of God's Word are activities. We are to be active in the process of becoming mentally tough. This is work, an exercise, not something we do when we are half asleep or distracted. We must come expecting to receive a blessing from God.

We must first deal with our sin through confession and repentance before God will listen to anything we might want to say to Him.

Not only do we need to be alert, but we must also come before God morally pure. It is an insult to God to ignore sin in our hearts or lives. A quiet time is fellowship with a holy God. Some people do not have a quiet time because they feel uncomfortable speaking to God because of their sin. If we harbor sin in our hearts, then God will not hear us when we pray (Psalm 66:18). We must first deal with our sin through confession and repentance before God will listen to anything we might want to say to Him.

We must plan the environment of our prayer time. Each morning Daniel opened the window toward Jerusalem and prayed to God. Jesus said, "When you pray, go into your inner room" (Matthew 6:6). Each of us needs a place where we can shut the door to the world and open the windows to heaven. We pray in private because we do not want anything to distract us from focusing on God. This place needs to be well-lit and well-ventilated. It becomes our special place of hope and trust in God. It is our tabernacle on earth where God meets us, and we meet God. It is the secret place that is the sacred place. The mark of a good prayer life is not how we pray in public but how we pray in private.

We must prepare the tools of meditation. There are several practical items that will make our quiet time more effective. First, you should have a readable Bible, large enough for you to write in the margins and easy to read. When you wear out a Bible, save it and buy another one. A well-read Bible will become a best friend. A person who reads the Bible so frequently that it is falling apart probably has a life that is not. Your Bible will become a chronicle of your spiritual journey marked by ink and tears on the passages where God spoke to you.

Second, you need a loose-leaf devotional journal. In this journal, write down truths you learned during your quiet time. Even if you think you have a good memory, the weakest ink is still better than the strongest memory. When reviewing the pages of the journal, it will be easy to see the pattern in which God is speaking to you. This is only possible if you record the intimate moments you have with the Master and view the entries collectively after the fact.

Third, a prayer journal is helpful to keep a list of those things for which you are praying. This will help to make sure you are praying about the things that are on your heart. A good prayer journal will keep you focused on your prayer needs on any given morning. In this journal, make a list of people and the needs you pray for each day. Ask God to help you to prioritize the list. Even while you are praying, there will be other people or things that come to your mind. Write them down and keep seeking the Lord on their behalf.

THE PERSUE OF THE WHOLE WORD OF GOD BEAUTIFYS CONFIDENCE

How big is your Bible? If God removed all the books of the Bible, you do not read, what size would the remaining portion be? The first activity of your prayer life should be to read and the study the Scriptures. Every minister needs to develop a systematic way to read and study God's Word in-depth each year. The Bible is the holy, inspired, inerrant Word that is filled with power.

If the Bible is not a vital part of your daily living and you are not feasting on the Word of God daily, you will never be the synergistic visionary leader that your local or the church needs today.

I encourage you to memorize Colossians 3:16-17:

"Remember what Christ taught and let his words enrich your lives and make you wise; teach them to each other and sing them out in psalms and hymns and spiritual songs, singing to the Lord with thankful hearts. And whatever you do or say, let it be as a representative of the Lord Jesus and come with him into the presence of God the Father to give him your thanks" (TLB).

For the study of God's Word, it is important to read manageable portions of Scripture daily. Reading a hundred psalms each day or only a short passage such as one or two verses rarely allows the full impact of the Scriptures to mold our lives. Many resources are available to categorize and assist the leader in studying God's Word. We suggest that a leader plan to read the Bible through each year. Organize your study by utilizing the divisions of paragraphs and chapters. Read the portion of Scripture more than once. Study the passage; do not merely glance at it.

It is often during the third of fourth time of reading through a passage that God gives special insights in the text. Read the Word first and pray second. God already knows everything about us, but we do not know everything about God. It is more important for you to hear from God than for God to hear from you. Read the Word carefully and systematically. Read from the Psalms for worship, and Proverbs for wisdom. When you read the Bible, use common sense. Do not jump all over the text with no thought or plan. Have a balance in your reading. Devotional books are wonderful, but this is not the place for devotional books; this is the time for the inspired words of God to become incarnate in your life.

THE PONDER OF THE WORD OF GOD BOLSTERS CONFIDENCE

After reading God's Word, stop and meditate on the words. Think through the concepts and truths presented. Apply them to your life. Do not be content with a casual reading of God's Word but mine the text for nuggets of truth and application. Pray the passage aloud and ask God to reveal Himself to you through the text. Many texts of the Bible are complex and require considerable meditation to "work through" in the human mind. This is not problematic but necessary for the Christian walk of faith. God wants us to trust Him and depend upon Him to speak to our hearts and our minds.

In Manna in the Morning, Stephen Olford suggests that we approach the text by asking the following questions:

1. Is there a command to obey?
2. Is there a promise to claim?
3. Is there a sin to forsake?
4. Is there a lesson to learn?
5. Is there a new truth to take with me?[2]

Think through each question carefully. As you meditate, the answers will come from God and His Word. In your prayer journal, record what God speaks to you about the passage of Scripture. This is not for others but for your own spiritual development. Make it personal. These moments with God and His Word are not the time for leaders to develop their sermon material. It is true that many of our messages and thoughts develop out of our personal time with God, but this is not the purpose of meeting each morning. During these quiet times, God may speak individually to the leader, addressing areas that are private and specific to the life of the believer. Often, the words revealed during the quiet time are not intended to be shared with anyone else.

THE PRACTICE OF THE WORD OF GOD BOOSTS CONFIDENCE

The visions and dreams given to us must be lived out. When God leads us to seek forgiveness of others, we must search out these persons and repent before them. Our spiritual train runs on two separate rails. One rail is insight, and the other is instruction. These rails make up revelation and obedience. If our lives get off the track, we will cease to have power with God.

Through His Word, God builds direction and faith in us. It is through His holy, inspired Word that we draw closer to Him. The church of the future is rooted in the Bible.

While many are disregarding it in the postmodern world, it is the commitment to God's Word that will separate the synergistic church from others and move it beyond the limits of relativism and powerlessness. A church that is not committed to the Bible will be grasping for truth in the days ahead. As moral relativism and religious pluralism invade the world, only those who have confidence in the Word of God will be able to live the life of faith.

THE PERSON OF THE HOLY SPIRIT BEFRIENDS CONFIDENCE

Jesus sent the Holy Spirit to comfort, convict, and empower the believer to be a fruitful witness for Him (John 16; Acts 1). The Holy Spirit is the particular person of the Trinity through whom the entire triune godhead works in us.[3] The Holy Spirit is God. He is an active member of the Trinity. People frequently react to distorted views and wrong interpretations of God's Spirit by saying things like, "We don't want the Holy Spirit," or "The

Holy Spirit is not for me." To say we do not want the Holy Spirit active in our lives is to say we do not want God in our lives. We see in God's Word that references to the Holy Spirit are interchangeable with references to God. In Acts 5, Peter confronts Ananias and Sapphira for lying to the Holy Spirit (v. 3). In the next verse he asserts, "You have not lied to men but to God." It is clear from verse 4 that Peter understood the Holy Spirit and God to be equal. We strongly affirm that the Holy Spirit is literally indispensable since no act of our Christian faith—birth, life, worship, fellowship, service, or mission—would be possible without Him.[4]

We should treat the Spirit as a person and regard Him as the infinite loving God within our heart, worthy of our worship.

The Holy Spirit is a person; He is not an "it" or a "thing." He is not an impersonal force as in New Age religions. In John 16:13-14, the Bible uses the masculine pronoun when speaking of the Holy Spirit. The Holy Spirit engages in actions and ministry that are only performed by people: He thinks, feels, teaches, speaks, commands, testifies, and reveals. The Holy Spirit is God just as fully and in the same way as are the Father and the Son.[5] In light of these truths, we should treat the Spirit as a person and regard Him as the infinite loving God within our heart, worthy of our worship. In addition to the person and work of the Holy Spirit, it is important to understand that God gave the Spirit as a gift to His people. We must receive this gift and allow Him to operate in our lives to accomplish what God has called us to do. In John 16:7, Jesus said, "I will send Him to you." Jesus states plainly that the Spirit's presence would be more advantageous than His own personal presence on the earth—meaning that when Jesus left His disciples, He would send them the Holy Spirit who would help them to grow more in Christ. This was the fulfillment of many Old Testament prophecies. Ezekiel recorded that God said, "I will put My Spirit within you and cause you to walk in My statutes, and you will be careful to observe My ordinances" (36:27). Joel spoke of a last-day outpouring of God's Spirit upon all flesh (2:28-32). Jesus' last instructions to His disciples were to wait in Jerusalem to receive the gift of the Holy Spirit (Acts 1:4-5).

THE POWER OF THE HOLY SPIRIT BECOMES CONFIDENCE

Jesus told His disciples, "You will receive power when the Holy Spirit has come upon you; and you shall be My witnesses both in Jerusalem, and in all Judea and Samaria, and even to the remotest part of the earth" (Acts 1:8). The nature of the power is evident. It is the coming of God to man for the accomplishment of a divine purpose in this sacred partnership. The natural result of the infilling of the Holy Spirit is power—power to serve and communicate effectively as leaders. Without the power of the Holy Spirit, leaders are unable to exert the effort, meet the responsibilities, and fulfill the ministry required of them. The Spirit of God turned the disciples from scared followers who denied their Master into sacred proclaimers of the gospel of Jesus Christ. When he was filled with the Spirit, Peter could stand before the multitude and proclaim the good news of Jesus Christ—the same Peter who had denied he knew Christ three times the night Jesus was betrayed.

Dwight L. Moody was an average young man, but at the age of 17, he made a commitment to Christ in the back room of the shoe store where he worked. His life was changed. He began inviting everyone he knew to his church. When he attempted to preach, one of the deacons assured him he could serve God best by keeping silent. Another member praised the young man for his zeal but recommended that he realize his limitations and not attempt to speak in public. Moody went on to preach to millions and to be used by God to draw thousands upon thousands into Christ's kingdom.

What made the difference in the life of this ordinary man? At the beginning of Moody's ministry, he accepted the challenge of Mr. Henry Varley: "The world has yet to see what God will do with and for and through and in and by the man who is fully consecrated to Him." As Moody reflected on these wise words, he thought, "He said 'a man.' He did not say a great man nor a learned man nor a smart man but simply 'a man.' I am a man and it lies within the man himself whether he will or will not make that entire and full consecration."[6]

That day D. L. Moody gave all of himself to his Savior and Lord. He invited Christ to live in and through him—and that made all the difference.

Our victory in Christ, like the victory D. L. Moody experienced, is possible only by living in Christ's power. Are you ready for your messages to be transformed? Are you ready to see hundreds, even thousands, introduced to Jesus Christ through your ministry? Are you ready to experience God in ways you have never before? If you want these benefits in your life and ministry, you want to be filled with the Spirit.

Paul's prayer in Ephesians 3:14-21 asks God to strengthen the Ephesians with power through the Spirit so that Christ could live in their hearts and they might better know and understand the love of God. When Paul came to Corinth and preached Jesus Christ, he did not come on his own. In 1 Corinthians 2:4-5, we read that when Paul preached, his sermons were accompanied by a demonstration of the Spirit's power. This was so that the faith of the Corinthians would not rest upon man but upon God. Jesus did not send His disciples into the world until they had first received the Holy Spirit on the Day of Pentecost. The result of that filling of the Spirit was a mighty harvest of souls for God's kingdom. When the apostles were confronted with adversity in Acts 4:29-31, they prayed that the Spirit would give them boldness to proclaim the message of truth. God answered their prayer, and the place where they were praying was shaken. The Holy Spirit's power will affect everything it comes in contact with, even the natural world.

THE PURPOSE OF THE HOLY SPIRIT BALANCES CONFIDENCE

We cannot live an abundant, effective, fruitful Christian life without the power of the Holy Spirit. Even Jesus Christ lived a Spirit-filled life. The Holy Spirit was present in every aspect of His life and ministry. The Holy Spirit caused Mary to conceive and give birth to Christ, thereby making His life on earth possible. The Holy Spirit descended upon Christ at His baptism and then led Him into the wilderness to be tempted by Satan. In a synagogue in Nazareth, Jesus began His ministry by declaring with a quote from Isaiah: "The Spirit of the Lord is upon Me, because He anointed Me to preach the gospel to the poor. He has sent Me to proclaim release to the captives, and recovery of sight to the blind, to set free those who are oppressed, to proclaim the favorable year of the Lord" (Luke 4:18-19). The Holy Spirit worked through Christ as He ministered in first-century Palestine.

We cannot live an abundant, effective, fruitful Christian life without the power of the Holy Spirit.

Ministers must also be filled with the Holy Spirit for their ministry. The leaders of the synergistic church are even more dependent upon God's power because they must guide God's people.

If the Spirit of God fell upon Jesus to enable Him to preach the good news, how much more do we need the Spirit of God to lead us and guide us?

The Spirit is the enabler, the one who empowers, the equipper, the counselor, and the helper. The Holy Spirit bears witness of Christ and reminds us of Christ's teaching (John 14:26). The Holy Spirit indwells and empowers every believer (1 Corinthians 6:19). It is the Holy Spirit who manifests Christ's nature within us; if we do not have the Spirit, we do not have Christ (Romans 8:9).

What an amazing privilege to have the same Holy Spirit who empowered our Savior living inside us. Only through the presence of the Holy Spirit can we experience a supernatural life because the Holy Spirit works in us to reflect Christ in our lives. From the moment we are born spiritually, He gives each believer the power to live a supernatural life and be fruitful for Him. The Bible assures us "His divine power has given us everything we need for a godly life through our knowledge of him who called us by his own glory and goodness" (2 Peter 1:3 NIV). Despite God's gracious provision, we may suffer power shortages and brownouts in our lives. We may fail to understand the power available to us. We may short-circuit the flow of that power in our lives by sin, unbelief, or a failure to spend time with God, the source of all spiritual power.

THE POSSESSION OF THE HOLY SPIRIT BLESSES CONFIDENCE

It is imperative that every pastor, evangelist, and missionary become a vessel of God's power. Every minister of the gospel, indeed every believer, is made "a servant of this gospel by the gift of God's grace given [us] through the working of his power" (Ephesians 3:7 NIV). It has been said, "God means business with those who mean business with Him." Make it your highest aim to live and serve God and your people in the mighty power of the Holy Spirit, drawing upon the supernatural resources of the triune God. There are moments when a single act says more than an encyclopedia could. Sometimes an entire life can be summarized by one significant action. The story of Elijah and Elisha demonstrates one of those scriptural events that say more than words ever could. It was when God's servant, Elijah, cast his mantle upon his successor, Elisha. The mantle was Elijah's divine logo or his identifying mark. It was a dramatic time when Elijah left Mount Sinai and traveled 150 miles north to Damascus in obedience to the voice of God. On his journey, God directed him to a young man plowing in the field. He veered off the road and, without a word, took his prophet's mantle and threw it upon the young man, and continued down the road. The biblical account of Elijah and Elisha illustrates several junctures on this journey that leaders need to traverse in order to impact their generation.

Synergistic Leaders Have a Priority to Practice (1 Kings 19:19-21)

When God calls us, He brings us to a point of decision. After Elijah had been renewed and revived in the cave, the voice of God told him to return to a difficult place. God told him to go back to where Ahab had a price on his head, back to the place where Jezebel wanted his life, back to the place where Baal worship still influenced an entire nation. It would have been easy to stay in the cave on Mount Horeb where there was an earthquake, wind, fire, and the voice of God yet God called him to go back to a place of difficulty. Elijah still had seven or eight years of dynamic ministry left. When Elijah placed his mantle upon Elisha, it was clear he was saying: "Follow me." We have been called to a Man, not a movement; to a Person, not a plan; to Christ, not a church. Jesus said, "Follow Me, and I will make you fishers of men" (Matthew 4:19 KJV). They immediately left their nets and followed Him. Elisha left his family and his yoke of oxen, and the disciples left their families and their fishing to follow Jesus. Have you prioritized your life? Are you truly willing to become what Christ has commanded you to be as a person and as a leader? At the end of 1 Kings 19:21, we see that Elisha began to follow Elijah and minister to him. We all must learn to minister *to* Christ before we can minister *for* Christ.

We are to become servants of Jesus Christ. It is the Holy Spirit who teaches us to live in humility serving Christ. In 2 Kings 3:11, we are told that Elisha poured water on the hands of Elijah. This passage indicates that Elisha took the place of a slave to serve Elijah. He ministered to his master. Is it your purpose and burning ambition to serve Jesus Christ?

We have been called to a Man, not a movement; to a Person, not a plan; to Christ, not a church.

After Elisha accepted the call to become Elijah's disciple, his name is not mentioned for another seven to eight years. During these years, he served God in the shadow of Elijah as a disciple. However, after those eight years of study, he spent 65 years in dynamic ministry for God. The Spirit of God often develops us in the shadows. We are prepared before our work is needed. It may take years of the Holy Spirit's work to develop us into the leaders we need to be.

We must be willing to take the long view, not the short view, understanding that the time in the shadows is not wasted time.

We need to be ready when the time comes to supernaturally lead others and impact our world for Christ. On the afternoon of June 2, 1925, the New York Yankees were preparing for a game against the Washington Senators. The veteran first baseman, Walley Pips, said to his manager, Miller Huggins, "I have a headache. I don't want to play." Huggins turned to a young man named Lou Gehrig and said, "Lou, you play first base." Lou Gehrig, a nobody, stepped out of the shadows and played 2,130 consecutive games, a record that stood for almost 70 years. One man stepped aside and another stepped into the spotlight. If Gehrig had not been preparing before the opportunity came his way, he would not have been ready and the chance would have passed him by. Leaders are not developed overnight. They prepare themselves daily for what Christ desires for them to be and do in their generation. You may be frustrated that you are living in the "shadow times." You have big dreams and grand plans, but your life seems not to be going fast enough. Do not let your ego or impatience limit what God can do for you. Live beyond the limits of your own pride and have faith in God.

Synergistic Leaders Have a Price to Pay (1 Kings 19:19-21)

Leading Christ's church will cost us something. Life is made up of tradeoffs. We cannot do everything. The leader who desires to live in the power of God's Spirit must be willing to abandon the things of this world. In Elijah's period of history, individuals who owned oxen were considered wealthy. Elisha had several servants and 12 oxen. It is obvious he came from an affluent family. God found Elisha working in the fields—in the midst of the ordinary, not the extraordinary. God does not usually call us in the red-hot heat of the dramatic. We do not live our lives in the sensational or the unpredictable. God's call usually comes while we are in the office, the home, the car, or our prayer closet. Then suddenly, the ordinary becomes the extraordinary; the natural becomes the supernatural. Elisha left his position to become a slave and servant to Elijah. Elisha gave up his professional responsibilities to follow his master.

Elisha was also willing to surrender his private relationships. When Elijah laid his mantle upon Elisha, Elisha ran to Elijah and asked if he could go back and kiss his parents good-bye. Elijah gave a concealed answer. "Go back again, for what have I done to you?" (v. 20). Did Elijah condemn or commend him? Elijah did not condemn him. He knew that this was a moment of decision. Elijah knew that God, not he, was calling Elisha to a life of discipleship. He simply laid the mantle upon him because God told him to do so. There are to be no earthly relationships that come ahead of our affection for Christ.

A life of service to God comes with a price. Elisha killed the oxen and sacrificed them on the wood of the plow he had been using in the field. He invited his family and friends and dramatically announced that he was burning his bridges behind him and becoming a disciple of Elijah. Is there anything you own that you would not give up to follow Jesus Christ? Is there a business? A dream? A possession?

The leader who desires to live in the power of God's Spirit must be willing to abandon the things of this world.

A disciple says there is no price too high to pay to be a follower of Jesus Christ. Elisha, who would have inherited his father's estate, was willing to sacrifice his personal riches. Are we willing to forsake all that God's power might be seen at work in our lives and ministries?

Synergistic Leaders Have a Perspective to Perceive (2 Kings 2:1-8)

We read in 2 Kings 2 that Elijah was taken to heaven in a whirlwind. There are only two ascension stories in the Bible—one in the Old Testament (Elijah) and one in the New Testament (Jesus). While Enoch walked with God and God took him to heaven, Elijah and Jesus are the only two who ascended into heaven in front of people. Only the personal disciples of the two who ascended witnessed these ascensions. Supernatural power is often most profoundly seen in private, not in the public arena. The empowerment of the Spirit is most often conferred in the prayer closet.

Some are trapped in the philosophy that bigger is better. They have fallen victim to a worldly view of power. They look for opportunities to showcase their leadership abilities and talents. They confuse spectacle with Spirit, announcement with anointing, publicity with power, and big with blessing. They limit the work of the Spirit because they are looking for an event rather than the Spirit's process. Synergistic leaders rely upon God's power to work in their churches and in other people's lives, not upon their own charisma.

If we are to be disciples of Jesus Christ, there are many things that can cause us not to stay focused. These are tests to see if disciples are resolute in their purpose. Elijah tested Elisha. He told him to stay while he traveled on, but Elisha would not be deterred. He pursued Elijah. Are you easily deterred from following Christ? Does it take very much to get you off track in your relationship with God? There are obstacles to becoming a disciple of Christ. Elijah was testing Elisha's determination to be a disciple. Many times, we are easily persuaded not to follow the Lord. God saves the best for those who are faithful to the end. Elijah was showing Elisha how to be prepared at all times to meet God. He led his fellow servants from Gilgal on to Bethel, then to Jericho, and finally to Jordan. In other words, if we are going to be ready to meet the Lord, we must be willing to move from the place of beginning (Gilgal) to the place of breaking (Bethel) to the place of battles (Jericho) in order to reach the place of beholding (Jordan). It is the Holy Spirit who enables us to pursue the vision God has given us. We must be careful not to be sidetracked by imitations.

Synergistic Leaders Have a Power to Possess (2 Kings 2:9-15)

We must possess the power that has been given to us. In his final moments, Elijah asked Elisha what he could do for him. Elisha said he wanted a double portion of the spirit of Elijah to be upon him. He had seen God's power working in Elijah, and he wanted that same experience. When we become a true Galatians 2:20 kind of disciple, our Master is able to work powerfully in and through us.

Christianity is not what we do for Christ but what He accomplishes in and through us.

When Elijah ascended in a whirlwind of fire, his mantle of power fell to the earth. Elisha bent over and put it on his shoulders. Because God had chosen Elisha to serve Him, God equipped him with all the power necessary to fulfill his tasks. Jesus promised His disciples the same power for service. He said: "'I am going to send you what my Father has promised; but stay in the city until you have been clothed with power from on high.'

When he had led them out to the vicinity of Bethany, he lifted his hands and blessed them.

While he was blessing them, he left them and was taken up into heaven" (Luke 24:49-51 NIV).

In Acts 2:4, the promised Spirit fell upon Jesus' disciples. Peter tells us that the gift is for all of us today. To be the leaders Christ has called us to be, we must humble ourselves to allow the Holy Spirit to work through us. Elisha's power was linked to the ascension of Elijah. Our power is linked to the ascension of Jesus. When Jesus ascended, He sent the Comforter to abide in us. When Jesus went up, the Holy Spirit came down, the disciples went out, and the lost came in. When the mantle came down, Elisha had to appropriate it—he submitted his life to God's will. Have we received the power that is potentially ours? The first time the mantle was placed on Elisha's shoulders by someone else; however, the second time, he had to put on the mantle himself. Though we are given the Holy Spirit when we are born again, we must choose to die daily to allow Him to have preeminence in our lives. If you get the full picture, you will see that just as God continued His work through Elisha, Christ lives His life in us and continues His work through us, His servants. Christianity is not what we do for Christ but what He accomplishes in and through us.

Nations have died for lack of leadership; corporations have folded because there were no successors to keep them going; institutions have withered after decades of prosperity because of a lack of new leadership.

When Elisha took that mantle and went to the Jordan River, he struck the water and asked, "Where is the Lord, the God of Elijah?" (v. 14). The power that had been on Elijah was now with Elisha. Some have the idea that the best days of the Church are in the past, but we are confident that the best days are ahead of us. The kingdom of God is not about to stop. We have confidence in God that He will continue to build the Church in the twenty-first century because we know that we have the power of the Spirit working within us to accomplish that task.

Nations have died for lack of leadership; corporations have folded because there were no successors to keep them going; institutions have withered after decades of prosperity because of a lack of new leadership. Yet after 2,000 years, the Church has moved from generation to generation with God raising up men and women called to supernaturally lead God's people. We do not have to worry about the Church. Jesus Christ will continue to raise up dynamic leadership until the end of the age. If we will only love and obey Him, He will empower each generation to fulfill the Great Commission and build His church.

In 1889, D. L. Moody asked Rubin A. Torrey to help him with his evangelistic work. Moody made Torrey the president of Moody Bible Institute in Chicago, Illinois. When Moody experienced a heart attack in Kansas City in 1899, Torrey took over the campaign and finished it successfully. Torrey influenced a young man named J. Wilbur Chapman. Charles M. Alexander, Torrey's minister of music, joined Chapman in a worldwide evangelism tour from 1909-1914. When Chapman finished his tour, he found a young man named Billy Sunday in Chicago. Billy Sunday became Chapman's associate. A year later, Billy Sunday was holding his own evangelistic meetings. He was an energetic baseball player who became an evangelist. Billy Sunday later influenced an evangelist named Mordecai Ham. In 1901, Ham began 50 years of itinerant evangelism. On the last night of a four-week crusade when he was in Charlotte, North Carolina, a clothing merchant named J. D. Prevette went to the back row where two young men were sitting. One boy was named Wilson and the other Graham. Prevette witnessed to Grady Wilson and Billy Graham about Christ that evening. Wilson and Graham came forward and gave their lives to Christ. A line can be drawn from the ministry of D. L. Moody of the 1860s to the present Billy Graham. Each of these men experienced the Holy Spirit's power. They practiced the right priorities, paid the price, perceived the right perspective, and possessed the power of the Holy Spirit.

Our Calling By God

It is amazing how many people, even in the ministry, struggle with a lack of fulfillment and doubts concerning their calling. They face seemingly insurmountable challenges and wonder whether they are truly fulfilling their calling in life. They desire a sense of mission, direction, and goal, so that when they have accomplished it, they can feel that they have truly heard and followed the voice of God.

If this sense of purpose and mission is not identified, they will struggle throughout their entire ministry. Until those in leadership know they are called by the Father to do His will, they will be filled with uncertainty and disappointment. On the other hand, those who follow the voice of God and finish the task set before them live a meaningful life. As Bob Buford said, their lives are not just a success; their lives were significant.[1] The calling of God provides direction and guidance for life and ministry. It gives a sense of "divine destiny."

THE TWOFOLD CALLING

Do you know what your mission is in life? How can you know if you are making progress unless you have a purpose? Do you worry that your life and ministry are meaningless?

Whether you are just beginning in ministry or have been in leadership for some time, you must consider the following question: Why do you do what you do in the ministry? Is it simply to have a full calendar, money in the bank, or a local or national platform? Do you preach without purpose and minister without mission? We must never forget that Jesus Christ could speak His mission in one clear, concise sentence: "I came that they might have life and have it abundantly" (John 10:10). He also said, "I have come to seek and save the lost" (Luke 19:10). This mission was passed on to His disciples. They knew what their purpose in life was for they had been sent out to point others to new life in Christ (Romans 6:23). Before Christ ascended into heaven, He gave them the Great Commission. Their goal was world evangelization and the creation of disciples for Jesus Christ.

We are each called to fulfill that same commission; but we also must realize that within the universal calling of God, there is a unique and special calling for each of us. The call to evangelize is complementary to the specific call upon an individual life. They are part and parcel of the same direction from God.

My prayer has been that the Holy Spirit would raise up unique, dynamic, synergistic leaders all over the world. Every snowflake is different and powerless on its own; yet when they get together, they can stop traffic as well as create beautiful scenery. Just like the snowflake, each of us has a unique mission and ministry—we look different from each other. However, when we work together, we can blanket the world with the gospel. This is the reason God gives us each individual callings. None of us is called to be just like another person. We have been given a mission that, when united with others, makes a powerful impact. The calling of God is more than a mission/

vision statement. It is more than a written set of core values and five-year goals although each of these is a reflection of God's calling.

Each of us has a role in the goal and a part in God's heart.

Peter was called to preach on the Day of Pentecost and to lead the church in Rome. James was to help the Jerusalem church through an early crisis. John was to record the great revelation of the end times and write letters of encouragement to the church. Each fulfilled the divine call upon their lives. They obeyed the Great Commission, but they also lived their own specific, God-given mission. Each of us has a role in the goal and a part in God's heart.

Leaders must listen to the voice of God to know what He would have them do and must submit to His direction. Many assume there is only one calling and that is to "go into all the world and preach the gospel" (Mark 16:15). While it is the calling of every believer to fulfill the Great Commission and evangelize the lost, He has chosen some to serve in full-time ministry. This calling is not distinct from the Great Commission; it is congruent with it. The general call to evangelize is complementary to the specific call upon an individual life. They are part and parcel of the same direction from God.

However, you cannot write your mission in the context of the Great Commission, until you have heard the voice of God clearly calling you. I cannot attempt to delineate the specifics of your own individual calling. Even if I could, I would not do it. The calling of God is so specific and so holy that it can be birthed and nurtured only through the inspiration of the divine. It can only come from God to you as you seek after Him; it cannot be created or derived from a formula.

In each of our lives, our mission is born from above while our vision is lived on earth. The leader's life is the expression of their God-inspired calling. We will, however, seek to help you understand the nature of God's calling and the way we should live in light of that calling.

Synergy is working together with others. It is the total collaboration of all parties involved in an adventure. The adventure of ministry is wrapped completely in the calling of God. If you are doing things you are not called by God to do, then you need to stop them immediately. Pursue God and pursue His calling upon your life. We challenge you to seek God's will through fasting and prayer.

THE MEANING OF GOD'S CALLING

God communicates and ordains the calling on an individual's life. Paul's calling began before the creation of the world (Galatians 1:15). God knew Jeremiah before he was formed in his mother's womb (Jeremiah 1:5). Leaders who desire long-term effective ministry must know without a doubt that God has called them into ministry.

This leads to a sense of providence in our lives and ministry. The word "providence" is derived from the Latin *providentia* which principally means "foresight or foreknowledge." When God calls a person into full-time ministry, He has foreknowledge of how this individual can make a unique contribution to the fulfillment of the Great Commission.

While the doctrine of providence means God's supernatural ability to see ahead of time, it also includes God's ability to govern all creatures, actions, and things according to His immutable counsel without violating man's free will. This is good news for Christian workers. God not only sees the potential we have for Him in ministry but also is at work using circumstances, both good and bad, to achieve His master plan for our lives and ministries.

When the pandemic of 2020-2022 arose, the Holy Trinity does not meet in an emergency session and say, "We did not see the pandemic coming. That one caught us by surprise." God sees everything ahead of time. Long before Adam and Eve fell in the Garden of Eden, God, in His mind, had already placed a cross on Calvary. Before you were placed in your leadership position, God already was working to help you during this time. Those who have been called into full-time ministry have providence attached to their lives. Understanding the importance of their calling will help them to better hear from God and allow the Holy Spirit to illuminate their mission in life.

Ministers need to know they have been called into full-time ministry and, by faith, move forward in their service to Christ and their community.

Without the assurance of this call, we will find the ministry we pursue difficult or impossible. Just as Christians in general need to have assurance of their salvation and move forward by faith in the Christian walk, so ministers in particular need to know they have been called into full-time ministry and, by faith, move forward in their service to Christ and their community. Ministers who question their calling to preach the gospel normally question almost everything else they do in the ministry. They become unsure of themselves and do not aggressively pursue ministry.

Life and ministry are filled with change. Nothing remains constant, even in ministry. Having an unchanging sense of who we are, what we are about, and what we value is the key to having the ability to change.[2] When the surroundings change and the strong winds blow, the divine providential calling is the anchor that will hold us. It is this calling that keeps us going despite the changing wind. It is knowing that God has providentially called us for such a time as this (Esther 4:14).

THE MYSTERY OF GOD'S CALLING

Although our calling in life is sacred and holy, most people have never spent time identifying their unique calling. It is amazing that most people spend more time planning for a two-week vacation than they spend planning for the rest of their lives. Our calling must be pursued through prayer and will develop inside of us over a period of time. It is not only through impressions or a sudden realization that God speaks to us, but the call and mission of leaders are also based on a lifetime of God's speaking and guiding them.

God does not want your calling to be perplexing. There are many sincere Christians who want to do the will of God but do not know how to go about discovering His will for their lives. By applying the "sound mind principle," we can better understand what God's will is for our lives.

The "sound mind principle" is based upon 2 Timothy 1:7: "For God hath not given us the spirit of fear; but of power, and of love, and of a sound mind" (KJV). This mind is being renewed and is under the control of the Holy Spirit when we offer ourselves to God as His servants (Romans 12:1-2). Christians who yield their lives fully to Christ can be assured of sanctified reason and a sound mind. Therefore, we can use wisdom and guidance to determine God's will for our lives. So many people are looking for a divine, cataclysmic event that they miss the plan God has laid out clearly for them. While all callings are unique, the call to leadership has characteristics that are universal.

THE MERITS OF GOD'S CALLING

When God calls us to His service, the calling is **purposeful.** God calls leaders to accomplish specific tasks. Moses was called to lead the Israelites out of Egyptian bondage. Joshua was called to lead Israel in the conquest of Canaan. The Old Testament prophets were called to proclaim the word of the Lord for their times. Paul was called to preach the gospel to the Gentiles. What is God calling you to do? What unique purpose do you fulfill in the kingdom of God? If you are an evangelist, why should a pastor invite you for a crusade instead of another evangelist? If you are serving as a pastor, what contribution can you bring to your community or city that other pastors cannot bring to your area? What is your local church known for? What distinguishes it from others? Is that distinguishing trait positive or negative? How does it relate to your calling? How do you differentiate success versus significance?

Each member plays a vital part in the kingdom of God. Each of us is divinely gifted and placed in the body of Christ to achieve a purpose.

Each member plays a vital part in the kingdom of God. Each of us is divinely gifted and placed in the body of Christ to achieve a purpose. Defining our roles and goals in life will help us to find and fulfill our purpose. Roles provide direction, and goals determine the destination toward which we are heading. Leaders understand that a vision becomes a goal when they place a date by it. A date gives a sense of chronology and progression in a person's life and mission.

The calling of God is very **personal.** God's hand was upon our lives long before we took our first steps as children. If we have been divinely called into a full-time preaching ministry, then God personally set us apart to preach the gospel. Preaching is much easier when preachers know that the providential hand of God has been laid upon their lives. Each of us has our own individual race to run. It would be tragic for our lives to come to a close and our personal race still not be completed.

In his book for business leaders, Business as a Calling, Michael Novak gives us insight on individual callings:

Each of us is as unique in our calling as we are in being made in the image of God. (It would take an infinite number of human beings, St. Thomas Aquinas once wrote, to mirror back the infixed facets of the Godhead. Each person reflects on a small—but beautiful—part of the whole.)[3]

Our calling is a reflection of God in us and in our ministries and is one more representation of God's beauty in the world. The call is not just a job or vocation but also a divine act of God. Each of our callings is a different expression of God. As we are each made in the image of God and are being formed more each day into the image of His Son, we are fulfilling God's call upon our lives.

The calling of God is also **practical**. The calling God places on our lives will match our God-given abilities and gifts. One of the reasons many people do not recognize their gifts is because they seem natural.[4] While the typical pattern in Scripture is that God calls and equips the least likely individual to accomplish His will, He can use our natural gifts and talents as well.

What is it that we "naturally" do well? Many times, the calling of God on our lives is very evident from what we seemingly do well naturally. It is our responsibility to recognize these gifts and use them in our service for God. Those who are natural organizers and administrators most likely are called to serve God in an administrative capacity. Those who naturally write well should allow that "natural" or "God-given" talent to fulfill their calling. God's calling on our life is practical. When lived out, it makes perfect sense in the life God has given us. God planned our calling before we were created, and He orchestrates the experiences of our lives and the talents that reside within us to achieve this calling.

Finally, the calling of God is **powerful**. The study of Scripture reveals that God-called servants are endowed with a special anointing to fulfill the task to which He has called them. A defined call provides both the passion for the necessary creativity and the renewed energies of the daily grind. Novak writes:

Facing hard tasks necessarily exacts dread. Indeed, there are times when we wish we did not have to face every burden our calling imposes on us. Still, finding ourselves where we are and with the responsibilities we bear, we know it is our duty—part of what were meant to do—to soldier on…there is an odd satisfaction in bearing certain pains.

The calling God places on our lives may not be easy. It may be filled with distractions and hardships, but the calling provides the energy and power to persevere. God's calling in our lives is something that will excite us. Enthusiasm comes from the root words "en" and "theos" which literally mean "in God." What are we enthusiastic or "in God" about? The calling of God for leadership is a calling that empowers.

THE MANIFEST OF GOD'S CALLING

Just knowing and understanding the nature and characteristics of God's calling are helpful in identifying and fulfilling that calling. However, each of us must determine whether success or significance is motivating the ministry we do. Success is timely and ends when we die. Significance is timeless and lives on after we die. The issue is not whether we are going to die or live forever. The latest statistics regarding death are fairly consistent. There are good odds that one day each of us is going to breathe our last breath and instantly be in the presence of God. When this happens, will we have lived a significant life? Will we have fulfilled the calling of God in our life? There are many successful people who never live significant lives because they have accomplished tasks, not fulfilled their calling. It must be the prayer of every leader to become who they are in Christ and to become the living fulfillment of the calling God has placed upon their life.

People frequently ask: "What is the secret to your success?" "What quality or characteristic can I incorporate into my life to make me a successful minister?" "What can I do that is new and invigorating that will help me become the minister God wants me to be?" Those who ask these questions are often well-intentioned men and women wanting to begin a powerful, fruitful ministry. Sometimes they are not seeing the results they anticipated when they first began the work of the ministry. They have been to every church growth conference, some of them twice or more. Their libraries are filled with the latest books and manuals of how to do church and how to do a relationship with Jesus, yet nothing is working. Their ministry and their walk with God are floundering in an ocean of turmoil and disappointments.

We are to be imitators of God, not man, not even righteous, inspiring, learned and experience, men.

While their questions are motivated by good intentions, people make the mistake of trying to copy what others are doing, looking for shortcuts to fruitful ministry. In Christ's work, there are no shortcuts and God does not make copies—He only makes originals. It is impossible to replicate the ministry of others. Leaders must seek to learn and apply principles and ministry techniques from others, not simply listen and copy.

When we are approached with questions and we sense a real hunger for more of God and a more effective ministry, we will ask some probing questions. It is amazing how so few of the principles presented here are active in the lives of those asking the questions. They are so busy looking for the new and catchy that they forget to exercise the basic components of Christian faith and ministry to find the answers. We ask them, "When did you last discipline yourself through prayer and fasting?" It is not the new things that are hard to do but the basic elements of the Christian walk with which they struggle. Simple things like prayer and Scripture memorization are often neglected. These leaders want to copy the methods of others without trying to become more like Jesus Christ themselves. The keys to leadership are not being used to unlock the difficult leadership positions in which they find themselves.

Sadly, many people cannot seem to see providentially or realistically what God is calling them to do. It is only through His work in our lives and His calling that we fully realize our potential. We must become who God intended us to be. When we ignore the calling of God upon our lives, we never fully become all God has called us to be. Instead, we settle for an incomplete picture of the life God has called us to live. We need to become who we are in Christ and not who we think we need to be. Our true identity or self-worth is much greater than any level of ministry we may have. In a sense, our uniqueness dies when we choose not to mature in our ministries. Everyone is young once, but we can be immature the rest of our lives if we so choose.

THE MINISTRY OF GOD'S CALLING

God has not called us to fulfill someone else's mission and ministry. Many ministers do not experience the life God wants for them because they are trying to copy others. There is a difference between learning from others, standing on the shoulders of giants, and imitating them.

We are to be imitators of God, not man, not even righteous, inspiring, learned and experience, men. God does not call an evangelist or a pastor to develop a ministry on the personality of someone else, but on proven eternal principles. We must be ourselves in ministry. Whether we serve on a large church staff or in a small church, God has a unique, personal call for our lives.

Vaclav Havel said,

"God is working in us to create a grand masterpiece of workmanship. He has created each of us as vessels for His honor and His glory."

When God sees us, He sees the completed work of Christ operating in the world.

We are God's "designer originals." We are each individually formed and created to achieve the purpose God has for us. Many leaders feel the easiest way to success and fulfillment is to copy others, but this is far from the plan of God. Each of us has been given the assignment to fulfill our specific mission in life.

"The real test of a man is not when he plays the role that he wants for himself but when he plays the role destiny has for him."[7]

Each of us has been given the assignment to fulfill our specific mission in life. To accomplish this mission, God has given us unique gifts and talents.

To accomplish this mission, God has given us unique gifts and talents. To imitate others is suicide and kills whom God made us to be. Are we fulfilling the life God has called us to, or are we living for our own personal desires? In one of his most quoted writings, Ralph Waldo Emerson discussed the importance of being original, of not becoming a mere copy of others:

There is a time in every man's education when he arrives at the conviction that…imitation is suicide; that he must take himself for better or worse as is his portion…The power which resides in him is new in nature, and *none but he knows what that is which he can do, nor does he know until he has tried…* Trust thyself: every heart vibrates to that iron string.[8] (Emphasis added.)

Emerson's understanding of self-reliance is based upon each person's innate ability to become better than they personally are, to personally succeed. The leader knows that through Christ, success—fulfilling our calling—is possible.

We need to learn from each other so that we do not reinvent the wheel in every ministry; however, we must not imitate others as the "easy" way to successful ministry. It may be "successful" on the outside, but it is not the plan God intended for us. It is not leadership.

Imitation violates essential uniqueness and damages creativity. When we copy others, we avoid using creativity. The plans of others have been worked out over time. Sweat, tears, disappointments, and commitment have created their model of ministry. When we imitate the process of others, we do not copy the commitment level of the process. We do not "own" the plan for our churches or our lives because we have not invested in it. This leaves us less committed to the system we are adopting because we have not spent the same amount of effort and energy in creating the system.

Imitation is, at best, a simplified version of the original. It is the synthesized, packaged resource version. Christian bookstores are lined with books on how to grow churches and leaders. Many have boiled down the ten or twenty years of hard work and history of their growth into 250 pages for only $19.99. While these resources may help leaders develop the plan to which God has called them, it is not a one-size-fits-all model for spiritual leadership. No one can show all the bends in the road, the detours that come, or the dangers of the journey. Leaders who copy others are cheap imitations of the original. Imitation rarely improves on the original product.

There is no motivation to increase effectiveness when the product is already successful. The innovative synergistic leader is always looking for new ways to live and operate in ministry.

When the leader and the church begin to copy others, their sense of innovation and destiny are lost. For those who copy, it will not be necessary to think big or create better ways because they can wait until someone else does it and then appropriate their improvements.

In this sense, imitating others means we are always behind the learning curve. When the imitator realizes there is a new way to do ministry, everyone else is already aware of it. The identifying niche of our church and ministry in actuality does not set us apart from others. The niche we copy makes us look exactly like everyone around us.

Why do so many preachers fail to implement their God-given calling in their daily lives and ministry? What is it that keeps them from moving forward in new areas of evangelism? What causes them to become stuck in ministerial ruts for most of their lives? The answer to all of these questions is the fear of failure. Fear will take the blue out our sky and the joy out of our heart. It is fear that dries up the well of innovation and locks the door of implementation. When preachers have completely grasped their divine calling to preach the gospel, many of the insecurities and fears fade away.

There are times in our ministries when the Lord will bring us to fearful situations in order to teach us how to handle them. We will never experience victory over fear until we have to face fearful things. However, we can face these fearful challenges with confidence when we know once and for all that God has called us to the preaching task. God gives us enough grace to fulfill our gift (Ephesians 4:7).

Remember that God does not create copies, but He designs originals to accomplish the Great Commission. We must not settle for anything less than complete inner peace regarding our divine call into full-time ministry.

THE MAP OF GOD'S CALLING

When we get where we are going, where will we be? The call God places upon our life enables us to live without fear of the future. God's providence helps us to see things as He sees them. Moses had the faith to see the invisible (Hebrews 11:27) and that enabled him to see the Promised Land in spite of Pharaoh's threats. As God-called leaders, we must creatively break out of the box around us and approach life through a system of understanding and values that may be foreign to others. Our faith in God allows us to see and operate differently than nonbelievers because, although the context and surroundings are the same, we have a different perspective—a different paradigm.

Vision: The Step Into The Future

On May 29, 1953, Sir Edmund Hillary raised the British flag atop Mount Everest, becoming the first human being ever to climb to the top of the world. Through sheer walls of ice, lack of oxygen, and bitter cold, Hillary and his companion, Tenzing Norgay, clawed their way between rock and ice to 29,028 feet above sea level. No man on earth will ever climb higher than that. Many have died trying to reach Everest's summit. All who had previously attempted this climb, including Hillary a few years before, had failed. Many believed Everest was not scalable because its twisting rock and dangerous cliffs provided no way of climbing. In fact, no one knew if the body could survive at such high altitudes. The paradigms of the day saw the feat as impossible.

Sir Edmund Hillary, however, lived under a different paradigm—one that saw the climbing of Everest as possible. He saw himself atop Mount Everest with the world at his feet months before he began the actual climb. For Hillary, he had already crossed the ice-capped peak in his heart and mind long before he got there.

Synergistic leaders are visionary. They are imaginative and constantly thinking of new ways to scale the heights. Hillary creatively approached each challenge in climbing the mountain. His ingenuity allowed him to go farther than anyone had ever gone. Since his remarkable climb, as of January 2023, 6,338 climbers have reached Everest's summit. All leaders have mountains in front of them. The challenge of leadership is to conquer the mountain creatively by following the vision God has placed in their hearts. Like Sir Edmund Hillary, we must see the summit long before we try to conquer it by beginning with the end in mind. The fulfillment of this vision is our passion and the definer of purpose in life.

Laurie Beth Jones says, "You are either living your own mission, or you are living someone else's."[11] On the road to where we are going, either we are accomplishing our own goals or we are accomplishing someone else's. Too many leaders of the church are not following the vision, mission, and goals God has given them. They have been sidetracked and now are led by the whims of someone else. They have been distracted from their calling and are pursuing other visions. When we have visions that are not from God, we pursue avenues that take us farther from His mission and will.

These distractions come from listening to other people rather than "seeing" through God's Spirit. Often our own desires lead us down paths that seem to be the "best" for us professionally. These false visions entrap us, but God's true vision empowers us.[12] Because we see with the eyes of the Spirit, we can accomplish more than we ever dreamed possible.

The synergistic church needs a vision for what God can do through it. Leaders help the church hear from God and see the vision God has for it. This vision is often stated through a mission or vision statement. The development of this vision or mission takes much time and prayer. It is not received and crafted in a day or even a week. It is a process where God speaks to the leadership of a church, and they carefully translate what God is revealing to them into a strong statement of vision and purpose. A word of caution, however, is needed for the leader. Leaders guide the church through the discovery and development of the God-given vision; they do not dictate what that vision is or is not.

George Barna wrote, "In every one of the growing, healthy churches I have studied, a discernible link has been forged between the spiritual and numerical growth of the congregation and the existence, articulation, and widespread ownership of God's ministry by the leaders and participants of the church."[13] To be an effective, healthy church, we must be operating in synergy with the vision God has placed in us because He has called us. This common vision articulates the ministry, Barna sees as vital to the growth and health of the churches.

Vision: The Systematic Effect on Ministry

Caleb lived a life influenced by the vision that was placed within him. He understood that God had called him to be a part of the children of Israel who would take the Promised Land. From the great exodus from Egypt to the conquering of Canaan, Caleb was a source of inspiration and vision. He saw what others did not. In Numbers 13:1-16, Caleb and Joshua joined ten fellow spies sent into Canaan to investigate the land God had promised them. The land they surveyed was full of challenges. The inhabitants of Canaan were giants—strong and numerous—living in the fortified cities of the mountains. The spies reported to the children of Israel that it would be impossible to conquer Canaan because of the giants. However, Caleb saw something different because he was a man of vision. He remembered the God of Israel who had defeated the Egyptians and brought them through the Red Sea. This same God had promised to give them this land. He saw past the challenges; he saw through the eyes of the Spirit.

Stimulated by the courage the vision inspired, Caleb declared that the giants they feared would become the very food of Israel (Numbers 14). Sadly, Israel did not listen or see what Joshua and Caleb saw. In fear and unbelief, they turned away and never set foot in the Promised Land.

Caleb, however, did see his vision fulfilled. After four decades, Joshua and Caleb found themselves at the same place facing the same enemies. The only difference was they were with a people who were willing to follow a vision and trust in God. At the age of 85, Caleb recalled the promises of God and asked to be allowed to lead the charge against the giants who had prevented them from possessing the promise of God years earlier. Caleb saw what others could not. His strength lay in the vision placed in him by God. What made him so special? As a man of vision, Caleb had already conquered the mountain in his heart. Just like Sir Edmund Hillary, the mountain had already been defeated.

We will never possess the vision God has given us physically until we have possessed it internally.

Before we can conquer a mountain with our hand, we must first conquer it in our heart. We will never possess the vision God has given us physically until we have possessed it internally. While Caleb wandered with Israel in the wilderness for forty years, the mountain burned within him. He never gave up on conquering the mountain; he could already see its defeat. Synergistic leaders have this kind of vision. Unlike others who are lost in the wilderness, they know they are only walking toward their eventual victory. While others have filled their hearts with compromise and complacency in the wilderness, leaders keep the mountain in their hearts. Caleb had a different paradigm than the rest of Israel. He and Joshua knew what God could do through them; they saw it through the power of God's Spirit.

Caleb had the courage to believe he could possess the Promised Land. He had the mountain in his heart from the moment he saw it. God had prepared him for this kind of faith. From where did Caleb's vision come? Caleb saw what others did not because his vision was based on God's promises, God's purposes, and God's perspective.

The vision of the mountain was in Caleb's heart because God had promised Israel a land flowing with milk and honey. He promised them that just as He had provided for them in the desert, so would He protect them in the new Promised Land. Caleb knew that the same God who had delivered them from Egypt had promised to fight their battles for them. God has enough power to keep the promises He has made. He never intended for Israel to wander in the wilderness for forty years. He promised Israel the conquest of Canaan; they simply refused to see far enough into the future to trust Him. Visionaries see the future in light of God's promises, and synergistic leaders trust in the promises of God.

Caleb's perspective was different from the other ten spies. He saw the mountain from God's perspective. He was standing on different, higher ground than the other spies. As leaders, we must have a different vantage point than those around us. Some look down at problems rather than looking up at them. Remember the spies' complaint about the giants of Canaan—that they made the Israelites feel like "grasshoppers." Many people fall victim to the grasshopper complex: they always seem small, and the trials of life always seem big. They always look up at the enemy instead of looking down on their problems. Israel made the mistake of comparing themselves to their problem rather than comparing their problem to God. They were willing to believe they could not do it rather than believing that through them, God could do all things. Because God was the source of Caleb's vision, he did not fear the giants. They seemed small in comparison to his God, and he saw them with a different perspective. This same vision was in the shepherd boy, David, as he faced the giant, Goliath. He, too, was not afraid of the enemy because of his view of God.

There are all kinds of giants challenging the church, but God is bigger than the giants. There will be some who will see the problems as too big; and just like the ten spies with the grasshopper complex, they will return to the wilderness and die. Rather than looking up at the obstacles, we must have a heavenly perspective and look down on the giants in our path. Even giants seem like ants when we are looking from heaven.

God was the source of Caleb's vision. He understood that Canaan belonged to the Lord. This is where the visioning of the secular, corporate world and church world diverge. As leaders, we do not create vision; we receive vision. This does not imply a lack of creativity on our part but acknowledges the source of all spiritual vision—God. Because God has called us, we must not be satisfied with the status quo. We see what can be accomplished through the eyes of the Holy Spirit, and we must see the vision fulfilled.

What vision has God given us? Can we easily state the mission of our life? If so, what kinds of obstacles are in our path? Do we view them from a biblical perspective, or do we suffer from the grasshopper complex?

Vision: The Scalability through Challenges

The capture of Caleb's Mountain would not be easy. Vision does not candy-coat the future. Although Caleb saw the giants from God's perspective, they were still giants. Vision does not see things that do not exist or make difficult things disappear. Caleb saw the same giants, walled cities, and mountain ranges the other spies saw; however, his vision was not limited to the physical realm.

Conquering Canaan would be a difficult but not an impossible task. Caleb knew that, most likely, some Israelites would die in the battles required to possess the land of promise; but he also knew that the God of Israel had promised to fight for them. Leaders are aware of the challenges ahead and are willing to face them because they know God will be with them. They survey the journey and see the obstacles in their way. The challenges that lie ahead only serve to strengthen the vision, and the vision stirs up courage in the heart of the visionaries.

Just like Caleb, leaders face challenges. Those others around them may doubt, but leaders know that it is God who makes the impossible possible. With vision, they see past the current situation to the end where God allows them to possess the promise, He has for them. The challenges they face are there to build the vision inside them. These challenges are the stepping-stones along the path that strengthen the visionary for the final destination. God has a purpose in every stage of the journey, even the bumps in the road. These challenges may look like giants to some but are small in comparison to the God who gives us the vision to accomplish the mission He has called us to do.

Vision: The Source For Victory

Caleb was forced to postpone conquering the mountain God had placed in his heart because of the failure of Israel. When Caleb finally saw his vision come to fulfillment, he was 85 years old. After wandering in the wilderness, Caleb found himself at the foot of the same giant-filled mountain that had frightened the children of Israel forty years before. Listen to his words to Joshua:

Now behold, the Lord has let me live, just as He spoke, these forty-five years, from the time that the Lord spoke this word to Moses, when Israel walked in the wilderness; and now behold, I am eighty-five years old today. I am still as strong today as I was in the day Moses sent me; as my strength was then, so my strength is now, for war and for going out and coming in.

Now then, give me this hill country about which the Lord spoke on that day, for you heard on that day that Anakim were there, with great fortified cities; perhaps the Lord will be with me, and I will drive them out as the Lord has spoken (Joshua 14:10-12). The mountain was still in Caleb's heart! The very mountain that caused others to turn back was the motivator for Caleb's perseverance. His vision was about to become reality. How did he keep that mountain in his heart for forty years in the desert?

The vision God gave Caleb inspired him to undying faith. His faith did not diminish in the wilderness. Through his forty long years of circling in the desert, the image of a conquered mountain only grew stronger. There is no way of knowing how many times Caleb fought and captured the walled cities of those mountains in his heart while walking in the desert.

Let others die in the wilderness if they want to, but we are going to take the mountain. He never gave up on the promised vision in front of him. Everything he did was in preparation for accomplishing the vision. When the going gets tough, leaders rely upon the vision God places in them for faith.

Though Caleb had not possessed the land physically, he had possessed the mountain in his heart. There are two ways to possess something: in your heart and in your hands. Even wandering in the wilderness could not take the mountain away from Caleb. He had already possessed it through the power of vision. Do we have a mountain in our heart? Do we live in victory while in the wilderness? While we are in the wilderness, we must never lose sight of the mountain in our heart. It will sustain us on our journey just like Caleb. A God-inspired vision allows leaders to walk in faith, devotion, and strength until they reach their goal.

Vision: The Strive Toward Our Vision

People of vision see what others cannot. Though others cannot make sense of the situation, it seems normal to leaders. God has birthed in them a vision that has been strengthened by challenges and will bring them to victory. They see how events are falling into place while others think they are falling apart. Their perspective is different; their current surroundings are the raw material of the future vision. They may be in the wilderness now, but the mountain is in their hearts. The leaders of the synergistic church live a life of faith and trust in God. They see the end of the journey and allow God to guide them on the path.

What is preventing us from realizing our potential, from accomplishing the vision God has given us? Are there doubts, discouragements, or distractions in our life? Do we feel like a grasshopper beneath the giant foot of adversity? Through the power of vision, we must see what others cannot. We must see the fulfillment of the promises of God in our life and see challenges as the building blocks of the future. We must possess the mountain in our heart.

Our Calling By God

Florence Chadwick was the first woman to swim the English Channel in both directions. She set records around the world for great feats of long-distance swimming. At the age of 34, her goal was to become the first woman to swim from Catalina Island to the California coast. On July 4, 1952, in freezing water and intense fog, she set out to accomplish this daring feat. For 16 hours, she swam in fog so thick she could barely see the support boats that followed her. Several times sharks were driven away by rifle fire. Within one-half mile of the shore, she asked to be pulled from the water. Her trainer assured her she could make it the final one-half mile, but all she could see was fog. In an interview after the swim, she said, "I'm not excusing myself, but if I could have seen the land, I might have made it." Two months later with the shore clearly pictured in her heart and mind, she attempted and accomplished the swim. What was the difference? She had a clear vision of the shore, and that was her strength.

If you are uncertain about your calling to be a minister of the Lord Jesus Christ, spend some quality time with some of God's choicest servants.

Through the power of the Holy Spirit, leaders enable people to see what they cannot see on their own. They help people see the shore ahead even when it is clouded by mist and fog. They help people realize that the mountain God has promised must first be conquered in their hearts. We are living our own vision and helping others discover theirs.

While the call of God is specific and personal, it may be hard to find at times. The journey of God's calling may be filled with false paths, experiments, and setbacks and require practice and prayer. If you are uncertain about your calling to be a minister of the Lord Jesus Christ, spend some quality time with some of God's choicest servants. Make plans soon to set some quality time aside and search your soul regarding the call of God for your life. If you are waiting until the pressures of ministry subside before resolving this important issue, you may have to wait the rest of your life. In this case, waiting time could be wasted time. It may take several years to know for certain that the calling rests upon your life.

As you are led by the Spirit of God to fulfill the calling of God upon your life, you will experience His power and purpose at work in you. You will be inspired by the vision He has given you so that, like Caleb, you can defeat the mountains in your heart before you even face them. Vision, calling, and power go hand in hand. God faithfully enables you through His Holy Spirit. It is important to understand that unless you know that you are called by God and are empowered by the Holy Spirit, you cannot reach a level of significance and fruitfulness in your ministry. Unless you fulfill that calling, avoiding the distraction of imitation, you will never achieve all God has for you in ministry and in life.

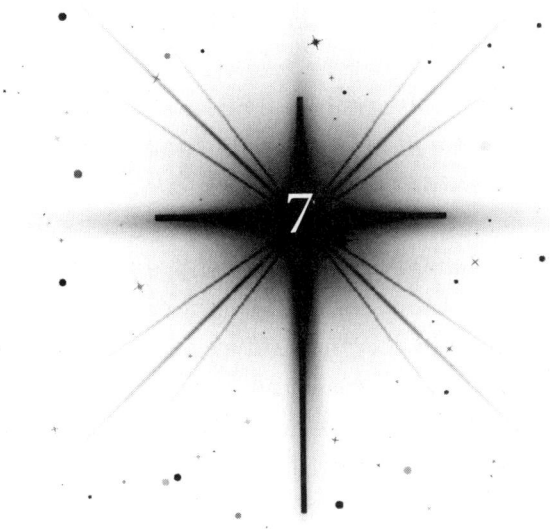

Our Character Before God

A Columbine High School student accurately summed up today's culture in a communication on the Internet during the Autumn of 1999:

- The paradox of our time in history is that we have taller buildings but shorter tempers, wider freeways but narrower viewpoints.
- We spend more but have less; we buy more but enjoy less.
- We have bigger houses but smaller families, more conveniences but less time.
- We have more degrees but less sense, more knowledge but less judgment, more experts but more problems, more medicine but less wellness.
- We have multiplied our possessions but reduced our values.
- We talk too much, love too seldom, and hate too often.
- We have learned how to make a living but not a life.

- We have added years to life but not life to years.
- We have been all the way to the moon and back but have trouble crossing the street to meet the new neighbor.
- We have conquered outer space but not inner space.
- We have cleaned up the air but have polluted the soul.
- We have split the atom but not our prejudices.
- We have higher incomes but lower morals.
- We have become long on quantity but short on quality.
- These are the times of tall men but short character, steep profits, shallow relationships.
- These are the times of world peace but domestic warfare, more leisure but less fun, more kinds of food but less nutrition.
- These are the days of two incomes but more divorce, of fancier houses but broken homes.
- It is a time when there is much in the show window and nothing in the stockroom, a time when technology can bring this letter to you, and a time when you can choose either to make a difference . . . or just hit delete.

Sadly, when it comes to the issue of character, most of us hit delete. Our world is cruel and brutal. The things that used to make us weep now make us laugh. The awful effects of sin have seared the conscience of our culture. We no longer govern according to what is right and wrong but according to what works and what makes money. Our culture has sold its soul to materialism, filled nearly every sector with liberalism, and has as its theme, "If it feels good, do it."

The church must stand against the attacks of the enemy. We must stand firmly consistent in a world that embraces moral relativism and abandons conscience and love. We must see God moving among the chaos of the world. Where others see death, real leaders see the potential for life. We are not bound by temporal circumstances because we can see the eternal creator. We see the potential in all people for knowing Christ and changing the world. People focused on the present world see the pleasures, treasures, and measures of the world, not the potential of Christ working in it (1 John 2:16). John says that in the world there are the "cravings of sinful man"—the world's pleasures. The person who is distracted by sin cannot focus on the Savior. God's Word says that in the world there is "the lust of the eyes"—the treasures of the world. Worldly people desire the temporary beauty of the earth rather than the eternal beauty of heaven. The Bible also says the world is filled with the "boasting of what man has and does"—the measures of the world. Worldly people trust in their accomplishments for advancements instead of boasting in the work of the cross. Worldly people cannot see the invisible world because they look only at the present world. Moses did not have a worldly view. He was able to look ahead and see the invisible reward because he trusted in God despite his circumstances (Hebrews 11:26-27). His eyes were on the creator, not the attractions of the world.

> *The Christian life must be lived in total, absolute surrender to our great God and Savior.*

We must rise up and help make a difference in the world. When the roof is removed from the church, our lives are laid open before God. We see Him in all His glory, and He sees us in all that we say and do. With the image of a powerful, loving God above us, we cannot help but live our lives in surrender to Him. The moral fiber of the synergistic church must be strong. Our character must match the volume of our rhetoric. Many people tell others what to do and how to do it. We must show people what to do through our godly actions and our Christlike character.

The Christian life must be lived in total, absolute surrender to our great God and Savior. We surrender to the lordship of

Jesus Christ, becoming His bondservants or slaves to His will and desires. The act of surrender strengthens our character, and our character enables us not only to live holy lives but also to persevere through the trials and adversities of life. We finish the course before us. Living a consistent life means we are committed to hard work. The difference between an effective, fruitful ministry for Christ and a mediocre ministry is hard work in the power of the Holy Spirit.

God's Word commands us "to work heartily, as for the Lord" (Colossians 3:23). Paul said, "I can do [not "I can sit or wait"] all things through Christ which strengtheneth me" (Philippians 4:13 KJV emphasis added). It is a principle that is only understood when seen through the eyes of potential. As leaders, we are not afraid to work hard or go the extra mile because we see what can happen from our hard work in the Lord.

SURRENDERING TO THE LORDSHIP OF CHRIST

Leaders must submit themselves to the lordship of Jesus Christ. When we surrender to the lordship of Christ, we follow Him in all that we do. He molds and shapes our lives, and we live for Him alone. As a result, we are conformed into His image.

One of the dangers of being a Christian leader is the misuse of authority. We must never forget that we are called to serve. If we are not careful, we forget that the source of our leadership is Jesus Christ. We are reminded of Paul's words, "I glory in Christ Jesus in my service to God" (Romans 15:17 NIV). As leaders, we must keep in mind that we serve those we are called to lead and that we live our lives in submission to the lordship of Christ.

Too many times, pastors fail because they become greater in their own eyes than they really are. They believe the compliments people give them. They assume that success and position give them privilege and license to do whatever they choose. Solomon warns us: "When pride comes, then comes dishonor, but with the humble is wisdom" (Proverbs 11:2). The leader who presides arrogantly over the church rebuilds the roof between himself and God. Our own pride is usually the major factor preventing us from surrendering to Jesus Christ. Pride becomes a limit we must move beyond.

The path of surrender takes three steps. To really surrender to Christ, we must **break** our pride, **bow** in humility, and **bear** our cross. When we follow these steps, we can prevent our character from being called into question, especially in the arena of leadership. Leaders must constantly remember to fight the fleshly nature within them and follow these steps to become a slave of Jesus Christ. Many individuals in positions of leadership or those aspiring to leadership roles have sensed a desire to make a significant mark with their lives and work. This motivation often comes from a sincere desire to serve Christ and His Church. We must be careful, however, to understand that any success that happens in ministry is only because Christ has chosen us to accomplish His plan. Jesus said, "Apart from Me you can do nothing (John 15:5).

To avoid the path that leads to a downfall in the life of the leader and to always remain a slave to Jesus Christ, we must follow these three steps: **Break our pride**. Pride seems to be one of the constant components of every human personality that irresistibly begins to drive us early in life.[1] The slave of Jesus Christ has nothing to boast about but Jesus Christ because we have submitted everything to God. We are to give our entire body as a tool for the glory of God, available for His use and the worship of Him (Romans 6:13). In the hands of the construction worker, the hammer never looks back at a finished house and thinks, "My, what a great hammer I am. Look at the house I built!" The hammer is just the tool. The effort, the ingenuity, and the credit go to the builder. This same principle applies to our lives. We are the tools God uses in leadership. Even in success, we have nothing about which to boast or be proud. God is the one who deserves all the glory and honor for the accomplishment.

Bow in humility. Paul encourages believers to be "slaves of Christ, doing the will of God from the heart" (Ephesians 6:6). We must submit our will to Christ. If we follow our own desires and path, we no longer serve Christ as Lord. Jesus is the perfect example of one who submitted His will to God: "I have come down from heaven, not to do My own will, but the will of Him who sent Me" (John 6:38). Submission is not a popular concept today, but our ability to submit to God determines whether we struggle through life or really live. Jesus submitted to His Father even to the point of going to the cross. As Paul admonished, we must bow before Christ and offer ourselves as living sacrifices:

The synergistic church must strive to make stronger, more mature Christians through discipleship programs. In fact, we are called as leaders to equip the body of Christ for service.

Therefore, I urge you, brethren, by the mercies of God, to present your bodies a living and holy sacrifice, acceptable to God, which is your spiritual service of worship. And do not be conformed to this world, but be transformed by the renewing of your mind, so that you may prove what the will of God is, that which is good and acceptable and perfect. (Romans 12:1-2)

In humility, we should acknowledge the lordship of Christ over our lives and the ministry He has given us. We must renounce our personal desires, needs, rights, and accomplishments.

Bear our cross. Many people are more interested in wearing a cross than bearing a cross. Jesus said, "If anyone wishes to come after Me, he must deny himself, and take up his cross and follow Me" (Mark 8:34). The essence of life as a slave is found in those last two words: "follow Me."

Leadership positions can easily rob us of our time with God. Leadership titles will tempt us to assert our own authority in different situations. Therefore, leaders can never leave the feet of Jesus. They must lead from a position of dependence upon God. When we are dependent Him, He will use us to further His kingdom. Leaders must never forget they are merely the tools God is using to build His kingdom. Paul admonishes us: "He who boasts is to boast in the Lord" (2 Corinthians 10:17).

SUBMITTING TO THE IMAGE OF CHRIST

Charles William Eliot (1834-1926), former president of Harvard University, had a birthmark on his face that bothered him greatly. As a young man, he was told that surgeons could do nothing to remove it. Someone described that moment as "the dark hour of his soul." Eliot's mother gave him helpful advice: "My son, it is not possible for you to get rid of that hardship . . . but it is possible for you, with God's help to grow a mind and a soul so big that people will forget to look at your face." Peter wrote about the beauty of "the hidden person of the heart" (1 Peter 3:4). Although he was speaking to women, the attractiveness of inner spiritual traits is equally becoming to men. Christlike character is more desirable than the finest external physical features.[2] The streams of life flow from our inner heart. And at the heart of one who ministers must be character. Financier J. P. Morgan once commented that "a man's best collateral is his character."[3]

While the character question applies to the leader of the church, it is also for everyone. The synergistic church must strive to make stronger, more mature Christians through discipleship programs. In fact, we are called as leaders to equip the body of Christ for service. The minister's purpose is clearly defined in Paul's letter to the Ephesians. Paul lists the fivefold ministry gifts of the church which are for the equipping of God's people for the "work of service, to the building up of the body of Christ" (Ephesians 4:12). The purpose of the leader is to equip the church.

The Greek term for "equipping" means "to put right" or "to put in order."[4] Equipping denotes "the bringing of the saints to a condition of fitness for the discharge of their functions in the Body, without implying restoration from a disordered state."[5]

The church leader is to set the church in order, making each member fit for the work of ministry. The Greek term for "building up" refers "to the act of building . . . to build on something, to build further."[6] We are to help God's people conform to the image of Christ, to help them through the Spirit of God become people of strong character.

After ministry's purpose—equipping—is established, Paul delineates the priorities of the gospel minister. There is a fourfold equipping or maturing function for the leader of the church. To function biblically, their message, motives, methods, and ministry must align with the Christ-given purposes outlined in Ephesians 4:13-16.

The Christian is to become mature in **stature**. We must be active "until we all attain to the unity of the faith, and of the knowledge of the Son of God, to a mature man, to the measure of the stature which belongs to the fullness of Christ" (Ephesians 4:13). This verse paints a picture of the Church maturing into a perfect, full-grown man. The whole body of Christ is viewed as one new man with one faith in the Son of God. The "faith" is the full message of the gospel. The "measure of the stature" indicates a level of spiritual perfection found in the fullness of Christ. The body of Christ is seen as progressing toward its future goal of perfection in the fullness of Christ. In short, as Christ inhabits our humanity, we are to display His deity more and more as we are being conformed to His image.

Second, we must help others become mature in **stability**. The Apostle Paul writes, "As a result, we are no longer to be children, tossed here and there by waves, and carried about by every wind of doctrine, by the trickery of men, by craftiness in deceitful scheming" (Ephesians 4:14). In verses 13 and 14, there is a purposeful contrast made between a perfect, full-grown man and children. Instead of spiritual maturity, the picture is of "spiritual infantilism."

The concept that Paul teaches is not of physical infants in a boat who are helpless to manage it in wind and waves but of physical men who know nothing about managing boats and are as infants amid wind and waves.

We are to help God's people conform to the image of Christ, to help them through the Spirit of God become people of strong character.

Paul warns of dangerous preaching that comes from "the trickery of men" and their "craftiness in deceitful scheming." Those who preach this false doctrine are seen as willfully undermining the body of Christ. These tricksters appeal to the immature Christian who is often deceived by unethical tactics and persuasive words. Leaders must take full responsibility for their message, methods, and motives in ministry. Their ethics and exhortations must cause the body of Christ to be stable in an unstable world.

Third, we can help the local church become more mature in **speech**. The Apostle Paul continues, "Speaking the truth in love, we are to grow up in all aspects into Him, who is the head, even Christ" (Ephesians 4:15 emphasis added). "Speaking the truth" means "truthing" or "doing the truth."[7] Mature Christians recognize the lies of religious tricksters by comparing them to the truth. They correct the error of these religious charlatans by speaking the truth in love. "Truthing in love" keeps "every joint" (v. 16) limber and flexible in the midst of a changing culture. It has been said, "Whatever is in the well of the heart comes out in the bucket of speech." When the heart of the body of Christ is filled with truth and love, Christians will lovingly confront all error in their society.

Fourth, we equip the local church to mature in **service**. Paul writes, "From whom the whole body, being fitted and held together by what every joint supplies, according to the proper working of each individual part, causes the growth of the body for the building up of itself in love" (Ephesians 4:16). The ultimate goal of an active, fivefold ministry is to have each member fulfilling their role. The whole body of Christ is being "fitted together" and "held together" by each separate "joint." It is only when every member is working together in synergy that the body of Christ receives the full support it needs to do the "work of service." The lifeblood of the body of Christ is "love." Each member is to have a loving heart toward the other members of the body of Christ.

STRIVING THROUGH TRIALS WITH CHRIST

Character is not just a matter of doing the right things; it is also staying consistent through adversity. Perseverance is a word seldom heard anymore. Our society is being programmed to want everything faster. If an activity requires time and effort, it is not worth doing. We must fulfill the calling God has placed upon our lives even in the hard times. We must live lives of integrity and consistency, persevering even when it is difficult to do so.

THE SECOND MILE LEADER

Among the many principles taught by Jesus Christ, the principle of "the second mile" completely highlights the dynamics of true discipleship. In the middle of the Sermon on the Mount, Jesus said, "Whoever forces you to go one mile, go with him two" (Matthew 5:41). It is the second-mile principle that will put a smile on our face, a spring in our step, and a song in our heart. The first mile is the trial mile, and the second mile is the smile mile. The key to living life with a smile is a Christ-centered life.

There are several reasons for going the second mile as a leader in the synergistic church. The second mile is **the character mile**.

What was Jesus talking about when He said, "Whoever shall force you to go one mile, go with him two"? In Jesus' day, the Romans had a practice that they had learned from the Persians about six hundred years earlier. This practice was to subjugate the people who had been conquered through war. A Roman soldier could command a Jewish man or boy to carry his backpack or burden for one mile. The Jewish person was required by law to oblige. Most Jews in this situation would carry the burden the requisite mile and not one inch more. The law caused terrible resentment among the Jews toward the Roman government.

Character is not just a matter of doing the right things; it is also staying consistent through adversity.

Can you imagine how the Jews felt when Jesus said, "Go the second mile"? The audience no doubt said, "He must be joking. Carry the burden for the Romans an extra mile? Who does He think He is? The law only says one mile, not two." It would be hard for most people to do more than the law required of them. Jesus was calling for ministry over and above the requirements. He was looking for people filled with love and servanthood. Jesus was looking for second-milers.

Second-milers do more than is required or expected. Jesus showed that any pagan or unsaved person could go one mile (Matthew 5:46-47). The first mile is to love those who love us. The second mile is to love those who do not love us. When a Jew was carrying the soldier's burden for the first mile, he was a slave. However, when he chose to carry the burden for a second mile, he then took control of the situation. The character mile moves us from slaves to masters. The first mile is the "have-to" mile, but the second mile is the "want-to" mile.

The second mile is the **commitment mile**. We go the first mile out of legalism but continue the second mile out of love. In order to live like Jesus, we must go the second mile when we experience *personal degradation* (Matthew 5:38-39). The first mile is to give place to revenge, but the second mile is to give place to love. Jesus said, "Whoever slaps you on your right cheek, turn to him the other also" (v. 39). For someone to strike us on the right cheek, that person must hit us with the back of their hand. If someone has treated us disrespectfully before others, this is an appropriate opportunity to go the second mile. As Abraham Lincoln stated, the best way to get rid of an enemy is to make that enemy a friend.

In order to live like Jesus, we go the second mile when others have wronged us, when we have wronged others, and when there are serious financial needs.

Furthermore, the commitment mile includes *personal defeat*. In Matthew 5:40, Jesus is talking about a legal settlement in which a brother has been found guilty. He is required to give his shirt. Jesus is saying that if we know we have done wrong, we should not simply try to rectify the wrong by fulfilling the law, but we should also go the second mile. If we are wrong, then we need to apologize, make things right with our brother and God, and then go the second mile.

Not only does the second mile include personal degradation and personal defeat but also *personal dedication* (Matthew 5:42). We are to have a giving spirit. We are not simply to pay our bills but also give to those who are in real need. In order to live like Jesus, we go the second mile when others have wronged us, when we have wronged others, and when there are serious financial needs.

Last, the second mile is the **commission mile**. Successful people live by the second-mile principle. The first mile is crowded, but the second mile is not busy at all. Imagine two different scenes. In the first scene, a Roman soldier commands a Jewish man to carry his burden for an entire mile. The man becomes extremely upset as he picks up the soldier's burden and begins to carry it. As he does so, he mutters in angry tones at the soldier. At the end of a mile, he throws the burden down and returns home, full of rage, hatred, and anger.

The second scene is the complete opposite of the first. As soon as the Roman soldier commands the Jewish man to carry his burden, the Jew responds with a warm, friendly greeting. In his heart, he truly wants to win this soldier to the Lord. Along the way, he converses with the soldier. At the end of the first mile, the Jewish man says, "If you do not mind, I would be honored to carry your burden for a second mile."

Can you imagine the incredulous look on the soldier's face when he hears these words?

The Roman soldier might say, "There is something different about you. Most Jews become angry when I command them to carry my backpack. What makes you different from the others?" The Jewish man says, "On one occasion, I heard Jesus Christ teach on the second-mile principle, so I am doing what He commanded me to do." The soldier responds, "Who is Jesus Christ?" The Jewish man answers, "He is the Messiah, the Savior of the world." By the time they reach the end of the second mile, the Jewish man has shared the gospel with the Roman soldier.

The second mile is the witnessing mile. More souls would be saved if we lived our lives on the second mile. Jesus went the second mile for all of us. Why would anyone want to live on the trial mile when we can live on the smile mile?

STANDING IN CHRIST WHEN WE DO NOT UNDERSTAND

In the 1990s, my wife, Sheri, and I spent a lot of time in the Greenlawn North Cemetery in Springfield, Missouri. Greenlawn North is a beautiful cemetery where maple trees create a magnificent show of vibrant colors in the fall. It is like a gorgeous park where many walk and run throughout the year. Our first pictures while we were dating were taken there in October 1982. We never imagined that our two precious children, Jennifer and James, would be born, live such a short time, die in Sheri's arms in the Cox South Medical Center, and be laid to rest at Greenlawn. Jennifer and James were born at 24½ and 29 weeks of gestation in 1991 and 1998, respectively. Our daughter lived for six weeks; and our baby son, born on Valentine's Day, died the following day. Even though we know our children are with Christ, the pain of helplessly watching our babies—with tiny features already resembling ours—die and burying them side by side was devastating to us.

We are not sinful for asking questions of God—only human.

On a spring afternoon in 1998, I stood by our children's graves pondering the most important priorities in life. As I read both the birth and passing dates on their tombstones, I began to reflect on the millions of children who are born each year around the world. Many are born in a Christless culture with very little hope of finding eternal life. If we do not have a worldwide spiritual awakening, the children will suffer the most in the years ahead. They will mature in a culture that has long forgotten the ways of the Lord.

How do we continue to serve God when we have such pain in our life? How do we continue despite the questions that plague us when we face such major trials? The prophet Habakkuk faced such a time in his life. The king of Babylon had conquered Palestine, and Jerusalem was plundered. Promising young men like Daniel, Shadrach, Meshach, and Abednego had been taken away while untold thousands were killed. Habakkuk wrestled to understand the ways of God. He agonized in prayer for answers.

Our Character Before God

To Habakkuk, it seemed that God was silent in the face of their adversity (Habakkuk 1:2). In addition, God appeared not to care that the righteous of Israel were suffering. The wicked Babylonians seemed to be prospering at the expense of Israel. God responded to Habakkuk with a revelation that works its way through scripture: "The just [righteous] shall live by faith" (Habakkuk 2:4 KJV). There are three components to that phrase: the just, shall live, and by faith. Interestingly, this phrase occurs three times in Scripture. In Romans 5:1, Paul writes that it is by faith that we have been justified and have obtained peace with God. In Hebrews 10:38, the author reminds us that the righteous will live by faith. In each of these sections, a different component is emphasized. Habakkuk is concerned about the righteous. He cannot understand why Israel is facing so much hardship. His questions sounded something like, "God, we are serving you, but all these bad things are happening and it does not make sense." God points out to Habakkuk that it is He who makes the righteous just and it is the ability to live by faith that makes them righteous.

Paul's concern is the living part of the righteous person's life. This quote is couched between instructions on holy living. It is not enough just to have faith; we must live it out and actively pursue what we have inside of us. The Book of Hebrews is teaching on faith. Hebrews 10:38 precedes Hebrews 11, the great chapter on faith. When each occurrence is viewed together, we realize that we must depend upon God in every aspect of our lives. We must trust in Him to lead us through adversity.

We are not sinful for asking questions of God—only human. It is a sign of character that we live through trials by faith. When we understand the love and faithfulness of God, we can rejoice and give thanks no matter what our circumstances (James 1; Romans 5; and 1 Thessalonians 5:18). When we do that as an expression of faith, Jesus reveals Himself to us (John 14:21).

FINISHING THE RACE: REALIZING OUR POTENTIAL

Within each Christian leader—indeed, within every one of God's children—lies the synergistic ability to transform a community, a nation, and the world. Oliver Wendell Holmes once said that most people die with the music still in them. They never let out what God has put in them. Their song was never heard because they did not know its potential. People of character are hardworking. They finish the race they are asked to run.

When we live our lives beyond the limitations of ineffectiveness and unfulfillment, we come to several realizations. These are very important to the workings of the synergistic church, and they are important to integrate into the local church. Leaders realize there are no shortcuts to long-term effectiveness.

"If building a great church were easy, there would be a lot of great churches." This summary of church leadership came from a discussion with George Sawyer, a pastor in Decatur, Alabama. His words captivated me for several months. After joining his church in worship and evangelism, I commented on how great a church he pastored. His response has stuck with me ever since. All the ideas, thoughts, creativity, and even potential amount to little if they are not acted upon. The greatest enemy to church growth is not a satanic attack but the laziness of the flesh. Too many leaders are looking for shortcuts to success, and there are no shortcuts in ministry if we want to be effective. While many long for successful ministries, it is the leaders who work hard over time, drawing upon the mighty power of God, who ultimately grow the greatest churches. While we cannot all be great, we can all at least be effective.[8]

George Washington Carver, a former slave, is considered one of the world's greatest agricultural scientists. This self-educated, African-American, discovered more than 300 by-products of peanuts, sweet potatoes, and soybeans. He received many awards for discoveries that affect our lives even today. Carver tells of a pivotal moment in his development. His foster parents were on a trip for several weeks, and Carver decided to help at home by repairing, cleaning, and polishing items in the house.

When his parents returned, Carver proudly listed all his achievements. Mariah, his foster mother, interrupted, "Now, George, don't tell me the number of things you have done but how well you have done them." It was a lesson he always remembered. This same work ethic continued throughout his life. While teaching at the Tuskegee Institute, he initiated strict rules for his students. He did not tolerate laziness or underachievement. Assignments not 100 percent completed or on time were rejected.

Within each Christian leader—indeed, within every one of God's children—lies the synergistic ability to transform a community, a nation, and the world.

He hated projects that were "about" finished and often told his students, "Remember, the more ignorant we are, the less use God has for us. There are only two ways. One is right and the other is wrong. 'About' is always wrong. Don't tell me it's about right. If it's only about right, then it's wrong. If you come to a stream five feet wide and jump four and a half feet, you fall in and drown."[9] Carver was able to accomplish great things because he was willing to work harder than most. Carver drew this work ethic not only from family but also from God's Word. He had a profound faith in Christ and daily sought God's wisdom for guidance.

Leaders realize that if they do not follow through, they have not really followed their calling.

When God told Israel to conquer Canaan, He promised them He would give them every place they set their foot (Joshua 1:3). He gave them specific instructions to possess the whole land and not let anyone remain (Joshua 1:4-5). As Joshua led them across Canaan, they destroyed every town except Gaza,

Gath, and Ashdod. For some reason, they allowed survivors in these towns (Joshua 11:22).

This lack of complete victory would haunt Israel in years to come. They did not follow through on what God told them to do. When leaders leave unfinished business in ministry, that unfinished business can finish their ministry.

It may not happen immediately; but eventually, the "enemies" we fail to conquer will attempt to conquer us. These Philistine cities and their presence caused much death and destruction throughout the history of Israel and Judah. They constantly caused problems for the children of Israel who failed to finish the conquest of Canaan. Goliath the giant came from Gath (1 Samuel 17:4). Is it a coincidence that the antagonist of Israel came from one of the cities spared in the conquest of Canaan? Goliath provided a political challenge for Israel, and the armies of the Philistines came through Gath.

It was in the Philistine city of Gaza that Samson, the great judge, met Delilah and fell victim to her temptations. As a seaport, Gaza provided many temptations and trials for the children of Israel and was a place of moral challenge. When leaders do not finish the work, they are called to do and completely destroy the hold the enemy has in their lives, the unfinished work will tempt them to fall.

The final Philistine city that Joshua's men did not destroy was Ashdod. When the Philistines captured the Ark of the Covenant, they took it to Ashdod (1 Samuel 5:1). Ashdod, which contained a great temple to Dagon, the Philistine god, was a spiritual challenge for Israel. When we do not fulfill the mission God calls us to do and we do not completely finish the task, the Ashdods that remain standing can steal the very presence of God from us. They become places of worship that are not ordained by God.

Leaders realize they are only as effective as the generation that follows them.

It has been reported that Martin Luther once said, "You will know whether or not your life was significant 500 years after you have died." Leaders take the long view, not the short view. Have you considered what your legacy will be? According to Max DePree, a legacy is created from the facts of our behavior that remain in the minds of others, the cumulative informal record of how close we came to the person we intended to be.[10]

Leaders realize they are only as effective as the generation that follows them.

This is not about setting and achieving goals but establishing and nurturing relationships. People with changed lives are the greatest legacy of a leader. In leadership conferences and in his personal study, John Maxwell has discovered that four out of five leaders emerged because of the impact made on them by a mentor.[11] Leaders lead for tomorrow, not for today. They understand that the best years of the church and their ministry are ahead, not behind. They influence tomorrow by investing in people today.

Real leaders find young leaders and train them for the future. They instill in them values, character, and the tenacity to accomplish their own goals. They replicate themselves over and over again in order to see the greatest impact. The leader must invest time and energy into future leaders. It is more than lunches and thirty-minute sharing sessions. Often it is a lifetime of sharing tears, laughter, ideas, and hurts with someone. A legacy is only created when leaders put their organization in the position to do great things without them.[12]

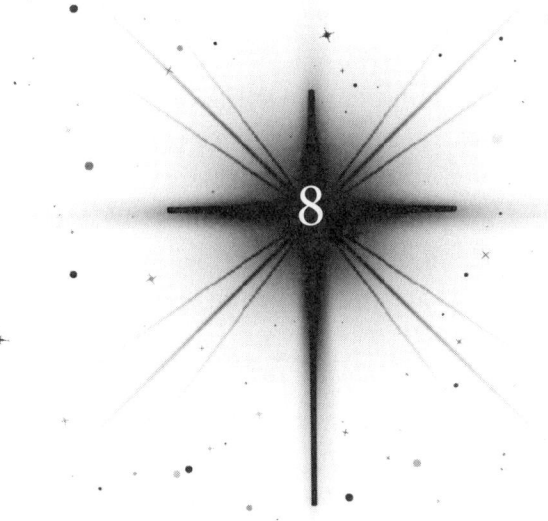

Our Commitment to God

It is not enough to receive God's call on your life and have your character formed by Christ. We must also demonstrate our commitment to God. The world is filled with people who claim to be committed but who do not follow through. Paul understood the necessity of being fully committed to Christ. Speaking to the Galatians, he wrote, "I have been crucified with Christ, and it is no longer I who live, but Christ lives in me; and the life which I now live in the flesh I live by faith in the Son of God, who loved me and delivered Himself up for me" (2:20).

When heaven is laid open before us, our only response is to commit our lives to God. We obey His commands and become like Peter and Paul, slaves of Jesus Christ. The synergistic church demonstrates its commitment to God through praise and worship, prayer and fasting, and its focus on helping to fulfill the Great Commission.

The prophet Daniel understood the importance of being committed to God. Few people in history have been as influential as this prophet. Daniel rose from obscurity in Jerusalem to be the advisor and confidant of some of the greatest kings in the history of the world. In fact, Daniel's influence was so great that, at times, he even ruled over all of Babylon. How could this Israelite exile rise from tragedy to triumph? How could this slave become a trusted friend of the king? Daniel never let his position in life or the pressures around him change his commitments.

The synergistic church demonstrates its commitment to God through praise and worship, prayer and fasting, and its focus on helping to fulfill the Great Commission.

Coupled with his faithfulness to God, his commitments enabled Daniel to become one of the greatest men of faith of the Old Testament. The exiled nation of Israel faced many temptations in Babylon. It would have been easy for them to forgo their commitment to God due to their circumstances. The temple of God in Jerusalem had been destroyed, thousands of men and women had been killed, and there was seemingly no hope left for Israel. Many believed that God had forsaken them. Because of this, many abandoned their faith and turned to pagan rituals. As slaves of the Babylonians, they left the laws of God and followed the gods of their captors. Daniel did not allow his circumstances to dictate his level of commitment to God. As advisor to Nebuchadnezzar, Belshazzar, Cyrus, and Darius, Daniel had many opportunities to reshuffle his priorities. His commitment to God often caused him to face death, but no matter the consequence, Daniel would not forsake the truths of his faith.

Daniel was committed to worshiping the true God of Israel and not chasing after idols. He was committed to maintaining his relationship with God through prayer and fasting. Daniel was also committed to advancing his faith and seeing people—even pagan kings—follow the one true God. These were priorities in Daniel's life. Underlying all of them was the understanding that God was sovereign. This trust in the power of God enabled Daniel to live a consecrated life.

WORSHIP AND PRAISE THAT LIFTS THE ROOF OFF

God explicitly told the children of Israel in the Law of Moses that He was the only true God. The Ten Commandments clearly indicated that Israel was to have no other gods before Him. Jehovah alone was to be worshipped. He gave them laws that governed the way He would relate to them and ways they could connect with Him. One way of worship was expressed through their eating practices. The Old Testament gave parameters on what God's people could and could not eat. This was an expression of their worship and allegiance to God. In addition to health reasons, many of the foods were banned because they were offered as sacrifices to pagan idols. Eating them would be worshipping gods other than Jehovah.

When Israel was defeated, Daniel and his friends were taken captive to the king's court. They were to be trained in the palace for service to the king. As part of their training, they were required to eat food from the king's table. This food was considered unclean in the Old Testament for it had most likely been sacrificed to idols. Daniel and his friends determined they would not eat this food because their commitment to God would not allow them. The Bible says, "Daniel resolved not to defile himself with the royal food and wine, and he asked the chief official for permission not to defile himself" (Daniel 1:8 NIV). His captors could change a lot of things but not Daniel's heart.

This brought Daniel into conflict with the chief official responsible for him. The official assumed that without eating from the king's table, Daniel and his friends would suffer from malnutrition or disease. If Daniel and his friends looked sick from lack of eating, the officials would be punished. Daniel, however, trusted in an all-powerful God. He believed that if He were faithful to God's Word, God would be faithful to him. The worship of God has been an integral part of how His people relate to Him. The Old Testament is filled with examples of God's people glorifying and honoring Him.

A revival of praise and worship has swept the church in the last 30 years. An emphasis on personal relationship and transformation has caused people to have a greater sense of connection with God and a greater desire to reverence and worship Him.

He convinced the chief official to allow Shadrach, Meshach, Abednego, and himself to consume nothing but vegetables and water for ten days. At the end of this time, the young men looked healthier and better nourished than those who ate the royal food (Daniel 1:15). The official then allowed Daniel to keep the Law of God. Daniel fulfilled his commitment to glorify only God. As the young men grew and were faithful to the God's Word, God gave them knowledge and understanding of all kinds of teaching and literature (Daniel 1:17). Their commitment resulted in blessing. Through a series of adventures and challenges, these exiles came to be some of the most powerful men in Babylon. Daniel became advisor to the king; and Shadrach, Meshach, and Abednego became governors of the province of Babylon, all because they were committed to God (Daniel 2:49).

From the early days of creation, Adam and his family built altars to God (Genesis 4:3-4). The Bible records songs of praise from Job, Moses, and many others (Job 1:20; Exodus 15:1-18). David, for example, wrote numerous majestic songs of adoration and praise to almighty God in heaven.

In the New Testament Church, worship was a vital part of life. Mary, the mother of Jesus, and Elizabeth, the mother of John the Baptist, both sang songs of praise to their God. Jesus also glorified His father in heaven, modeling the way His followers should worship God. If anyone deserved to be worshipped on earth, it was He; but He lifted up the name of His Father God. In teaching the disciples about prayer, He began with the holiness of God (Matthew 6:19). Even the Holy Spirit came to glorify God (John 16:14).

Early Christians often went to the temple to pray and worship (Acts 3:1). They spent time together fellowshipping and praising God (Acts 2:46-47). Worship of the one true God separates God's people from the world around them. This worship is not only the necessary response to our loving Savior but is also a message to the world about who God is. Our worship of Him expresses the elements of His character and attributes (Psalms 119 and 145), the power He has in the world (Psalm 47), the work He has done for us (Psalm 66), and the future we have when trusting in Him (Psalm 87). From these declarations of love to God, we reveal to the world how important it is that they also follow Christ.

The Impact Of Praise And Worship On Today's Church

A revival of praise and worship has swept the church in the last 30 years. An emphasis on personal relationship and transformation has caused people to have a greater sense of connection with God and a greater desire to reverence and worship Him. Praise and worship music makes up more than one-fifth of all Christian music sales. Spiritual formation and devotional books are filling the shelves of Christian and secular bookstores. People desire to show their devotion to and worship of God in tangible ways. They are redefining what it means to personally worship God. Just like Daniel, people are committed to honoring God through worship, and this worship is not confined to a Sunday service.

Dr. Elmer Towns, a leading historian of church growth, sees the emphasis on worship as indicative of the churches that are growing in this new decade. Through research, he has identified several methods that have been used in the last few years to reach our culture for Jesus Christ. The fastest growing churches in the 1970s were churches that emphasized bussing. In the 1980s, the "seeker-sensitive" model became the standard method for growing a church. In the 1990s, churches that emphasized small group and cell ministries were attracting people. Towns now sees the churches that emphasize praise and worship music as the churches that will see the most growth. The church is turning its eyes on Christ and desires to worship Him.

The church of the twenty-first century is a church that has the roof off. The roof is off in our churches because the praise of God has knocked it off its hinges. Interestingly enough, the term "worship service" is being used more and more to describe the times when God's people corporately gather together. In her book, Extravagant Worship, Darlene Zschech, said that true worship is extravagant worship. She defines extravagant worship as "worship that is beyond the limits...excessive, extremely abundant, over-generous, costly, precious and valuable."[2] As a church, we focus on our God in heaven and worship Him.

Worship songs today are filled with personal references to God and each individual's relationship to Him. Some have explained the difference like this: In the past we sang about God, but today we are singing to God.

Worshipping God—Glorifying God in All We Do

In this renewal of worship, it is important to realize that our worship of God is not just confined to fifteen to thirty minutes of singing at the beginning of each service. True worship is more than listening to the current best-selling track. Our entire lives should be lived as an expression of true worship to God. Paul wrote, "I urge you, brethren, by the mercies of God, to present your bodies a living and holy sacrifice, acceptable to God, which is your spiritual service of worship" (Romans 12:1). Paul was saying that our lives are a total expression of worship. We lay our

Our Commitment to God

lives on the altar and sacrifice who we are to acknowledge Him. When we obey God's commands and live righteously, we do it as an act of worship to God. True worship goes beyond the limits of song or time and pours into every aspect of life. Unlike previous decades of church growth techniques or distinctives, praise and worship is near and dear to the heart of God. This is more than a niche idea; it is the way God desires for us to live and move in His presence. As we glorify Him in all we do, we will find He continues to conform us to the image of Christ.

Our entire lives should be lived as an expression of true worship to God.

The people who exalt the name of the Lord on Sunday in song but do not live lives of holiness the rest of the week are not worshipping; they are just singing. We must engage our whole being—heart, mind, and soul—in our worship to God. We can praise God with our lips but not serve Him with our hearts. In the time of the prophet Joel, God's people acted like they were repenting. They had all the outward signs; but in their hearts, they did not mean what they were saying or doing. God rebuked them and said, "Rend your heart and not your garments" (Joel 2:13).

Churches and individuals who argue and fight about form and style in music and worship are spending more time in the works of the flesh than the works of the Spirit. True worshipers, extravagant worshipers, are not concerned about form but about the object of their worship, the Lord Jesus Christ. In fact, true worship has little to do with style or music form. Many people are convinced that a certain style of music is why God is moving today. These people have missed the point. God inhabits the praises of His people, regardless of the style. He inhabits praise, not tempo. A theology of worship that glorifies only one worship style is a narrow view of Christ's inexhaustible riches.[3] If we limit our expression of faith to God by only our preferred means, we will never fully grasp the vastness of God's presence and work in our lives. It is often from others that we see and learn more about God.

True worship always results in synergy. If there is one thing the body of Christ should be able to agree upon, it is the worship of Jesus Christ. To sing hallelujah to the Lord, it does not matter our theological persuasion or distinctive doctrine, traditions, history, race, social status, or view of baptism. We need not argue about whether a form of expression is or is not worship. Everything we do in life should be done as an expression of love and adoration to our Savior and King. When we take the stories of what God has done in Scripture and in our lives and retell them through art and music, we are glorifying God and testifying to others about who our God is. The beginning of synergy in a church or group of churches is always the worship of God. When we focus on Him, our differences become less and less significant. Let us take to heart the word of this hymn:

> Turn your eyes upon Jesus
> Look full into His wonderful face
> And the things of earth will grow strangely dim,
> In the light of His glory and grace.

As we grow closer together, may we look into His face and worship extravagantly.

PRAYER AND FASTING KEEP THE ROOF OFF

Not everyone loved Daniel's worship of God and God's subsequent blessing on him. While serving as advisor to King Darius, Daniel distinguished himself so much with his leadership skills that Darius desired to place him over the whole kingdom (Daniel 6:3). The other leaders were jealous of Daniel and tried to come up with ways to discredit him (6:4), but Daniel lived such a holy life that they were unable to find any corruption in him. Daniel's integrity and fairness were known throughout the land. The only area of his life they knew they could challenge was his commitment to the law of God (6:5).

Everything we do in life should be done as an expression of love and adoration to our Savior and King.

These men knew Daniel was committed to prayer. Three times a day, Daniel prayed and thanked God for all He had done for him. This worship and communication was a priority for Daniel. Every day, no matter the circumstances, he would go to the upper room of his home where the windows opened to Jerusalem and would pray three times a day (6:10). King Darius loved and respected Daniel which caused the other leaders to hate Daniel even more. These jealous leaders approached Darius to trick him into decreeing Daniel's death. Through flattery and manipulation, they convinced Darius to write a decree that for thirty days no one was to pray to any god or man except King Darius. The punishment for praying to another god would be death in the lion's den.

Daniel had a decision to make. He was the servant and advisor of the king and was soon to oversee the entire kingdom. The law did not require Daniel to pray to the king; he just could not pray to his God. Would Daniel follow the decree and not pray to God for thirty days? What would be most important for Daniel: personal advancement or commitment to God? Daniel's priorities would not allow him to follow this decree because he was committed to prayer.

When Daniel learned of the decree, he immediately went home to the upper room and prayed to his God (6:10). He was a man of conviction, a man of priorities, and a leader. The law of the king was not as important as God's law.

Daniel's enemies were waiting for him. They saw him praying and immediately went to the king. When King Darius heard their report, he was greatly disturbed. In fact, he made every effort to save Daniel from the lion's den, but his law was binding. Daniel would be thrown into the lion's den and a stone placed over the entrance. The den was sealed so that no one could get in or out. Darius did not sleep all night as Daniel remained with the lions. At the first morning light, the king raced to the lion's den and called into the den, "Daniel, servant of the living God, has your God, whom you constantly serve, been able to deliver you from the lions?" (6:20) Daniel's voice answered from the black cave, "My God sent his angel and shut the lions' mouths, and they have not harmed me, inasmuch as I was found innocent before Him" (6:22). God had saved Daniel! God had been with Daniel in the darkest and most dangerous of moments because Daniel had not compromised his commitment to prayer.

Like Daniel, we must be committed to prayer. Prayer and fasting were his strength in captivity. Christians who are called to live beyond the limits in this world must be plugged into God, the source of their strength. Prayer must saturate everything we do. It must permeate every new idea and old habit. It must be the first thing we do before beginning and the last before concluding. A church with no roof is a praying church.

EFFECTIVE PRAYER OF THE SYNERGISTIC CHURCH

Many people pray, but the Bible tells us we must have effective prayer: "The effective prayer of a righteous man can accomplish much" (James 5:16). The Greek term for "effective" means "stretched-out prayer." The implication is not in length but in intensity. This is comparable to the athlete stretching for the finish line.

With the roof off our church, there is a constant connection to God. We should pray without ceasing (Luke 18:1; Matthew 7:7-11; 1 Thessalonians 5:15). In Luke 18:1, Jesus told His disciples "not to lose heart." Moreover, Jesus constantly reminded them never to cease praying. Those who search for God with all their hearts will find Him (Jeremiah 29:13). Jesus illustrated this kind of "effective" prayer in the Garden of Gethsemane. Christ was in agony while praying fervently (Luke 22:44). The same word is used again to describe these kinds of prayers. Jesus was in agony, and His soul was "stretched out" to the point that His sweat became like drops of blood. The synergistic church must pray fervently, without ceasing or losing heart.

If leaders are going to have the mighty anointing of the Holy Spirit upon their message and ministry, they will have to agonize in prayer before God.

We need to understand that it is harder to pray than it is to preach the gospel. It is harder to intercede before God than it is to inspire others to serve God. We cannot fail in our commitment to prayer. If leaders are going to have the mighty anointing of the Holy Spirit upon their message and ministry, they will have to agonize in prayer before God.

Prayer must begin with the leadership of the church. Sadly, too many churches and pastors depend on the prayers of a few retired ladies for spiritual renewal. It is not enough to have several people praying. The entire church, including the pastoral team, must be praying. The synergistic church will budget time and money into the week for prayer. Pastor Jim Cymbala of the Brooklyn Tabernacle has seen the power of a church built upon prayer. Brooklyn Tabernacle spends hours each week in prayer and fasting.

If you are the pastor of a local church, how important is prayer to you? Do you systematically plan for periods of prayer during the week? Many church staff spend hours each week preparing the building for worship but do not prayerfully prepare their hearts for worship. Leonard Ravenhill summed up the issue well:

If we are ever to see a real revival of God's Spirit in our churches, if we are ever to live in synergy with His will and power, we must be praying churches.

No man is greater than his prayer life. The pastor who is not praying is playing; the people who are not praying are straying… We have many organizers, but few agonizers; many players and payers, few prayers; many singers, few clingers; lots of pastors, few wrestlers; many fears, few tears; much fashion, little passion; many interferers, few intercessors; many writers, but few fighters. Failing here, we fail everywhere.[5]

If we are ever to see a real revival of God's Spirit in our churches, if we are ever to live in synergy with His will and power, we must be praying churches. This commitment to prayer is necessary for the growth of the church. Before we can advance into the marketplace of ministry (where the church walls are down), the roof must be off in preparation.

A praying church undergoes **spiritual conditioning.** The spiritual muscles of the pastor and people grow as they "stretch" and "work" them out through supplication before God. The quality of our quiet time will result either in spiritual strength or spiritual weakness. Many pastors are failing in ministry because they are busy preparing messages or developing programs rather than praying for people. It is hypocritical to preach to people before first praying for them. The source of strength is our connection to God. Without this conditioning, we will not be able to finish the course.

A praying church is being **spiritually cleaned.** The journey of leadership consists of dirty, muddy roads. Each day the soul of the minister is soiled by the world. We will make mistakes as we move past the limitations that come against us. If we are not careful, the grime of life will create non-Christian attitudes in the heart and sin can be committed—even in the ministry. Thus, the prayer life becomes a time of spiritually washing the heart, mind, emotion, and will before God. The more time the leader spends each day in prayer, the more adjustments will be made in attitudes and actions in ministry.

Every great revival has been characterized by confession of sin to God and one another. Revival also comes when confession replaces criticism. There is constant temptation in the ministry to criticize fellow ministers. The humble servant leader is careful to listen and understand before commenting about various issues and individuals in the church. A praying church acknowledges it is in spiritual conflict. The evangelist and pastor are in a spiritual war for the souls of men and women. We must all realize that we wrestle not against flesh and blood but against principalities and powers of the air.

The most effective way to fight the enemies of God is on our knees in prayer. When the time of prayer is neglected, the battle is left unfought. How many victories have been won by the hordes of hell because God's people never entered the field of battle? How many battles have been lost because the Church of God never bowed its knees in prayer? When we neglect prayer, we are weakening our defense before Satan and his kingdom.

FASTING DEMONSTRATES DEPENDENCE

The committed Christian must be committed to prayer and fasting.

In 1994, God spoke to Dr. Bill Bright instructing him to fast for forty days. During that time, He revealed to him the need for a book on fasting. In that book, The Coming Revival, he identifies several benefits of fasting and prayer:

- It is a biblical way to truly humble oneself in the sight of God (Psalm 35:13; Ezra 8:21).
- It brings revelation by the Holy Spirit of a person's true spiritual condition, resulting in brokenness, repentance, and change.
- It is a crucial means for personal revival because it brings the inner workings of the Holy Spirit into play in a most unusual, powerful way.
- It helps us better understand the Word of God by making it more meaningful, vital, and practical.
- It transforms prayer into a richer and more personal experience.
- It can result in dynamic personal revival—being controlled and led by the Spirit and regaining a strong sense of spiritual determination.
- It can restore the loss of one's first love for our Lord.[7]

Elmer Towns points out that in fasting, we are not manipulating God but obeying His commands.[8] Fasting is not an end in itself but a means by which we can practice humility before God. In fasting, more than any other discipline, we are denying ourselves so that we might be filled with God. By humbling our souls, fasting reduces the power of self so that the Spirit can do a more intense work within us. As a result, He can accomplish His will in us and do even more than we can ask or imagine.

The synergistic church must be a fasting church. I strongly recommend reading the book, Fasting Can Change Your Life, by Drs. Jerry Falwell and Elmer Towns. This book is a collection of insights on fasting and the local church, from pastors and church leaders such as D. James Kennedy, Dutch Sheets, Jack Hayford, and others. There are chapters on leading the church through forty-day fasts, fasting for miracles, how to teach fasting, and several other relevant topics for the church that wants to emphasize fasting and prayer. It shows the need for personal and corporate times of prayer and fasting.

This often means the leadership of the church should call the church to fasting. There were definite times in the Bible when God's people were corporately called to fast. When doing this, it is necessary to teach and preach on fasting for several weeks to prepare the people.[9] It is very important to be led by God during these times along with using God-given commonsense. It is unrealistic to attempt a forty-day fast if a person has never fasted before. Begin with a one-day fast and follow the instructions from the Bible and other helps that are available. Those with medical conditions who cannot fast entire meals should never feel guilty or "less spiritual." They should consult a physician on what they can do. Perhaps they could fast from a certain food or abstain from a particular activity.

It is so important to seek God's face through fasting and prayer. The leader must be connected to God through prayer.

It is impossible to exaggerate the importance of prayer. Jesus said, "If you ask Me anything in My name, I will do it," (John 14:14).

It is absolutely necessary to keep this line of communication with God open in order that the roof of the church stays off.

EVANGELISM FLOURISHES WHEN THE ROOF IS OFF

Daniel was committed to more than just prayer and worship. He was committed to sharing God with his captors. It is interesting to note that Daniel influenced the key leaders of his day. By his testimony and faithfulness, he led King Nebuchadnezzar to acknowledge Jehovah as the Most High God (Daniel 4:2-3). Later in his life, Nebuchadnezzar declared Daniel's God as the majestic King of Heaven (Daniel 4:34-37). When Daniel's enemies tried to slander him, his testimony was so strong that they could find no area in which to accuse him. They therefore determined to accuse him regarding his commitment to God. As Daniel was being thrown into the pit, King Darius said to him,

"Your God whom you constantly serve will Himself deliver you" (Daniel 6:16). Daniel's priorities led to a powerful testimony.

He served God continually, even in the face of death. God delivered Daniel, and King Darius had Daniel's enemies thrown to the lions. Because of the testimony of Daniel, King Darius issued a new law protecting Israelite exiles from persecution when they served God. Darius also decreed that all the men of his kingdom should fear and reverence the God of Daniel. Daniel's commitment to his priorities allowed him to have a powerful testimony before the king and before all of Babylon.

EVANGELISM CREATES SYNERGY THROUGH RECONCILIATION

What is the meaning of the term "evangelism"? The Lausanne Covenant of the International Congress of World Evangelism (1974) provides a comprehensive definition:

To evangelize is to spread the good news that Jesus Christ died for our sins and was raised from the dead according to the Scriptures, and that as the reigning Lord, He now offers the forgiveness of sins and the liberating gifts of the Spirit to all who repent and believe. Our Christian presence in the world is indispensable to evangelism, and so is that kind of dialogue whose purpose is to listen sensitively in order to understand. But evangelism itself is the proclamation of the historical, biblical Christ as Savior and Lord, with a view to persuading people to come to him personally and so be reconciled to God. In issuing the gospel invitation, we have no liberty to conceal the cost of discipleship. Jesus still calls all who would follow him to deny themselves, take up their cross, and identify themselves with His new community. The results of evangelism include obedience to Christ, incorporation into His church and responsible service in the world.[10]

World evangelism is the supreme goal of the Church. Evangelism is to bear witness to the gospel with the soul aflame and to teach and preach with the express purpose of making disciples of those who hear.[11]

Even though Christ has commissioned every Christian to participate in world evangelization (Matthew 28:19), the leader must be focused on the cause of evangelism.

In the last one hundred years, the Church has witnessed positive movement on this front. Virtually every branch of the Christian church is being blessed with growth through evangelism. According to one estimate, the Pentecostal movement—which had its humble beginnings in Topeka, Kansas; and Azusa Street in Los Angeles, California, in the early 1900s—now numbers nearly one billion people. The total Christian population is approximately 2.4 billion at the time of this writing.

Despite these encouraging figures, it is estimated that unreached people groups still number as high as 2.5 billion people! Unquestionably, leaders must continue to be passionate about bringing men and women to Jesus Christ, taking seriously Christ's command to "go into all the world and preach the gospel to all creation" (Mark 16:15).

The fundamental mission of Jesus Christ was to seek and save that which was lost (Luke 19:10). Christ died on the cross in order that He might draw all men unto Himself (John 12:32). Paul calls Christ's work at Calvary "reconciliation" (2 Corinthians 5). He then tells us that we, as Christ's ambassadors, have been given the ministry of reconciliation (v. 5). What does it mean to have a ministry of reconciliation and what is the message of reconciliation? Paul writes that reconciliation is the work of Christ drawing men and women to Himself:

Remember that you were at that time separate from Christ, excluded from the commonwealth of Israel, and strangers to the covenants of promise, having no hope and without God in the world. But now, in Christ Jesus you who formerly were far off have been brought near by the blood of Christ (Ephesians 2:12-14).

The Bible contains God's plan for reconciliation and understanding. Some scholars believe that this word, reconciliation, is the ultimate message of all of God's work in the Bible—the restoration of a right covenant fellowship with God.

We must be sensitive to the needs of the seekers as we point them to Christ, but we must also be Savior-sensitive, not neglecting our message: Jesus Christ, reconciler of the world.

Reconciliation means the bringing together of things that are apart. The Bible's opening picture portrays humanity separating from its creator and God working to reconcile this divide. From that first break in communion with God, God's plan for reconciliation unfolds in Scripture and climaxes in the work of the cross.

The great paradox of Christian ministry is that we who were unable to reconcile ourselves to God are given the ministry of reconciliation. The goal of the Great Commission is not to establish an institutional church or denomination but to share the gospel and make disciples of all men. We are not so bold as to think that we as individuals can save others, but we can initiate their reconciliation by pointing them to Jesus Christ. Jesus Christ is the center of our faith and the center of our message.

Since we fear the Lord, we try to persuade men... Christ's love compels us because One died for all, therefore all died; and He died for all that those who live should no longer live for themselves but for Him who died for them and was raised again. So now we regard no one from a worldly point of view" (2 Corinthians 5:11, 14).

We must persuade men to embrace the Savior who died for them. We must challenge sinners and give them opportunity to accept the risen Savior. Through this message of reconciliation, Christ has torn down the walls between God and man. This is the passion of the leader. We must be sensitive to the needs of the seekers as we point them to Christ, but we must also be Savior-sensitive, not neglecting our message: Jesus Christ, reconciler of the world.

Connecting to the Culture

The Church must connect to the culture around it in three ways to be effective in the world in which we now live. These adaptations will enable the church with no roof to knock down the walls that have hindered the evangelism of the world.

First, we cannot **debate** minutia but must focus on essentials. A post-Christian world wants to know if there is a God and how He can be experienced. They are not concerned with the debated details of Christianity because they have not bought into the big picture yet. Arguments over Calvinism and Arminianism, the Eucharist, or modes of baptism are irrelevant when people do not know if God exists. By focusing on the essentials of the Christian faith (there is a God, man is a sinner, and Christ died to allow a relationship with God), we can help the world come to know Christ. We must not allow denominational trappings to limit the ability of anyone to receive and follow Christ.

Second, we cannot **condemn** those who reject our Lord but must reason with them in winsome gentleness, love, and respect. The greatest sign of desperation in any argument of debate is to fall to personal attack. For centuries, Christians have fallen into the trap of name-calling. Rather than reaching out in love, we have attacked those who did not immediately embrace Christ. We must tone down our verbiage and strengthen our love so that we might better lead them to Christ.

McClaren points out that it was easy to dismiss Buddhists and Muslims when they lived on the other side of the world, but the reality is that they now live next door to us. They will know we are Christians by our love, not by the volume of our speech. We must find ways to interact with those around us who do not follow Christ. We do not compromise our message or our passion, but we must model the love and humility Christ practiced on earth. Remember, Christ's harshest words were not for the pagans of His day but for the self-righteous Pharisees who treated others with contempt. It is a very important fact learned from many surveys and years of experience that Jesus is usually respected and admired even by non-Christians while His followers are often held in low esteem. Why? Because we fail to obey His teachings and follow His example.

The last component in reaching our culture is **patience**. We must not rush people but help them come to Christ at a healthy pace. We are programmed for a major conversion event or an instant salvation experience. However, the history of Christianity has been more process-centered than event-centered. Conversion for many people is a long process of commitment and understanding. Too many people have been rushed to commit to Christ before they have fully accepted the message of the gospel and are ready to fully commit to the life of faith. As a result, they have abandoned their faith. In this new period in history, we must enable people to understand what they are committing to as the Holy Spirit works in them.

BECOMING PURPOSEFUL IN OUR WITNESS

The greatest mode of evangelism in the world today is still personal evangelism. Every member of the body of Christ, from leadership to laity, is to be a personal witness who takes the initiative to share the most joyful news ever announced about our Lord Jesus Christ. Leaders do not just train others for evangelism; they do evangelism. They are personal witnesses for Jesus Christ. The greatest thing any follower of Jesus Christ can do is win someone to Jesus Christ.

Witnesses are those whose life and words are Christlike. They demonstrate that Christ is in control of their life. The Holy Spirit came to glorify Christ and to bear witness to Him;

therefore, Spirit-directed Christians will glorify Christ and tell others about Him. This will help fulfill the Great Commission given by our Lord Jesus Christ before He ascended into heaven (Matthew 28:19-20).

Many ministers can comfortably explain Christ's message to thousands at a time but struggle telling an individual the plan of salvation.

People express themselves to the world around them through actions and words. This communicates to others who we are and what we believe. To have an impact on other people, our words and actions cannot be in conflict. Our walk must be consistent with our message.

If we tell others about the love and lordship of Christ yet they see actions that do not reflect His love or lordship in our lives, we communicate a contradictory message to them.

Carnal Christians communicate disturbing and confusing messages to others. If we are not totally surrendered to Christ and His lordship in our lives, we can destroy our witness to people and hinder the work of God in their lives. Passionate leaders guard their actions and monitor their words.

Many people feel inadequate when it comes to personally sharing their faith. Many ministers can comfortably explain Christ's message to thousands at a time but struggle telling an individual the plan of salvation. Many have the passion for evangelism but do not know how to personally evangelize. This problem results from several causes. It may be a reliance on self and a lack of reliance on the Holy Spirit. Remember, Jesus told His disciples not to go witnessing until they received the infilling of the Holy Spirit. He knew that human ability alone was inadequate for the spiritual task of evangelism. We need to make sure we have appropriated the fullness of the Holy Spirit, confessed any known sin in our lives, received forgiveness and cleansing in accordance with 1 John 1:9, and expressed our reliance on Him. This will inject a new spiritual power into our witnessing.

The sense of inadequacy in personal witnessing could stem from fear or a lack of boldness. This can also be overcome by the Holy Spirit. God has not given us a spirit of fear but of power, love, and a sound mind (2 Timothy 1:7). Our love for God cannot help but overflow in our witness to others. The individual who struggles in this area should consult my (Bill) Gold Medallion-winning book, Witnessing Without Fear, where these issues are discussed at length. The leader must overcome the fear factor in witnessing through prayer and practice.

Our faithfulness in our commitment to God keeps the roof off the synergistic church. When the roof is off, we will wholeheartedly praise and worship our Creator God. Through prayer and fasting, we keep our connection to God open through earnest conversation with Him. This commitment to listening and speaking to God is what keeps the roof off. When we are committed to following the Lord, God knocks down the walls that would limit us in reaching out to others. Just like the children of Israel outside the fortified city of Jericho, God will use our shout of praise to knock the walls down, enabling us to evangelize the world. In the synergistic church, the roof is blown off with praise and the walls are brought down by our desire to introduce others to Christ.

PART THREE

A CHURCH WITH NO WALLS

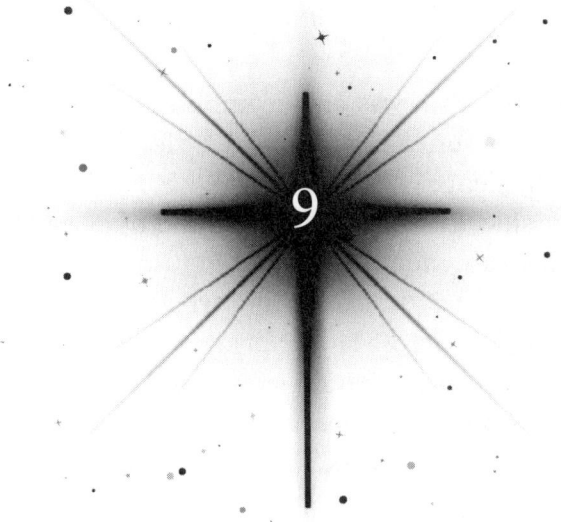

9

Our Interdependent Cooperation

"Look around," Jeff Evans said to Erik Weihenmayer. "Just take a second and look around." His words were simple; there was nothing special about them unless you understand the context in which they were said. Erik Weihenmayer is blind, completely blind; and the two men were standing on top of the world, Mount Everest.[1] On May 24, 2001, Erik and his team of 19 climbed 29,035 feet to reach the summit of the world's tallest mountain. Only a few brave explorers have accomplished this incredible feat, none of them blind. Almost 90 percent of all climbers fail to reach the summit; many fail to return home. After several months of climbing treacherous ice fields, fighting bitter cold and wind shear of over 100 miles per hour, Erik Weihenmayer became the first blind man to conquer Everest, achieving the seemingly impossible.

This Herculean achievement has caused people to compare Erik to Helen Keller. How did a blind man from Colorado make it to the top? The answer is simple: teamwork. Mountain climber Pasquale Scaturro assembled a team of climbers that helped Erik reach the summit. Erik was an accomplished climber who had already climbed Mount Kilimanjaro in Africa, but Everest would be a greater challenge. Across ridges with 10,000-foot vertical falls on either side, Erik followed the sound of a bell fastened to the back of the team member in front of him. He listened to his fellow climbers' verbal directions and trusted them to lead him to safety. He walked across ladder bridges that spanned chasms hundreds of feet deep. He fought snowstorms and temperatures 30 degrees below zero while wearing oxygen tanks to breathe.

Many wondered how Erik would contribute to the expedition. Would he put people at risk and slow down the expedition? Apparently not. Eric Alexander, a fellow climber, called Erik the "heart and soul of the team...he won't let you quit." Although Erik was an experienced climber, he needed Alexander, Scaturro, Evans, and the others to make it to the top. It takes the whole team to climb Everest. These men became the eyes for Erik as he climbed. He became their heart. They enabled him to do the impossible because they were a team, but they needed Erik as well. He kept them motivated to keep going as they helped him make his way. He would not let them quit!

The partnership these men formed over the months of climbing is incredible. How many times did Erik entrust his life to those around him? How many times did they entrust their lives to Erik? It took each of them working together to make it to the top. It took a team to accomplish the goal. It was a team that was greater as a whole than any individual person alone—a team built on synergy.

NO CHURCH IS AN ISLAND

The days of ministry in isolation are over. The church must form strong, viable partnerships if it is to make an impact in the twenty-first century. We must work together with those around us if we are to make a difference for the gospel. While it has been sufficient in the past to create individual churches or ministries, the new age of ministry requires collaboration. Those called to lead the church must unite with other leaders to accomplish the task. It will take all of God's people working together.

Many churches have thrived in this isolation. Like little islands of refuge in their community, these churches rise up from an ocean of evil around them. Long distances of philosophy and theology separate some churches from each other. Those who choose to interact with these different islands (churches) are forced to use great effort.

The Bible's picture of effective ministry and leadership is built around the concept of Holy Spirit-inspired teamwork and partnership.

Many are happy as long as their island is growing and are supportive of others as long as it does not require extended effort. Some churches are not even separated by beliefs; they simply have not taken the time to work together with other churches around them. The church beyond the limits must unite with those around it to form a strong force to reach the community.

Models for strong leadership have often been built around strong, magnetic personalities. People like Henry Ford, Andrew Carnegie, Aimee Simple McPherson, and D. L. Moody are considered models of successful leadership. They were rugged individualists who attracted followings and achieved great results. They were the great leaders of their day. Their legacy is felt even today.

The Bible's picture of effective ministry and leadership is built around the concept of Holy Spirit-inspired teamwork and partnership. Jesus selected the twelve disciples, the early Christians chose seven deacons, and Paul chose partners for his missionary journeys. Just like these early Christians, we must realize that it will take strategic partnerships of mutual respect and admiration to achieve the leadership task we are called to accomplish. Just like Erik Weihenmayer, we will need a team to help us reach the summit.

This truth is reflected even in corporate America. In recent years, the importance of teamwork and cooperation has risen to the forefront of the leadership culture. Old paradigms are collapsing, and people now see the value of teamwork. Businesses and organizations are realizing that old, antiquated forms of authority are not working. People today are interested in words like synergy, network, sharing, and community. "Hierarchy is out—it slows everything down," says Betsy Morris of Fortune magazine. "The conventional desk job is out…employees think of themselves as knowledge workers—their office is the information they carry with them…a CEO on a pedestal is definitely out; a CEO as a platoon servant leader is in."[2]

PAUL, THE MODEL FOR SYNERGISTIC MINISTRY

The Apostle Paul understood the necessity of synergistic ministry. His ministry was filled with examples of teamwork. Relationships were vital to Paul. To accomplish his mission in life, Paul needed fellow workers such as Luke, Timothy, Barnabas, John Mark, Titus, and others. Each of these individuals collaborated to create a more effective team. However, Paul was careful; he did not align himself with everyone. In fact, he often warned against collaborating with those who would shipwreck the faith (1 Timothy 1:18-19). Even though Paul knew there were dangers, he realized it would take everyone in the body of Christ, each doing their part, to fulfill the Great Commission. Just like Paul, we also need to work together to accomplish the work of God.

Paul and Barnabas: Partners in Ministry

Paul and Barnabas were one of the first missionary teams. After Paul's conversion experience on the road to Damascus, it was Barnabas who brought him to the elders in Jerusalem. Barnabas's name means "son of encouragement," and he lived up to his name in Paul's life.

Barnabas went to Antioch to investigate a report that many were coming to the Lord (Acts 11:21-22). Upon arriving, Barnabas, full of the Holy Spirit, saw God's hand at work and knew that Antioch needed someone to help them in their journey of faith. He sought out Paul, and for a year they ministered together in Antioch (Acts 11:25-26). Together they formed a powerful ministry partnership. They understood that their effectiveness was doubled through teamwork, and together they launched a missionary crusade that brought the gospel to all of Galatia. The Antioch church sent Paul and Barnabas to evangelize the region. The Holy Spirit instituted this ministry team: "Set apart for Me Barnabas and Saul for the work to which I have called them" (Acts 13:2). God Himself had brought Paul and Barnabas together. Today, God divinely directs certain organizations and groups to join together. He sets apart groups that will work together for the task to which He calls them.

At Iconium and Lystra, Paul and Barnabas faced death together (Acts 14:5-19). On the island of Cyprus, they saw a Roman proconsul come to Christ (Acts 13:12), and in Antioch Pisidia, a great many believed (Acts 13:48). They appointed church leaders where they established churches; and upon returning to Antioch, they reported all that God had done (Acts 14:23-27). Together they achieved more than they could have done alone. Their partnership provided both accountability and fellowship as they ministered for God. It is God's plan for His ministers to cooperate in ministry and evangelism. Paul did not face death alone at Lystra; the Holy Spirit provided Barnabas to encourage him. Barnabas did not have to evangelize Cyprus alone; the Holy Spirit provided Paul to help him. As God directs us, we must cooperate with other leaders to form ministry teams that provide fellowship and accountability as we work for God.

Paul and Silas: Partners Through Adversity

In later missionary journeys, Paul traveled with Silas because he and John Mark had a disagreement (Acts 15:39). Even in God-ordained partnerships, disagreements can arise. The disagreement was later resolved between Paul and John Mark (2 Timothy 4:11) so the division did not stop the ministry of Christ. They separated and continued to minister the gospel. Barnabas and John Mark returned to Cyprus, and Paul took Silas into Syria and Cilicia.

We wish we say that you will never face adversity or trials. The reality is that we all face trials, and at times many find themselves in chains at midnight. However, we can still worship God by faith, even in the darkest hour.

Soon after, a young disciple named Timothy joined Paul and Silas (Acts 16:1). These men traveled to Philippi preaching and teaching the gospel. Here we see the relationship of Paul and Silas being tested. Among other miracles they performed, the apostles cast an evil spirit out of a fortune-telling slave (Acts 16:16-24). Upon finding that their livelihood was gone, the girl's owners seized Paul and Silas and cast them into prison where they were flogged and then chained inside the prison overnight. Despite their pain and humiliation, Paul and Silas trusted in God and in each other and began to sing and worship while bound in chains.

As they praised the Lord, God sent an earthquake that opened the doors of the jail and broke the chains that bound them (Acts 16:26). How could Paul and Silas, bruised and bleeding, worship God and see past this trial? It was a direct result of their view of God and their partnership. Leaders need each other in order to stay focused during adversity. Synergy creates shared strength that enables a team to stand in the face of difficulty. Paul and Silas drew strength from each other to persevere in the face of danger. Trials and tribulations will come in ministry; but by forming strong partnerships, we can better face adversity. "Iron sharpens iron, so one man sharpens another" (Proverbs 27:17). By joining with others, we can increase our effectiveness, especially when we confront the struggles of life.

We wish we say that you will never face adversity or trials. The reality is that we all face trials, and at times many find themselves in chains at midnight. However, we can still worship God by faith, even in the darkest hour. This can be done by surrounding ourselves with fellow leaders who help keep us focused and on target. We can hold each other mutually accountable and lift each other up in various ways. We can then watch the chains fall off together as we worship through the trials and fight the attacks of Satan through the enabling power of the Holy Spirit.

Paul and Timothy: Partners for the Future

Timothy proved to be a great friend to Paul. From Paul's two letters to this young minister of the gospel, it is clear he deeply loved Timothy, calling him his "true child in the faith" (1Timothy 1:2). Timothy also respected and listened to Paul, even following his direction regarding circumcision (Acts 16:3). Their partnership was that of mentor and student. Paul knew that every successful leader must have a successor. Just as Jesus mentored the disciples, Elijah mentored Elisha, and Moses mentored Joshua, Paul helped young Timothy become a leader. Paul's understanding of ministry allowed him to see past his own life. Synergy is not only for the present but also for the future.

Paul encouraged Timothy to serve as an elder despite his young age (1 Timothy 4:12). He also instructed Timothy in the essential doctrines to which the church should adhere (1 and 2 Timothy). It is apparent from Paul's writings that Timothy was an important part of his life.

He understood that it is the responsibility of leaders to pour themselves into the generation that follows in order that they might continue the work of God when they are gone. Just as Paul partnered with Timothy for the future, every leader should be mentoring someone for the future. Leaders who invest themselves in the lives of younger leaders create a legacy that will survive long past their lifetimes.

Paul and Demas: The Dangers of Partnerships

Demas was a fellow worker of Paul. While imprisoned in Rome, Paul wrote letters to the church at Colosse and to Philemon who was a part of that church. In both letters, Paul sent greetings from his coworker, Demas, who was with him. Very little is known about Demas other than these passages. He apparently followed Paul and Luke into the Roman prison, yet something happened between the writing of Colossians and the writing of Paul's second letter to Timothy. During this time, Paul learned that partnerships sometimes break your heart.

Exactly what happened we do not know since Paul did not give us the details. "make every effort to come to me soon; for Demas, having loved this present world, has deserted me and gone to Thessalonica" (2Timothy 4:9.10). In the darkness of a Roman dungeon and dependent upon the help of friends for his nourishment and protection, Paul found himself deserted by his fellow worker, Demas. His only explanation was that Demas loved this world.

Partnerships can be dangerous. The interdependence we achieve by relying upon one another makes us vulnerable if one party deserts the other. Paul was alone. He learned firsthand what it was like to be left in a time of need. What is interesting is that Paul does not condemn Demas or complain about the problem. He simply acknowledges that Demas is gone and tells why. Demas had fallen victim to worldliness. Perhaps the dungeon and adversity were too much for him or the temptations of the world overpowered him. Followers of Christ are not to love the world because everything in the world does not come from the Father (1 John 2:15-17). Demas could not see past his present world and see the potential world as Paul did. While Paul fixed his mind on things above, Demas could not see past the darkness of the Roman dungeon. Demas saw the present defeat; Paul saw the potential victory.

Paul and Demas's partnership did not work out as planned. Demas defected, and Paul was alone. However, this did not sour Paul on relationships and partnering in ministry. In the same passage in which he announces Demas's defection, Paul calls for Timothy and John Mark to join him (2 Timothy 4:11). Remember, it was John Mark with whom Paul had problems earlier in his ministry. Paul was willing to mend fences and continue to partner with others because he still saw the potential of working together.

Even though his present situation was marked by Demas's leaving, Paul saw the potential of cooperation based upon synergy. We must expect dangers and even heartbreak when we work with others, but the reward of synergistic ministry is far greater than the danger.

BUILDING BRIDGES TO CREATE SYNERGY

People separate themselves politically, socially, racially, and economically. This same separation has also worked its way into the body of Christ. Many Christians live isolated from each other, never working together. Even worse, they are often competing against one another. Even though human beings are made for fellowship and community, we build walls between each other and portray fellow Christians in a bad light because of pride and ignorance. We are at our best when we are connected with others; we are at our worst when we selfishly compete.

Despite technology's advancement in travel and communication, we still alienate ourselves from others. While information is at an all-time high, compassion remains at an all-time low. We have developed marvelous new means of communication which have enabled us to yell louder and more quickly at each other than ever before; but for all his ingenuity, Bill Gates cannot teach us to love each other.

People are separated, and we are called to unite them to God and to each other. Leaders are called to bridge the divide of stereotypes, unbelief, and lack of faith.

Paul writes that we have been given the ministry of reconciliation (2 Corinthians 5:18). This ministry involves taking the message of reconciliation—that Christ is drawing men and women to Himself through the cross—to a world in need of His love and forgiveness. Paul also says that reconciliation is the bringing together of different groups of people (Ephesians 2:14-16).

The ministry of reconciliation is the work of God's people to build bridges between people and Christ and between each other. As leaders concerned about effective ministry, we are called to be bridge builders.

Dr. Randy Jumper, who serves at First Assembly of God, Little Rock, Arkansas, years ago spoke at a gathering of church leaders about the necessity of building bridges. During his message, he emphasized:

"The ministry of reconciliation in one sense is bridge building. People are separated, and we are called to unite them to God and to each other. Leaders are called to bridge the divide of stereotypes, unbelief, and lack of faith. The bridges we will be called to build will be different for each of us. We each have a unique calling, but there are certain bridges we are called to build. They leap from the pages of Scripture and the context of life. Christ has torn down the walls that separate us. The rubble is at our feet. What will we do with the stones in front of us? Will we build more walls, or will we build bridges?"³

Whatever the ministry in which we are involved, we must make it a priority to connect with others around us. If we want to build synergistic church communities, we must begin to build bridges toward each other. Christ has torn down the walls of separation (Ephesians 2:14). We must now build bridges that allow us to partner together. It will require effort and sacrifice on our part, but we must work together. As Christ has reconciled the lost to Himself, we must mirror that same Christlike quality to the world as we work together.

SYNERGY BEGINS INSIDE THE LOCAL CHURCH

The local church is the first place the principles of synergy and cooperation need to be present. It would be interesting to learn how many people have been turned away from the gospel because the church to which they were exposed was filled with backstabbing and politics. How sad it must make Christ to see His church filled with division and mistrust. When the local church cannot function due to a lack of cooperation, how do we expect the global Church to make an impact for Christ and the glory of the Father?

To create synergy in the local church, each member must realize the value of cooperation. This begins with valuing the people in the church. Everybody is a somebody in the body of Christ. When we view each other as fellow members of the Christ's body, we will treat each other as such. This means that pastors will view themselves as Christ's servants to laity and will not manipulate them or view them as less important to God. The members of the local church all contribute vital spiritual gifts that make a healthy church grow (Ephesians 4:16). When members do not do their part by utilizing their gifts or they neglect the gifts of others, the church will never achieve all God has for it.

Whether we realize it or not, it is imperative for the local church to grow together internally before expanding outwardly. Healthy churches are not just growing in number; they are also growing in strength. A tree with many branches and no roots or a thin trunk will not support its own weight. This interdependence and synergy will create new avenues of ministry as we unite. Just like Paul and Silas, we will call upon each other in the night to help us to stand strong. There will be times when it will be necessary to rely upon the strength of others because our strength is gone. The church that is interdependent can do this.

Building Bridges Across the Generational Divide

As synergistic church leaders, we must build a bridge that connects the various generations. As the prophet Joel explains, God is seeking to work through old and young alike:

It will come about after this, that I will pour out my Spirit on all mankind; and your sons and daughters will prophesy, your old men will dream dreams, your young men will see visions (2:28 emphasis added).

A trend has been developing for some time in our churches and in our ministerial ranks that is alarming. It is the disenfranchisement between the younger generation of the church and the older generation. The greatest point of conflict is in worship styles, particularly music. The older generation feels threatened because what they have created seems to be slipping away due to a lack of respect. The younger generation feels threatened because their opinions and perspectives seem irrelevant to their leaders. The younger generation sees no value in the old ways, and the older generation sees no need for newer methods. This same disparity is found even among church leadership. In most cases, both groups are committed to the same beliefs and convictions; they just express them differently. They remain fragmented because they would rather separate and blame than communicate and love. This is a direct result of the cultural shift that is taking place in the world. As discussed in Chapter 1, the information divide is rapidly changing the landscape of the world and thus the church. We cannot fall victim to its results.

> **The older generation needs to seek input from the younger generation, allowing them to become the eyes and ears of the culture around them.**

What if Paul had not discipled Timothy? What if Timothy had dismissed Paul as antiquated and useless? Where would the early church have been if these men had ignored the leading of God? We cannot allow cultural bias and personal dislike to infect the church. We must bridge this divide if we are to see Joel 2 become a reality in our churches.

How can we bridge this gap? It will come with work and cooperation. It will take trust and time. It means that the younger generation must get past their suspicions of institutions and participate in the church structure. It means they cannot demand change overnight. They must learn to respect and understand the heritage of their faith. Why? Because even though they love independence, we need each other to accomplish the Great Commission.

In return, older leaders must meet them in the middle. They must understand the need for change and the updating of methods and must look to youth for counsel and advice. They cannot look down upon new ideas because their ideas were new once also. They must mentor and guide young Timothies to see past their suspicions so the younger can benefit from the experience of the older. The older generation needs to seek input from the younger generation, allowing them to become the eyes and ears of the culture around them.

They need to prepare the younger generation for the day, Jesus should tarry when they will be the older generation. Do not allow choice in music or service style to become barriers to cooperation. Unite to advance the kingdom of God.

Building Bridges Across the Racial Divide

Global Church Network has always sought to bring the message of Christ to all people. On many occasions, we have been privileged to work side by side with ethnic groups as we help evangelize the world. This is God's plan for world evangelization. Since the early days this ministry has grown and expanded with great blessing. The melting pot of America is turning into a mosaic of many different cultures and groups. In a postmodern world, diversity is celebrated and, in a sense, better resembles where the church should be.

It is time that the Church of Jesus Christ take the lead in combating the sins of racism that infect our communities.

The value of different ethnicities and heritages is not a threat to Christianity. Creativity and variety are characteristics of the world God created, and He saw that it was very good. The leader must recognize this and create ways to partner with those of different ethnicities. It will take healing and restoration between races that have been separated for years. The bridge of love and compassion must be built. It is the will of the Father.

The result of reconciliation (our bridge building) is the picture of true community—a community in Christ where there is no Greek and no Jew, no circumcision or uncircumcision, no slave or free, no male or female, no rich or poor, no white or black; just Jesus Christ as the all in all. We cannot ignore the years of sinful racial separation and profiling that have existed in the church. In your community, it may be necessary to join with others in confession of these sins and restoration of destroyed relationships, but do not allow this effort to consist merely of superficial marches and "reconciliation lunches." It is time that the Church of Jesus Christ take the lead in combating the sins of racism that infect our communities. Partner with other churches to reach your community through joint outreaches and service projects. One of the easiest ways to do this is to join together in worship and missions. Combine services with other churches in your town and sit together. Model to the children the importance of worshipping together with different ethnic groups. In your church, do not be afraid to have staffs that are ethnically diverse. Encourage people to grow past racial bias in the community by allowing them to use the leadership gifts God has given them. In your own church and community, build bridges across the racial divine.

THE ART OF SYNERGISTIC PARTNERSHIP WITHOUT COMPROMISE

There are many bridges that must be built in the life of the leader. There is not time or space to list all the different organizations or groups that could work together in the kingdom of God. What is essential to realize is that leaders must partner together to reach the world for Jesus Christ. Global Church Network has been privileged to work with tens of thousands of different churches, denominations, and organizations over the past twenty-two years. It has been amazing to find so many brothers and sisters in Christ in so many different contexts. We all serve the same God, and we all need each other to fulfill His plan without compromising our biblical commitments.

However, we cannot forget Paul's models in the New Testament. There are Demases out there who can cause us trouble and heartache. There may even be some relationships that, like Barnabas and Paul's, will start off well but will have the potential to end in disappointment. How can we protect our churches from these hardships and at the same time follow

Christ's command to take the gospel to the whole world? Is it possible to avoid the problems? Probably not, but the few trials along the way are worth the glory of working in synergy. Jesus asked Peter to be His disciple, knowing he would deny Him.

Many are afraid of sharing ministry with those who have doctrinal differences. Some of these differences are major tenants of faith. While we do not suggest that anyone abandon what they believe, there are always areas of commonality in which we can work together. Through the years, I have spoken in hundreds of churches to thousands of people. These groups have represented many different denominations and beliefs. Despite of the differences, there were always areas where we could agree. These areas of agreement became the center of our working together.

St. Augustine coined this axiom as a basis for agreement between believers of different Christian communities whenever questions of doctrine arise: "In essentials, unity; in nonessentials, liberty; in all things, charity." This is excellent criteria to use when judging the legitimacy of a call to church unity. In cooperating with other believers, it is important to follow seven steps to make the partnership the most effective. Leaders who rush into partnerships with others without planning often end up doing more harm than good. It is necessary to grow together before groups can work together. Each of us brings a truckload of baggage when we partner together. It will be necessary to walk through the initial stages of union carefully so that expectations are understood, and no feelings are hurt. The one component to synergistic relationships that most ignore is time. It will take many hours of working together to create the trust and goodwill necessary to create strong relationships.

1. **Know yourself**. The first step before any partnership can be formed is for leaders to know who they are and what they are called to do (as discussed in Chapter 4). If leaders are confused about their mission, their mission will be lost when they combine forces with those who have a clear mission. It is important that each individual's distinctives stay in place as they collaborate. In

working together, they should not compromise who they are. Value each other's differences as they are inevitable in life. It is the mosaic of faith that allows the message of God to be communicated to many different kinds of people. The goal of teamwork is not homogenization; it is cooperative fellowship.

2. **Initiate cooperation.** Someone has to start a relationship. Just like Barnabas, we must show initiative in starting partnerships. Working together does not start in a vacuum or overnight. It will take hard work and perseverance so leaders must step forward with their hand out to join with others in leadership roles.

When we model synergy in our churches, we show the world that we value each other. We must not only talk about cooperation and interdependence, but we must also start the process of building it.

Many people talk about reconciliation and teamwork, but very few actually join a team. Great leaders move past talk into action. Seek out groups in your community that may need your help and groups that may benefit your ministry. Join ministerial alliances and prayer gatherings. Sponsor racial healing services with different ethnic groups. Allow your church to contribute its time and resources to the work of the kingdom in cross-denominational events. Remember the laws of God: "Whatever a man sows, this he will also reap" (Galatians 6:7), and "Give, and it will be given to you" (Luke 6:38). What you choose to invest in as an individual and as a church determines what will take place in you.

When we model synergy in our churches, we show the world that we value each other. We must not only talk about cooperation and interdependence, but we must also start the process of building it. There are many different components to the body of Christ. Do not neglect Jesus' prayer that we would all be one in Him (John 17:21). Begin the necessary partnerships in your community in order that we might better reach the world for Jesus Christ.

3. **Listen and understand others**. The greatest tool of any leader is the ability to listen. Marriage counselors have pinpointed the number one cause of divorce as a lack of communication. Communication means listening and understanding each other. It is vitally important that we seek to understand the people with whom we want to cooperate. Most people do not listen with the intent to understand; they listen with the intent to reply.[4] When we work as teams, we must know where each party is coming from and what their expectations are. Many times, great churches and ministries have joined together to accomplish ministry goals but have dissolved in failure. It is sad to see these united forces torn apart over misunderstandings and inadequate communication.

4. **Share ideas; share power**. In partnerships, authority must be shared. If one party has ultimate authority, there is no cooperation; there is a dictatorship. When the principles of synergy are in operation, each partner plays a vital role in the idea and power structure. Each member of the relationship should be able to contribute to the planning and execution of the ministry task. While resources and abilities will often require one member to be in the forefront, there will be times when other people's gifts will necessitate their involvement and leadership.

In sharing ideas, the group empowers each member to achieve the goals God has placed before them. Everyone has "ownership" of the ministry because everyone was active in creating it.

In an information-rich society, those who know how to collaborate and share will be the leaders. Effective cooperation requires humility and patience. Sometimes it will be necessary to place our personal agenda on the shelf for the greater good of the partnership. When we share with others, we must be willing to let others step into the spotlight as we step back.

5. **Emphasize essentials.** Global Church Network synergizes and mobilizes in order to finalize the great commission. The answer is simple. We emphasize essentials rather than majoring on minors. Let everyone else argue minutia while we work together to reach our world for the Lord Jesus Christ. This does not mean we allow just anyone, regardless of their personal beliefs, to be a part of the Global Church Network. We are committed to the essentials of faith. We believe in the lordship of Christ, man's need for a Savior, and the necessity of a life of holiness. These beliefs are found in our statements of faith. These statements of faith are our standard for working together in ministry. In areas in which we disagree, we follow the direction of Jesus and Paul: In all things, we must love each other. We can have the greatest knowledge in the world, the greatest methods of evangelism, and even miraculous signs and wonders; but if we do not have love, we are nothing (1 Corinthians 13). These truths are what allow us to work together despite differences in other areas of faith.

6. **Be sensitive to others' needs.** When we partner with others, the primary purpose cannot be our own gain. The self-centered, greedy, and self-consumed leader will become obvious to everyone. We have all been approached by an "overly helpful" individual who seemed to want to "be there for us." Usually these "helpers" turn out to be wolves in sheep's clothing. They want a relationship with us because they want something from us. We must learn to be givers, not takers. Being sensitive to our partner's needs is a vital part of teamwork.

Take into consideration all aspects of partnerships, not just ministerial tasks. Evaluate the impact on the family, finances, and other relationships in which we are involved. This is another expression of God's love in the world. When we work together, there will be situations that will arise where we can be a blessing to others. As leaders, we are gifted with talents and abilities that others will not have. When we are sensitive to our team's needs, those gifts and talents can be used for others, not just ourselves. They prepare us for the time when we will need help from others and their gifts come to the forefront. Be sensitive to the needs of others by helping them where they need it the most, not where we can benefit the most.

7. **Praise others and accept blame**. General George Marshall once said there was no limit to the amount of good people could accomplish as long as they did not care who received the credit.[6] Synergistic churches defer praise. Their leaders build others up; they do not promote their own success. No one enjoys working with someone who demands the spotlight. These people often do very little work and a whole lot of talking. It is these kinds of people who are not team players. When synergy is in place, we constantly try to find ways to lift other people up by acknowledging their contributions. This is not self-serving humility but true thankfulness for the people who make things possible. When we honor those around us, we increase their potential for doing more by increasing their self-respect, proactive living, and loyalty.[7] As members of a partnership, leaders should never gossip or pull down team members but point out the positive things they have accomplished. When mistakes are made, it is important to accept blame. We cannot avoid taking responsibility when things go wrong.

Those in leadership are ultimately responsible for the mistakes and setbacks that occur. Rather than pointing the finger at others, we should assume responsibility for our mistakes. Those who work with us will appreciate our care and concern when we shoulder the load of responsibility. Nothing sours relationships like the blame game. In these partnerships, it ultimately does not matter whose fault it is but who will fix the problem.

Dennis Waitley, a renowned author and much sought-after speaker, has often said, "You can always spot losers in life. The losers in life spend all their time making others look bad while making themselves look good. Instead of painting their house, they spend all their time throwing mud on their neighbors' houses."

We must work together in synergy if we are to evangelize the world. Remember, synergy is when "the sum is greater than the parts." Fellow leaders must work in tandem with other churches of different denominations and ministry organizations to reach their communities. By working together, we increase our effectiveness, supply accountability for each other, and help each other through difficult times. These relationships are vital to church life. The church is not only the sum of all its parts but also the relationship between the parts.[8] The way we work together greatly affects the work we do in the world. Synergistic churches' greatest value is seen when they are a part of something greater than themselves.

We must work together in synergy if we are to evangelize the world. Remember, synergy is when "the sum is greater than the parts."

The church must present a unified force to the world. It is sad that many in the world see the church as a bickering, infighting organization. We have allowed petty differences in church government and structure to fracture us into hundreds of pieces. Let us work together to reach our communities and create positive change in the world by helping to rebuild Christ's kingdom.

To do this will require trust and transparency which are foundational to all relationships. Our character must never be in question. If the people you partner with cannot trust you, it will be impossible for you to work together. Part of honesty and trust is being open and transparent. The relationship must be built upon cooperation and openness. Working together requires a level of knowledge about each other. If it is apparent that we are hiding something from the team, there will be less unity.

This kind of synergistic cooperation was seen when Global Church Network launched from the Beyond All Limits Conference (now called Synergize Conference, www.Synergize.tv) in Orlando, Florida, in January 2002. Various leaders from around the world gathered to focus the attention of the church world on working together for training. Together we can achieve more than we can ever achieve on our own. Southern Baptists, Methodists, Pentecostals, African-Americans, Hispanics, and a host of other groups and their leaders joined together to form strategic partnerships for effective ministry. We were privileged to spearhead this new endeavor.

Leaders from various ministries and denominations have been meeting to determine what will be the most effective way to train harvesters for the harvest field. Through cutting-edge Internet technology and direct broadcast television, a new wave of opportunities presents itself to the synergistic church. We must capitalize on these new means of fulfilling the Great Commission and expanding the Church of our Lord Jesus Christ. To God be all the glory.

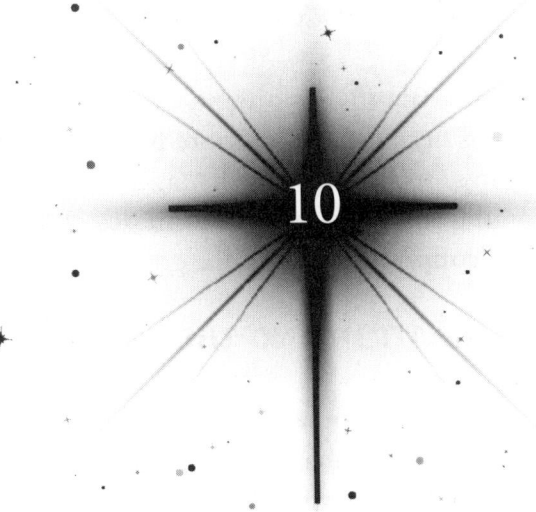

Our Impactful Communication

In 1960, President John F. Kennedy delivered this memorable challenge: "I believe that this nation should commit itself to achieving the goal, before this decade is out, of landing a man on the moon and returning him safely to earth." A computer scientist with the Apollo space program describes the impact this clear, focused, and demanding goal had on his colleagues:

> I have never seen a group of people work with such absolute focus and fervor as these people who saw it as their own personal mission to send astronauts to the moon. They worked incredibly long hours, under intense pressure, and they loved it. They had something that added meaning and value to their own lives, and they gave 200 percent to make it come true.[1]

Kennedy announced a vision that was in the heart of the American people. While many knew that America was behind the Soviets in the space race, Kennedy transformed that knowledge into motivated work by challenging America and the space program. John Glenn's giant leap for mankind was possible because of Kennedy's short statement years earlier. Kennedy was able to communicate the vision and desire for America to reach the moon. His declaration was more powerful than all the committee meetings, reports, programs, and even the process to reach the moon. Kennedy motivated America by focusing its resources through communication of the goal.

PROCLAMATION AND THE CHURCH

Powerful churches are preaching churches. Most times, preaching does not fail because of logistics but because the preacher does not know his audience. People need to have their ears turned into eyes so they can see the truth. We must always remember that a person's mind is not a debating hall but a picture gallery.

Too much communication only presents facts to make people intelligent. Twenty-first century leaders must present the truth to set people free.

Leaders create great pictures in the minds and hearts of their followers. Through effective communication, they enable the people around them to see what they could not previously see. Great churches are built upon solid biblical preaching.

As I have crisscrossed America and ministered in more than one hundred forty countries, I have discussed the subject of preaching at length and have perused hundreds of libraries belonging to pastors and churches. I have concluded that vibrant, evangelistic churches consistently hear Spirit-anointed, Bible-based preaching. The pulpit is no greater than the preacher who fills it on a weekly basis. Some pulpits have style without substance while others have substance without style. Today the need in preaching is for substance with style. The Christian and non-Christian alike are searching for truth in a generation filled with a valueless preoccupation with self and greed. Even though we believe "that everything rises and falls on leadership," we contend that every great church is led by a pastor who knows how to communicate the gospel effectively. The primary means of communication in the church is preaching; everything else is subsidiary to this.[2] Too much communication only presents facts to make people intelligent. Twenty-first century leaders must present the truth to set people free.

John the Baptist Came Preaching

John the Baptist was one of the greatest preachers of his day. Thousands of men and women in Palestine came to hear him proclaim the message God had given him. John the Baptist became the anticipated herald of the coming Christ, calling wayward Palestine to repentance. His ability to communicate and connect with people was matched only by the preaching of Jesus a few years later. Why did all of Israel, even their Roman masters, come to hear this eccentric prophet from the wilderness? What was it about John that was different? What made him a powerful preacher?

Looking at John's proclamation, he mastered three important components of communication: His message connected with the crowd, was centered on Christ, and called for a commitment. We must understand and master these three components if we are to communicate the gospel effectively.

Connecting With the Crowd

The man whom Jesus called the greatest man born of woman (Luke 7:28) captivated the thoughts of an entire region. His message was strong and convicting. His caustic words revealed sin in each listener's heart and brought conviction on all who came to hear him. Most of the people who heard him repented of their sins and were baptized. John the Baptist connected with the common men and women of Palestine unlike the Pharisees and chief priests of his time. This ability to connect and persuade the masses eventually became his downfall with the powerful religious elite. How did John the Baptist connect with the crowds that came?

1. **His message was practical.** Unlike the complicated laws of the Pharisees and Sadducees, John preached down-to-earth, realistic faith. He was not concerned with how many miles a person could walk on the Sabbath or how many times one should wash to become ceremonially clean; he was concerned with how people treated each other and the condition of their heart. John was questioned about how to live without sin (Luke 3:10-14). His response was not profound but practical, not complicated but clear, not extreme but easy. If you were a tax collector, do not extort money but do your job honestly and fairly. If you were a soldier, do not use your authority to take advantage of others but protect the helpless and defend the weak. Everyone should love each other and help those who are hungry or cold. John's practical message resonated with people who were burdened under the weight of religious jargon and seemingly impossible religious requirements.

2. **His message was also easy to understand.** He was more concerned about communication than oratory. His message was clear and concise: "Repent! The kingdom of God is at hand." There was no mistaking the content of John's preaching. Through metaphor and analogy, John created word pictures to illustrate the message God gave him that anyone could understand. He compared hypocritical Pharisees to snakes and vipers and talked of stones, barns, wheat, and fruit. John illustrated the power of God's cleansing with baptism and water.

We must learn how to connect with our audience as well. If there is no connection during our sermon, there will be no response to our invitation. When Jesus spoke to the woman at the well in Samaria, His point of connection was, "Give Me a drink" (John 4:7). He began with physical thirst before moving to spiritual thirst. What are our points of connection today? We can connect through stories of hardship and personal struggles and through stories of family and friendships. By understanding the times, we can better connect with the audience.

The ability to make the difficult appear easy is the primary indicator of an effective preacher.

Jesus demonstrated this principle. He engaged His listeners through common expressions and points of contact. He used stories, dialogue, questions, comparisons and contrasts, common experiences, metaphors, creativity, and imagination to connect the gospel to His generation. Just like John the Baptist, He was able to take complicated, abstract spiritual matters and turn them into simple concrete pictures that anyone could understand. The ability to make the difficult appear easy is the primary indicator of an effective preacher.

We must enable every member of the church to understand God's Word and the vision God has given them to accomplish the Great Commission. Jesus often connected with His hearers by stories or parables (illustrations). "He did not speak to them without a parable" (Mark 4:34). A descriptive story helps people see the truth in everyday life. Thirty-three percent of all the recorded teachings of Christ were parables or stories.[3] Everyone loves a good story. They should be used to illustrate and clarify the truths of Scripture; however, sermonizers must be cautioned not to make the basis of their sermon's contemporary stories. Stories move people, but the Word of God changes people. There must be a balance between meeting the needs of people and teaching the precepts of Scripture.

On the one hand, people determine the starting point of the sermon. On the other hand, the Scripture determines the subject and substance of the sermon. This is not abdicating the supremacy of Scripture or the biblical basis for the sermon but simply underscores the simple truth that preachers must begin where the people are and not expect them to first come up to their level. John connected with his audience, but he was also centered on Jesus Christ.

Centering on Christ

John proclaimed the coming of the Messiah. Though it was not until after Jesus' baptism that he identified Jesus as the Christ, he constantly pointed to the time when the Messiah would come. John did not fall into the temptation of promoting himself. He knew his calling was to prepare the way of the Lord. When others tried to lift him up and asked if he were the Messiah, John quickly pointed to the one who was higher than he, the one for whom he was preparing. He did not let his message become distracted by current issues or the popular topics of his day. John did not try to overthrow Roman oppression. He did not rail against the tax collectors. He simply called people to prepare themselves through repentance for the coming of Jesus Christ.

In humility and a servant-like manner, John proclaimed the coming of the Lord.

When Jesus came to the Jordan River to be baptized, John knew he was not worthy to baptize the Messiah. Only after Christ's command did John agree to baptize Him. He knew he was standing before the man he had been chosen to proclaim. The Apostle Paul declared to the Corinthians: "I determined to know nothing among you except Jesus Christ, and Him crucified" (1 Corinthians 2:2). Philip preached Jesus Christ to the Samaritans (Acts 8:5, 12) and to the Ethiopian eunuch (Acts 8:35). The Seventy preached the kingdom of God in the name of Jesus (Luke 10:9-11). Peter proclaimed "peace through Jesus Christ" to Cornelius and his household (Acts 10:36). The central thrust of the fivefold ministry of Ephesians 4:11-16 is the maturing of the body of Jesus Christ. Jesus is not simply "an issue" in evangelistic preaching—He is the "main issue." While many abandon the preaching of Jesus Christ today, we cannot neglect the Savior of the world.

True biblical teaching does not take place unless the hearers of the message have learned and then acted on the new knowledge.

Sadly, most preaching today reflects the self-help movement or financial seminars more than the message of Jesus Christ. We must never neglect the centrality of Jesus Christ in the messages we preach. Through our preaching, we must glorify and magnify Christ. Jesus Christ changes men's lives and brings salvation to the world. Preach Jesus Christ and Him crucified.

We should be known for the content our message rather than the crafting of our message.

Calling for a Commitment

John's intent was not to share information and send people on their way; he called people to a commitment. Information that is not acted upon has no value. John knew he must call his hearers to interact with his message and commit it to their hearts. Rather than being a dispenser of facts, John led people to truth. The tax collectors would have to change their practices, Pharisees must quit their prideful acts, and everyone must repent of their sin before God. Without the commitment to change, the preaching of John the Baptist was worthless.

Teaching is not simply talking. Learning is not simply listening. What does it mean to communicate? The term "communication" comes from the Latin word communis, meaning "common." According to Howard Hendricks, commonness or commonality must first be established before effective communication can take place between people.⁴ The more we build a commonality between the message and the listeners, the higher the level of communication between the audience and us. It is our responsibility to make sure the audience understands and applies the message to their lives. True biblical teaching does not take place unless the hearers of the message have learned and then acted on the new knowledge.

We will never see the fulfillment of our vision and goals if we cannot communicate them to others. We will lead only as long as we can communicate. As Christ's ambassadors to the world, we must model our preaching after John the Baptist's. Our preaching should connect with the crowd, be Christ-centered, and call men and women to repentance. It must be focused and powerful through preparation and the Spirit's anointing. The most powerful sermons are the ones that clarify, communicate, and stay consistently within the context of the author's intended communication.⁵

THE PINNACLE OF PREACHING

For most pastors and church leaders, preaching is the primary vehicle for expressing leadership and communication. It is the conduit through which Christ calls humanity to repentance and fellowship with God. Through the foolishness of preaching, God has chosen to save the world (1 Corinthians 1:21). It is the means by which the leader can cast vision and cause others to grow in Christ. Our communication helps foster and create the synergy that is necessary to carry out the plans and priorities of the church. It sets the tone for the effectiveness of the local church. Without solid communication, it will be difficult to nurture the synergistic spirit in the church.

In our attempt to communicate through preaching, it is important to understand completely the principles of effective communication.

I have identified an eight-step process for constructing an effective sermon based on the principles of communication. We will highlight these eight steps here but suggest you study them further in the books *The Preacher's Summit* and *The Pastor's Best Friend: The New Testament Evangelist*.[6] This preaching process can be applied to many different kinds of sermons (topical, textual, expository, etc.), but it was designed with the expository type in mind. Expository sermons put content, power, substance, and authority into our preaching.[7] Haddon Robinson defines expository preaching as:

The communication of a biblical concept derived from and transmitted through a historical, grammatical, and literary study of a passage in its context, which the Holy Spirit first applies to the personality and experience of the preacher, then through him to his hearers.[8]

Each of the eight steps of the preaching process builds upon the others. They unite to create a powerful message that communicates Christ's gospel. They lead the preacher upward to the pinnacle of proclamation. Each step is intertwined with the others to create a message that is empowered and practically constructed so that the leader might adequately communicate the gospel.

Intercession

The first step in the process of proclamation is intercession. The leader or "proclaimer" is to be a praying person every day, not just when messages are being prepared for a church or crusade. Prayer should always precede preparation and preaching. At every juncture in sermonic preparation, a "spirit of prayer" should be in the minister's heart. A preacher who is not praying in the ministry is playing in the ministry.

One of the most important of all disciplines is to "pray without ceasing" (1 Thessalonians 5:17). He does not stop to pray; he simply does not stop from prayer.[9] It is interesting that Jesus commanded the disciples to go forth and preach the gospel, but He did not teach them how to preach. He did, however, take time to teach them how to pray. Many today emphasize the mechanics of preaching rather than the power of preaching—that is, prayer. Pray over and through all the steps of preparation and pray for the lost and the believers who will hear your sermon. Ask the Lord to direct every thought during your sermon preparation for the purposes of connecting, communicating, and converting the lost to Christ as well as strengthening the walk of the believer. Pray that God will enable you to communicate the vision He has given you.

Ask the Lord to direct every thought during your sermon preparation for the purposes of connecting, communicating, and converting the lost to Christ as well as strengthening the walk of the believer.

The priority of the leader's prayer life will determine the power of their preaching. In studying the biographies of ministers God used in the past, you will find the common denominator was their priority on prayer. Mighty men and women of God will have a consistent quiet time with God.

Illumination

The second step upward in the process of preaching is illumination. The unseen spiritual world is just as resourceful as the seen world of precise research and study of a Scripture—if not more so. In addition to practical exegesis, we must allow the Holy Spirit to illuminate God's Word to us. John MacArthur writes:

No clear understanding of Scripture leading to powerful preaching is possible without the Spirit's work of illumination.

Powerful preaching occurs only when a Spirit-illumined man of God expounds clearly and compellingly God's Spirit-inspired revelation in Scripture to a Spirit-illumined congregation.[10]

There is a difference between inspiration and illumination. Inspiration is the process by which men "inscripturated" the revelation of God. The Apostle Paul needed inspiration in order to write the revelation of God (things previously unknown). While inspiration was the needed vehicle to reveal eternal truth from God to us in the Bible, illumination is needed today to fully ascertain the correct interpretation and application of a particular passage of Scripture. The anointing or illumination of the Holy Spirit teaches the meaning of the Word of God (1 John 2:20-27). The Word of God comes alive for the minister when illumination becomes a part of the preparation of effective evangelistic sermons.

While some preachers tend to ignore the role of the Holy Spirit in ministry or go to extremes in manipulating people, we must understand the balanced role of the Holy Spirit in preaching.

The Holy Spirit is a gift, not a toy. There needs to be biblical balance both in the private area of preparation and the public area of proclamation. Only the Holy Spirit can inspire a message and transform a carefully prepared manuscript into a message.

Interpretation

The third step upward to the pulpit of proclamation is interpretation. In order for exegesis to produce a thorough biblical theology, the minister must have a high view of scriptural authority. Scripture must have the final authority in all aspects of evangelistic ministry. Author David Larsen put it well: "If there is no difference between the Bible and Aesop's fables or Joseph Smith's tablets, we are abandoned with a hopeless mixture of truth and error calculated to foster hesitation and equivocation in the pulpit."[11] Our view of the Bible will determine how we preach it in the pulpit.

The meaning of the passage is achievable when the minister researches all the data.

Before we can make proper application of Scripture, we must know what the original writer through the inspiration of the Holy Spirit wanted to convey to his readers and understand the unique challenges the modern hearer faces every day.

Evangelists and pastors must keep in mind that we are not called to make the preaching text relevant but to show its relevance. If Scripture is not already relevant, then the most gifted preacher cannot make it so.

How does an evangelist or pastor make the Bible relevant to the churched and unchurched? How do ministers communicate a relevant message from Scripture to the present culture?

Historical-cultural research focuses the preacher back to the times and events of the original writer and compels them forward to a current context. If modern leaders wish to transfer the relevant message of the past to the present, then the historical-cultural gap must be bridged. The historical-cultural gap is not crossed by allegorizing, spiritualizing, and moralizing the preaching text. Relevance is lost in a long, didactic discourse on the details of the preaching passage. People want to hear the message of the passage. Before we can make proper application of Scripture, we must know what the original writer through the inspiration of the Holy Spirit wanted to convey to his readers and understand the unique challenges the modern hearer faces every day.

The total framework within which the biblical authors communicated and how that message relates to our own times is accomplished through grasping the whole before attempting to dissect the individual parts of a text. It is the total message that contains propositional truth. The sermonizer needs to look beneath the "surface structure" (grammar, semantics, and syntax) to the "deep structure" (the message behind the words). Answering why the text was written is at the heart of interpretation in order to apply the text to the present situation.

Last, the interpreter "principalizes" meaning into timeless truths.[12] The text sets the agenda for the sermon. Grammatical-syntactical exegesis (understanding what the text means by examining its word choice, sentence structure, and placement) and a historical-cultural background of the text (what events are taking place in the text that affect its meaning and presentation) reshape the preacher's understanding of the text. Expository preaching serves as the tool that evangelists and pastors should use to carry them from a biblical concept discovered through serious exegetical study to appropriate application for the congregation. A sermon constructed out of honest exegesis and sound hermeneutics will be true to the Bible in its purpose.[13]

Imagination

The fourth step to effective preaching is imagination. We live in a rapidly changing world. The attention span of most people continues to get shorter and shorter, and prolonged concentration of one idea is no longer effective. People are programmed to see and experience many different bits of information quickly. Too many speech teachers are teaching that speaking is a medium of words rather than a medium of sight and sound which happens to use words. People are asking, "Is your message worth the price I am paying?" We need to remember that they do not see the world as other people see it but as they see it. Thomas Troeger wrote: "We assume that the world is the way we speak it, that reality matches the metaphors we live by."[14] Effective communicators understand how listeners imagine or view their world. The sacred responsibility of the preacher is to use biblically guided imagination to cross the bridge from the past to the present.

The imaginative mind sees how different facts and ideas can be mixed together to build a sermon. Just as a contractor knows how to pull together blueprints, brick, sand, and wood in order to build a house, the creative preacher knows how to tie together the parts of exegesis to form a "meaning" and the different aspects of homiletics to form a "message."

It is often helpful to give "life" to a passage by retelling the story using our imagination and creativity, interjecting various cultural and historical realities into the story.

The creative evangelist or pastor powerfully connects every word of the message to the next, forming sentences packed with pictures for the modern mind to understand eternal truth. Imagination arouses faith in God and His Word. Imagination makes history come alive today. Imagination is one of the strongest allies of the sermonizer to change lives forever.

It is often helpful to give "life" to a passage by retelling the story using our imagination and creativity, interjecting various cultural and historical realities into the story. This allows people to connect with characters in the story as well as the message.

Imagination and creativity are to be used all throughout sermon preparation. Just like prayer keeps the proclaimer in tune with God, imagination and creativity will keep the minister relevant to the world. In order to be effective communicators of the gospel, preachers must stay in touch with the eternal world above them (God), the temporary world around them (nature and humanity), the pragmatic world within them (the body, mind, and spirit) and the life-changing world of the Bible.[15] The imaginative evangelist or pastor has the distinct ability to pull all of these worlds together into an effective preaching ministry.

Those who are the most creative have a structure to their presentation. Those who do not have a structure are slaves to chaos. We must be focused on our destination. How many times have we listened to a sermon and said at the end, "What was the main point?" "What did he really say?" When this happens, the speaker failed to create a powerful message.

Every message must be packaged in some creative way in order for the audience to grasp its meaning and be motivated by it. The biblical text determines the substance of the sermon. The sermonizer determines the structure of the sermon. Rick Warren states,

"The crowd does not determine whether or not you speak the truth: The truth is not optional. But your audience does determine which truths you choose to speak about."[16]

Illustrations

The fifth step upward to the effective pulpit of proclamation is illustrations. Creative communicators are aware of the world around them and can find illustrations in many different walks of life. Just as the Holy Spirit illuminates the mind during the exegesis phase, illustrations paint pictures in the minds of the listeners during the preaching phase. Illustrations are not to be a substitute for solid scriptural substance; they are to illustrate various truths or principles throughout the evangelistic message. Illustrations allow the audience time to catch its breath mentally before diving down again for deep truth. Learn to use illustrations at the right time and the right place during a sermon to reach the maximum impact in the listener's heart.

Stories stir the emotions, open the mind, paint pictures, help the memory, and keep the attention. Use a variety of illustrations in each sermon. Timely illustrations can be found in books, magazines, newspapers, conversations, television programs, technology, the arts and sciences, sports, and most arenas of life. Look for them. Listen for them. Think about them. File them. Cultivate them. Practice them before preaching them. Illustrations are the "spices" that awaken the five senses of a person and make the sermon easier to swallow mentally, emotionally, psychologically, and spiritually.

The goal is to make the message relevant to as many people as possible every time you speak. We need to engage the whole person, or we will miss the opportunity to persuade them and motivate them at the conclusion of the message. The more involved the listeners, the more likely we are to convince them of our message.

Introduction

The sixth step upward to the pulpit of proclamation is the introduction. When does the introduction begin? The introduction begins before the sermon ever starts; people are "sizing up" the preacher before the sermon begins. They are judging sincerity, integrity, mannerisms, and believability. The experienced preacher knows the audience is watching during praise and worship, the special singing, and the offering. It is extremely important for the evangelist or pastor to set the tone of the message long before the actual sermon.

What are the qualities of a good introduction? Haddon Robinson has clearly described them as: (1) commands attention, (2) surfaces need, and (3) introduces the body of the sermon. The introduction needs to be long enough to capture attention, focus on needs, and orient the audience to the subject, the idea, and the first point. Until this is done, the introduction is incomplete; after that, the introduction is too long.[17]

There are limitless ways to craft an introduction. The speaker can use an illustration, statistics, rhetorical questions, a paradoxical statement, a song, the Scripture passage, humor, authoritative quotations, or anything that grabs the hearers' attention. The speaker should view the introduction "not in terms of what begins your presentation but in terms of what will open up the audience."[18] This prepares the heart and mind to receive. The purpose of an introduction is to invite people into the arena of ideas with us.

Do not underestimate the impact of a powerful introduction. Remember, "the first ninety seconds of any presentation are crucial."[19] If the preacher does not capture the attention of the congregation at the very beginning of the sermon, the audience may never enter into the heart and soul of the sermon.

It is imperative from the beginning and throughout the sermon that the preacher understands the audience's DNA: Demographics, Needs, and Attitudes.[20]

Begin to craft your introduction, illustrations, and applications by first discovering your audience's demographics. Whenever possible, make sure your content is relevant to the age group and socioeconomic structure of your audience. Know the general make-up and typical occupations of those to whom you are speaking.

We must also know the dominant needs of our target audience. What are their interests? What challenges do they face? The good communicator scratches where people itch. Be prepared to deliver relevant messages to people by knowing their needs.

Finally, understand the attitudes of your audience toward ideas and challenges. How do they feel about the subject? What motivates them? What is their perception of you as a preacher and as an authority? Do not change your message just because of their concerns but be aware of their opinions.

Impartation

Personal power and charisma to persuade are not mysterious things that are only available to a privileged few. Some believe they cannot be earned or learned. This is not true. The effectiveness of our communication determines the effectiveness of our life. Leaders whom people respect and follow are those who are able to communicate effectively. They have a dynamic presence. If we desire to make a difference, we will have to learn to communicate with a powerful presence.

We must be able to communicate what we desire to be accomplished in the church, in the ministry, and in life. There is a certain amount of style in the packaging of a sermon. Jesus said, "I did not speak on My own initiative, but the Father Himself who sent Me has given Me commandment, what to say, and what to speak" (John 12:49). In other words, Jesus was led by the Father in all aspects of His speaking engagements. Attention must be given to the delivery of the sermon as well as its content.

The verbal persuasion of the sermonizer will be greatly determined by the choice of words and phrases. Emotive words drive home the theme of the message.

What do we mean by the delivery of a sermon? It simply means to deliver "into the possession of the person for whom it was intended."[21] Lani Arredondo describes delivery as "the methods by which you communicate 'what' you have to say to the 'who.'"[22] Many people do not receive Christ because the sermon was not properly prepared and communicated with the nonbeliever in mind. It is possible for the preacher to speak the message, use up a portion of time, give an altar call, and still not accomplish the intended purpose of the sermon. It may be necessary to change the style of delivery for a particular sermon based upon the region of the world in which it is preached. Style may not be the major priority of preaching, but it is a major component of the preaching event.

The evangelistic message is delivered through the means of the verbal, vocal, and visual. Many ministers of the gospel spend most of their time thinking about what they are going to say to the audience, yet studies have concluded that the decision-making process of people is determined first by visual cues

(55 percent), second by vocal (sounds and tones account for 38 percent), and third by verbal (actual words of the presentation account for only 7 percent).²³ This data reveals that the average person is persuaded more by feelings than by facts. The visual cues the speaker gives to the audience are positively or negatively persuasive. Mannerisms, gestures, head movements, facial expressions, platform movement, eye contact, and clothing project the overall presence of the presenter.

The vocal effectiveness of the presenter is determined by the quality and variation used during the preaching event. The voice should project the different "landscapes" of the sermon. There should be changes in volume, speed, and tone according to the content of the message. Pauses help the preacher and the audience to catch up with the message. Often these pauses are more powerful than words because they enable the listener to think through what was just said. Fillers should be avoided at all cost as they are distracting to the congregation. Stay on target with your message and do not become distracted.

The verbal persuasion of the sermonizer will be greatly determined by the choice of words and phrases. Emotive words drive home the theme of the message. The communicator must be enthusiastic about the message. Since only seven percent of the impact in the decision-making process is composed of actual words, every word and phrase of the speaker should be chosen carefully for maximum impact. We must always remember we are not called merely to impress people but to influence their decision-making for Christ. We should know our audience at all times during the preaching of the sermon. This is crucial to effectiveness. A sermon is not too long because the clock says so; it is too long if the audience says so.

Invitation

The final step upward to the pulpit of proclamation is the invitation. The invitation phase is listed last because it is viewed as taking place at the end of the sermon. However, effective communicators begin their invitations in the interpretation phase, looking for bridges of persuasion. The end is viewed from the beginning. Life-changing invitations do not just happen at the close of evangelistic messages.

There must be interpretation, application, and then invitation. The invitation brings into focus the answer to the question: *What do I want to accomplish by delivering this message?* This is the objective actualized. When preachers have accomplished the objective, they can shout, "Bulls eye!" If thoughts, words, and actions do not support the objective or main thrust of the sermon, then do not include them. The invitation causes the audience to make a decision regarding the objective. By the conclusion of the message and invitation, people will _____. It is the presenter's responsibility to fill in the blank. As a result of hearing a sermon, people will be able to understand something or be able to do something. What is an invitation?

Allen Street defines it as follows:

The invitation is that act by which the preacher of the gospel exhorts his hearers and instructs them how to appropriate the content of the kerygma in their individual lives. Any sermon that does not include an invitation as well as a proclamation is not New Testament-style preaching. Every sermon should aim to stir the human will. Truth is something that must be obeyed. It is the gospel invitation that presses home the claims of Christ and calls for an immediate response.[24]

Just as the first century evangelist concluded the message with an invitation for people to repent of sin and place their faith in the Messiah for salvation, the twenty-first century evangelist/pastor should strive to invite people at the close of the sermon to receive the Lord Jesus Christ for eternal life.

How does a minister prepare and give an effective public invitation? For an invitation to be persuasive, it must "be tied in closely with the major thrust of the sermon. In other words, it should grow out of the main theme of the message so that the people will not be surprised when it is given."²⁵ It should also be implicit throughout the sermon to prepare people for their response. The effective evangelist or pastor looks for ways to imply the invitation throughout the entire development of the evangelistic message. For some pastors, invitations flow naturally; for others, much practice is needed before the presentation of powerful invitations.

When we preach, we are to proclaim God's Word with God's breath upon our words. We must inhale God's breath (His Word) during our study.

When the invitation is at hand, the preacher must plan to issue an effective call for people to act upon the truth. If we fail here, the rest of the invitation is useless. The key to a successful invitation is persuading people to place their faith in Christ.

Emotions can be aroused, and the intellect stirred, but unless sinners are challenged to exercise the will and are given the opportunity to do so, it is unlikely they will do it on their own. This is why the public invitation is the hub of the evangelistic sermon. One of the greatest tragedies is the person leaving the service with the anticipation of accepting Christ but not being given the opportunity to do so or not being told how to receive Him into their lives.

After fasting and praying for forty days, Jesus announced, "The Spirit of the Lord is upon me, because he anointed me to preach the gospel" (Luke 4:18; Isaiah 61:1-2). Do you desire to be appointed by God and anointed by the Holy Spirit before and during your preaching ministry?

Though some say the preaching event is no longer important, it is impossible to overstate the value of a solid pulpit ministry to the life and health of the local church.

When the preacher follows in the footsteps of Christ, they will experience the anointing of the Holy Spirit. When we preach, we are to proclaim God's Word with God's breath upon our words. We must inhale God's breath (His Word) during our study. Then we will be able to exhale God's breath when we preach His Word to a lost and dying generation. Ask yourself, "Did I take time to inhale today?" The leader and the church that are not communicating with the people who attend and the community around it are not taking their mission seriously. In fact, Time magazine profiled the importance of preaching in America in an issue on the most important influencers in America. It showed that the priority of preaching is surging in American churches. Duain Claiborne says that search committees for pastorates only want to know one thing: "Can the candidate preach?"[26] These churches have realized that dynamic programs are necessary for the local church in order to keep people involved; however, it takes dynamic preaching to attract them initially. It also takes dynamic preaching to keep them coming. Does preaching matter? Obviously. It matters so much that even secular news magazines recognize its importance. We fundamentally believe that great churches are built on great preaching.

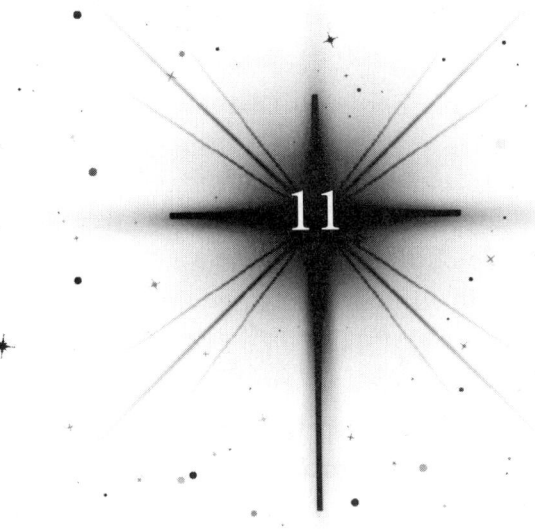

Our Ingenious Compassion

The greatest fuel for creating synergy is love. Nothing else makes the mutual cooperation of individuals possible. Paul said we could have the greatest miracles and events happen in our lives and ministries; but without love, we are nothing (1 Corinthians 13:1-3). This love for others permeates all that we say and do. Our churches must demonstrate heartfelt compassion for people if we are to make an impact for God. The walls of our churches can only come down when they are pressured to fall by the power of love—a love for people.

This love for people comes from Jesus. Jesus Christ died on the cross for people. He came to seek and save the lost, not set up an earthly kingdom or a religious organization. Jesus was not interested in launching a movement or starting a denomination. He was not concerned with politics or the elite leadership. He was interested in people, all kinds of people. He did not try to stay with the wealthy and popular. We find Him with beggars and the sick, sitting by a well talking to a Samaritan woman, or looking up in a tree to find Zacchaeus, the tax collector.

We find Him concerned about a rich young ruler and Jarius's daughter but still making time for children to sit upon His knee. Jesus spent time with lepers and prostitutes, showing them the compassion and love they had not felt in many years—if ever. He loved people, and so should we. As ministers of the gospel, our lives should be filled to overflowing with love for people.

The greatest fuel for creating synergy is love. Nothing else makes the mutual cooperation of individuals possible.

As members of His Church, we must show the love and compassion Christ gave to the world. We must be active in helping restore people who are in need. One of the greatest avenues for showing this compassion in the local church is the emphasis on family. As society pulls down the family structure and sin wreaks havoc in the lives of men and women, we must rise up and protect the family, enabling it to become the center of love and compassion in communities. The love inside the church will never surpass the devotion of the home. In our interview with Dr. James Dobson regarding the church and the family, he said, "The church and the family are the only two institutions left in America. If these two institutions crumble, western civilization, as we have known it, will fall apart." We must teach people the importance of loving their own families according to God's Word. We must also reach out to those in our communities who may be less fortunate and embrace them.

The church must be active in evangelism. Through love and compassion, we must reach out from the church and reach around the slumped shoulders of those who walk our streets. Moving beyond the limitations of insensitivity and apathy, we can show the love of Christ to those who are in need.

COMPASSION FOR THE FAMILY

Most church calendars contain a confusing mixture of events, prayer times, programs, and services. In most churches today, we have taken the command to assemble together very seriously. In our desire to provide as many avenues of involvement as possible, we have often overloaded the church member's schedules. The greatest compassion the church can show is the protection of family time. We can do this not only by preaching and teaching on the family but also by scheduling and planning for a time where the family can be together.

One local church does not allow any activities to be scheduled on Monday nights. This is family night. This church values time with the family and protects it by not scheduling anything to conflict with it.

As Christian leaders, we must model this compassion in our own families. Too many families are morally bankrupt and emotionally drained because the minister's priorities are not correct. It almost sounds cliché to say, "We can win the world but lose our family in the process." Everyone is aware of the danger, but few do anything to prevent it from happening. We may think we are winning the world to Christ; but in reality, we have not won the world because we have not given proper attention to our families. Though Noah preached for 120 years that the flood was coming and no one listened, God allowed Noah's family to be included in the ark. It is in the ark of salvation that we are to shelter our families from the storms of life.

God has given us a responsibility to minister to and nurture our families. Anything, including church work, that harms or hinders this ministry is not from the Lord.

It is a distraction to our primary, God-given responsibility. It has been said before, but leaders must have the following order of commitment and devotion in their lives:

- We must be committed to God first.
- We must be committed to our spouse second.
- We must be committed to our children third.
- We must be committed to our ministry fourth.

As synergistic leaders, we must have the private (God), the personal (family), the professional (ministry), and the public (world) spheres in order. We cannot allow an imbalance in these areas. When these priorities are out of order, something will go wrong. Sadly, there are many sons and daughters of "powerful" ministers who will suffer eternal damnation because their fathers did not make time for them. God has called us into union and fellowship with our families before our ministries. God has given us a spouse to love and cherish, and our spouse's spiritual well-being is our primary ministry in this world. God has given us children that we might raise them to honor and love God. They are the primary mission field to which we are called to labor and disciple.

The minister's life is a complicated maze of responsibility. We are often pulled in hundreds of directions that seemingly make us choose between our family and other people. However, ministers must always strive to put family above the ministry. We must never let the work of God be the reason our spouse and children do not follow Christ. This will be difficult, but God will give us grace to accomplish His will and purpose in life as we give Him first place in our lives. When we live compassionate lives that include our families, people will see and understand what we are doing. They will know why we are not able to be at every event and why we cannot always "be there" for them. We are being there for our families. When leaders put their family first, the community benefits; when leaders put the community first, both the family and the community suffer.[1]

THE MINISTRY TO YOUR SPOUSE

God said, "You shall love your neighbor as yourself" (Mark 12:31). The closest neighbor we have is our spouse. Most of us will be married as long as fifty or sixty years. My parents were married for over seventy years. If couples are going to spend that much time together, they should work at making marriage a lifelong romance. A relationship built on arguing and fighting is unrewarding and pointless.

A marriage should be filled with love, laughter, prayer, worship, and service. It should be an adventure.

A marriage should be filled with love, laughter, prayer, worship, and service. It should be an adventure. Too many wives of church leaders hate their husbands and the ministry of the church. Their husbands are willing to help and serve anyone but their own children and spouse. Is it any wonder these precious, mistreated women turn their back on the calling of God? Pastors often unknowingly communicate to their spouses that they love others more than they love them.

We must be sensitive to the needs of our spouse and heed Paul's words: "Husbands, love your wives, just as Christ also loved the church and gave Himself up for her" (Ephesians 5:25). We are going to be together as long as we are alive; therefore, we should serve one another in love. Husbands are to love their wives sacrificially and steadfastly. Though we are responsible to love and care for our children, we should never allow our children to come between us. Our spouse is far more important to us than our children are. Children will be born, grow up, and leave home to start their own families centered on Christ. God has given our spouse to us for the length of our lives together.

The most important person in each of our lives is our spouse. Just as Christ loved His church, so we are to love our spouse.

Do not even allow problems to occur if possible. Plan ahead and guard the time together; do not allow situations to get out of hand. By doing this, we avoid having to constantly "make up" for mistakes. Many people think they can make up for missed dinners and forgotten appointments with gifts. Do not fall into the trap of substituting material love for time together. Because of the demands of ministry, many ministers will try to replace the time they lost with flowers and gifts. These are wonderful, but flowers wilt and fade; memories never do. All the gifts in the world cannot replace the joy our spouse feels when we cancel an appointment to take a walk in the park together. All the flowers in the world become insignificant when we turn down a speaking opportunity or cancel a counseling session to spend time alone with our mate.

There are many times when we failed by not holding our wives' needs higher than the needs of the ministry. When this happens and we realize our mistake, we must take steps to rectify the situation.

Sheri and I have traveled millions of miles in ministry together. From the jungles of the Far East to the inner city of Chicago, we have worked for Christ. Along the way, there have been many trials and testing times, disappointments, and even despair. However, the synergy we have as a couple is the sustaining power of our ministry. We all make mistakes; Sheri can never be thanked enough for her sacrifices. There are not enough flowers in the world to make up for missed opportunities, but the couple committed to ministering to each other will be the couple that will make it through the hard times.

Does this mean everything is easy? Absolutely not! We all fail somewhere along the way.

Dr. Bright, in his wisdom and insight, taught me a practice I call the "twelve words." These can be the most powerful words spoken when uttered sincerely and from a position of humility:

"I was wrong. I am sorry. Please forgive me. I love you." These combined statements take us through a process of reconciliation. By saying "I was wrong," we recognize our mistakes. Saying "I am sorry" allows us to reflect on our mistake and show our sorrow. "Please forgive me" is the process of repentance before our spouse; and when we say, "I love you," we renew our commitment to each other.

We should work on our marriage together by reading books by leading counselors and attending marriage retreats once a year. Do not leave family issues unconfronted. Use the twelve-word formula or whatever is needed to be open and honest with each other and quickly admit mistakes. Sometimes the most important thing we can do is admit we were wrong. We should not avoid mistakes or ignore them. We defuse potential problems by not allowing them to continue to develop and get bigger. We must schedule special time away from other family members and friends to talk and develop our primary relationship in life. As we do this, we will fall more in love each day, and our ministry will be strengthened as we obey the commands of God.

THE MINISTRY TO YOUR CHILDREN

The greatest gift God gives people is the joy of parenting. God gives us a heritage in the children He brings into our life. Children can bring great joy or immense frustration into our lives. They make trips to the zoo and the park more exciting. The tears of a three-year-old can humble the greatest of kings, and the smile of a two-year-old can brighten the darkest moment. We invest ourselves in our children by spending time with them and participating in the important events in their life.

Our children are gifts from God that have been entrusted to us. We are to teach them about God and how to live a life of faith. They are the first mission field to which we are called. It is sad that so many ministers' children are far from the Lord. We must guard against this tragedy at all costs by pouring ourselves and God's Word into their lives from an early age.

We should schedule our travel and meetings around their important events and performances. There is no substitute for being there.

Our children are gifts from God that have been entrusted to us. We are to teach them about God and how to live a life of faith. They are the first mission field to which we are called.

When disciplining our children, we should not keep scolding and nagging them, making them angry and resentful. Parents often are too busy to give their children time to interact and talk. Listen to them. Do not be so busy serving God that there is no time to speak with them. This will cause them to become resentful, not only toward us but also toward God. Instead, bring them up with the loving discipline the Lord Himself approves. We must love our children and communicate with them, teaching them to love, trust, and obey the Lord our God above every other consideration in life (Ephesians 6:4).

ORGANIZING THE CHURCH AROUND FAMILY NEEDS

The church itself must have compassion for the family. Many times, we ask so much of the members of our church that they do not have time to be together. According to George Barna, the average family in America is pressed for time together. Of the 168 hours available each week, adults spend 56 hours of that asleep. With the remaining 112 hours, the average American family devotes 50 hours a week to job-related events. This leaves only 62 hours a week for other activities. If the family attends church twice a week and is involved in a small group or some other activity, they can spend an average of 6 hours a week at church. This does not include any other extracurricular activities or involvement in youth activities or groups. This leaves the family 56 hours a week to eat, attend to errands, and take care of any other matters in the home. The church must proclaim God's view of the family.

We must create opportunities to guard this time for family learning and time together. The family should be the place where intimacy and fellowship take place. The family is where children should learn their ideas about God, relationships, philosophy, sexuality, and education. The family should be the most synergistic institution on earth.

To accomplish this, we must be careful not to make too many demands upon people's time and energy. The members of our churches should not feel guilty for spending time at home together. We can help accomplish this objective through purposeful planning and teaching. Some churches have dropped a Sunday night service once a month and replaced it with a family night. Families meet at home together and worship in their own "small group." However, we must help people understand the importance of this special family time so they will give it the priority it deserves.

Many churches have developed extensive, elaborate, age-based Christian education programs. These programs are testimonies to the creative power of a local church, but sometimes these incredible teaching machines can cause more harm than good because families are constantly segregated from each other. In some churches, there is never a time for corporate worship. One churchgoer expressed dislike of this situation by saying, "I would love it if our church would put on things that I can do with my kids, not simultaneous to what my kids are doing. Sometimes I need a break, and I am grateful for the things they offer which allow me to think and interact like an adult for a change; but more often, the problem for me is that I do not get to share these times with my kids because I am talking about kids with an adult class while my kid is off somewhere being a kid with the children of the other parents." Compassionate churches provide opportunities for families to worship together. In Joel's prophecy of an end-time revival, he calls for a time when all of Israel would join together for repentance (2:15-17). The old men and the young people, the babies and senior citizens were all to join together. When God's Spirit moves, He encompasses all of God's people—young and old. We need to facilitate the learning of one generation from another.

We can create family times by scheduling healthy, uplifting, entertaining activities for the whole family. Synergistic churches can also create support groups and workshops to help singles, divorcees, abuse victims, and those with addictions. Pastors can preach a series on the family and have people sit together during these sessions. Many families feel stretched thin by commitments and responsibilities. The church must learn to accommodate family needs compassionately and teach them to value their families.

COMPASSION FOR THE LOST

Christ's love inside us compels us to love the world around us. While we can create loving families and communities inside the church, to be obedient to Christ's command, we must also love those outside the church. Pluralism and tolerance are sweeping the world. For the first time, Christianity in America is "competing" with many other faith systems. Islam and Hinduism are on the rise. New Age cults, witchcraft, and satanism are attracting members every day. However, our compassion and love for people can separate us from these other groups.

Our world is reachable for Jesus Christ. If this is true, why has the Church failed to evangelize the whole world after two thousand years? The lack of world evangelization is not due to the size of the world, a growing population, false religions, political systems, or cultural barriers. When the Lord Jesus Christ was on earth, He did not plan to reach the world with the gospel single-handedly. The Master's plan was to equip His disciples for world evangelization. We have failed because we have not synergistically joined in a unified force of love to reach the world through personal and mass evangelism. We must passionately take the gospel into a dark world and train others to evangelize as well.

We must passionately take the gospel into a dark world and train others to evangelize as well.

The Church has not accomplished the Great Commission because we have failed to equip both the minister and the parishioner for evangelism and discipleship. The walls of our church will be down as long as we allow the love of Christ to knock them down. For too long, the Church has endeavored to reach the world through addition and division rather than by multiplication. If a leader had the physical stamina to preach every night for 34 years to a crowd of fifty thousand people and at each meeting, at least one thousand conversions were recorded, the leader would win more than one million people to Christ. He would have conducted the greatest revival in church history.

However, if that same minister reached and trained just one person for evangelism in one year and then that person and the minister each reached and trained one more person during the next year, there would be four people equipped as evangelizers after two years. If each of these four also reached and trained one person, there would be eight more trained at the end of three years. At first, this would seem to be a much slower process of world evangelization; however, after 34 years of each convert winning one person to Jesus annually, the total number of conversions would be more than 16 billion! If each person would win one person per year to Jesus Christ, the entire world would be touched by the gospel. We live in a reachable world.

Open-air and citywide crusades are effective tools for winning the lost. Local church campaigns are still vital in the overall life of the church. However, the greatest means of church growth and evangelistic revival is personal evangelism. Biblical revivals turn saints into soul winners. Spiritual awakenings cause cities and even entire nations to turn to God. In each of these events, leaders have led the way in cutting-edge evangelism, leaders who know how to surf the spiritual waves of revival for the purpose of evangelism and discipleship. Brian McLaren defines the mission of the church as "to make more Christians, and make better Christians."[4]

This is the role of the truly missional community in the world. Will the rest of the world be told the good news of Jesus Christ? If not now, when? Will we make more, better Christians? If we as leaders will not lead the way, who will? We will never find a better time and better place to accomplish this global task. Therefore, let us arise together, ministering hand in hand in order that everyone might hear the gospel.

THE MISSIONAL CHURCH: AN ARMY OR A SOCIAL CLUB?

The synergistic church with its roof and walls removed turns into a "missional community." Mission means "sending," and it is the central biblical idea describing the purpose of God's action in human history.[5] The idea of missional churches in North America draws attention to the essential nature and vocation of the Church as God's called and sent people. Leslie Newbigin explains a missional church as a church that understands that God's mission calls and sends the Church of Jesus Christ to be a missionary church in its own society and in the culture it is in.[6]

Missional churches are passionate about evangelism. They seek creative ways to influence the world around them with the message of Jesus Christ. Through love and compassion, they break through the barriers in men's hearts with the gospel. They understand their role in their community is to shine the light of the gospel. It is their job to reconcile the world to God through His work on the cross of Calvary. They purposefully target people for evangelism.[7] They are passionate in their efforts to become missional communities reaching people for Jesus Christ.

Missional churches are passionate about evangelism. They seek creative ways to influence the world around them with the message of Jesus Christ.

Along with several other evangelistic leaders in the mid-1990s, I was privileged to meet with Dr. D. James Kennedy to discuss worldwide evangelism strategies. During that time, Dr. Kennedy shared with us a powerful concept that has affected my understanding of evangelism ever since. He said, "Many people begin to complain when a local church begins to grow. They often say their church is too big, that there is no way they can ever know everyone." For Kennedy, if your goal were to know everyone, then you would probably prefer a social club. However, if we are trying to raise an army, then every church is too small. It will take a large army to touch and transform this world for the glory of God.

What kind of church do you want? A church with walls is isolated and will always want to remain small. When we have a church with no walls, the limits are removed, and we are eager to grow. We need to view the size of our church not by the numbers who choose to worship with us but in light of the task of the Great Commission.

We are an army of passionate lovers—lovers of Jesus Christ and lovers of the world. We can expand only as far as the love we have inside us will allow and that love is unlimited: "The love of God has been poured out within our hearts through the Holy Spirit who was given to us" (Romans 5:5). Through love and compassion, we call men and women to a greater life that can be lived by walking daily with Jesus Christ.

COMPASSION FOR THOSE IN NEED

In response to God's love, we will want to share it with others. We must become channels of God's love to the world. "Beloved, if God so loved us, we also ought to love one another" (1 John 4:11). The world will know we are Christians by our love. We must be the hands of God extended in a world that has a false understanding of true love. As imitators of Christ, it is our responsibility to love a lost world to Christ. If we do not love others, our faith is bankrupt and John calls us a liar (1 John 4:20).

As sin wreaks havoc on the world, the plight of the less fortunate becomes worse and worse. Leading research agencies tell us that of the 8 billion people in the world, almost half live on less than $2 a day. Over 1.8 billion people live on less than $1 per day. In developing countries, almost 50 percent of the children are malnourished.[9] As followers of Jesus Christ, we have been called to minister to those in need—the hurting and less fortunate. We must have compassion for the hurting around us. True leaders are not arrogant or hateful because the ultimate goal of leadership is to reflect the love of God in a loveless world.

The Importance of Compassion Ministry in the Twenty-First Century

Jesus said, "When you give to the needy, do not let your left hand know what your right hand is doing" (Matthew 6:3 NIV). Compassion ministry should never be seen just as a tactic of evangelism. It should not be trumpeted as our efforts for God. Jesus commanded that we love people and serve them for their sake, not our own. When we help people, our motives will show. If the people we help feel they are being tricked or used, any chance of ministering to them will be lost. We must love the people around us even if they never join our church. Ministering to them is the command of Christ, not a strategy of church growth. Many will see the love we share with God and want that same love in their lives, and this will make them want to come to Christ. While not all will seek to find Jesus Christ as their Savior, our loving them fulfills His command. We help those who are longing for love to find it in God.

A church without walls is not confined to a set location but goes wherever necessary to help someone connect with Christ. The greatest testimony any church can have is that it gives back to the community it serves.

Compassion for the hurting is more than soup kitchens and Thanksgiving baskets. Our churches must become centers of love for everyone who needs it. Communities are filled with people who have deep wounds that no one is trying to heal. Synergistic churches connect with those around them by ministering to these needs. Churches like the Brooklyn Tabernacle have begun support groups and workshops for people struggling with addictions. Our society is filled with divorced people. Rather than ostracizing them, it is possible to minister to their specific hurts and help them through their crisis. It is the love we show to the lost that separates us from false religions and belief systems. Large segments of our communities are shut off from hearing the gospel because of their circumstances. As the average age in America continues to climb, hospital and nursing home ministries will become increasingly important. Sending CDs of sermons, or connecting people to YouTube streaming, and other church activities to shut-ins are keyways to bless those who are less fortunate. The physically handicapped such as the blind and deaf should not be neglected in our ministry outreach. Compassion for these groups of people is more than just having a place for them to worship with us. It involves identifying their needs and seeking practical ways to minister to them.

A church without walls is not confined to a set location but goes wherever necessary to help someone connect with Christ. The greatest testimony any church can have is that it gives back to the community it serves. Churches should involve every member in compassionate outreach. For example, Pastor Tommy Barnett integrated and encouraged the simple theme, "Find a need and meet it" in the life of his church, Phoenix First Assembly of God. The faithful service of the members has led to phenomenal church growth.

The synergistic church not only connects with its own community but also sends its people and its dollars to connect with those around the world.

World missions is integral to the growth of the church. The synergistic church not only connects with its own community but also sends its people and its dollars to connect with those around the world. We can be active in the rebuilding of struggling, war-torn nations through worldwide relief organizations like Samaritan's Purse, a ministry led by Franklin Graham; Convoy of Hope, led by Hal Donaldson; or Global Hope, a ministry of Campus Crusade for Christ. We must teach the body of Christ that it can be connected with other members of the body even when separated by great distances. Believers in earthquake-shaken India are intimately tied to believers in America. The Apostle Paul said, "If one member suffers, all the members suffer with it" (1 Corinthians 12:26). Because we are compelled by love, we must rise to help those around the world who are hurting.

Missionaries must be sent to those who have not heard the gospel, the hungry must be fed, and the naked must be clothed.

The local church can be a most powerful force to achieve lasting change in the lives of members of third-world countries. They can do this because they are compassionate churches that serve in obedience to our compassionate Lord and Savior.

SYNERGISTIC EVANGELISM

As we journey into the new millennium, we now live in what some church strategists are calling a "post-Christian" or "postmodern" era. We can no longer assume that everyone has a basic understanding of faith and the gospel. Whereas much of the evangelism efforts of the last century were to turn nominal, Christianized people into full-fledged followers of Jesus Christ, evangelism now consists of turning professing atheists and biblically ignorant people into followers of Christ.

Each group of people did not know God, but the manner in which we make the gospel known to them may be different because they begin at different levels of understanding. The love inside us compels us to help them come to Christ. There are more unchurched people in North America than ever before. They do not understand the religious jargon (Christianese); practices; rituals; and in some cases, the purpose of the Christian faith. Elementary Christian concepts and beliefs once known by all are foreign to them. The individual at athletic events holding a sign that says "John 3:16" makes little impact. Few people even know what it stands for anymore, assuming the sign refers to "John" sitting in row 3, seat 16. Some may know the reference but are unable to understand the truth of the Scripture because they are alienated from the concept of a loving God. This lack of understanding has created hostility between the church and the world.

Traditional methods of evangelism are not working. The gospel is in tension with a world that is unable to hear the message because of a dramatic difference in philosophical mindset and is unwilling to hear what we have to say because of false perceptions of who we are as Christians. We know that because followers of Jesus Christ are not accepted. They are even hated by the world because they are not of the world (John 15:18-23). Because of our love for others, however, we must reach past the world's stereotypes of unloving Christians and let the love of Jesus Christ flow through us as He reaches out to the unsaved person. Some churches' answer to this growing problem has been to become more aware of the needs and concerns of the unchurched.

Their efforts are to make the church of Jesus Christ more easily accessible and understandable to those in the unchurched culture. The world around us must not be viewed as the bad outsiders with whom we fight but as hurting neighbors who need love and grace. We must find creative ways to be a true missional community. We must find ways to make more and better Christians. We can do this because of Christ's love in us which can be reflected through us.

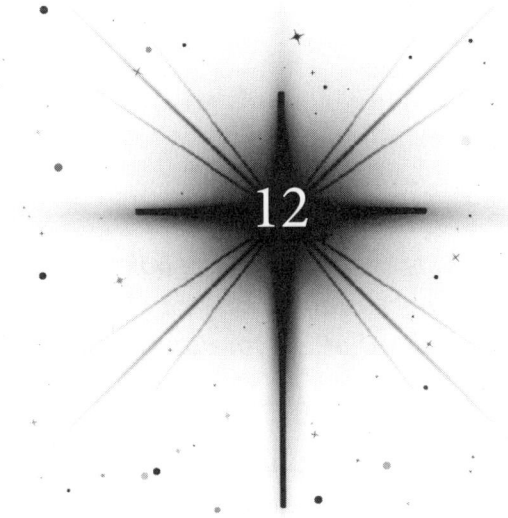

Our Innovative Creativity

One of the greatest limitations we will face in establishing a thriving ministry and church is not an attack of Satan or people who may come against us. Rather, it is found inside our mind. The ability to think creatively and to move beyond the limitations that stand in our way is the greatest catalyst to synergistic ministry. Leaders creatively break out of the boxes around them and approach life through a system of understanding and values that are foreign to others. Creativity fuels synergy because it enables the different elements of the church to find new ways to connect with each other. Synergistic leaders see and operate differently than others around them although the context and surroundings are the same. They have a different paradigm. Once of the different elements of the church are connected, it is imperative for the church to seek and implement creative ways to reach the world with the gospel. One of the great challenges all church leaders face is how to minister the gospel in a post-modern context without compromising essential biblical truths. The ways God communicates His love and will for our lives can assist us here. The fact is that words are the outward expression of inward thoughts.

***Leaders creatively break out of the boxes around them and approach life through a system of understanding and values that are foreign to others.**

God communicates His inward thoughts to the world in two ways:

First, He communicates His thoughts to us through the written Word—the Bible. Scripture itself tells us that the Bible is "God-breathed" (1 Timothy 3:16). God communicated His inspired Word to us by means of His very own breath.

Second, He communicates His inward thoughts to us through His incarnate Son—Jesus Christ (Hebrews 1:1-2). The person and work of Jesus Christ is the principal way God speaks to us in these "last days." To be successful at reaching a postmodern audience, the minister of today must follow the pattern of communication that God has set. Leaders must be empty vessels, a mere suit of clothes for Christ to fill so God can speak His inward thoughts of love and forgiveness to the world lost in sin. We must allow God to speak His Word through us using His breath. This spiritual dynamic happens only as we are fully surrendered to Christ.

As empty vessels full of Christ, leaders are free to cross the bridge to a new world through the use of creativity and imagination without violating scriptural standards. A great misconception among many pastors is their belief that reaching the world with the gospel requires worldly paradigms. In Judges 18, the Danites learned the folly of using the world's methods to accomplish a spiritual task. They took Micah's idols in their foolish belief that his idols would assist them in conquering the city of Laish. Unfortunately, instead of achieving something great for

God, the tribe of Dan managed to introduce idolatry into the other tribes of Israel by setting up the idols to commemorate their victory. It was this act that many years later led to God's judgment of the houses of both Israel and Judah.

Rather than depend on the world's tactics which can only lead to idolatry, church leaders must develop and use a biblical worldview as the grid for all they do in ministry. A synergistic church requires leaders who are dead to self and full of Christ, thus being free to use imaginative and creative ways to connect with a world in hyperchange. In Chapter 4, we discussed Sir Edmund Hillary's ability to see Mount Everest conquered. He had the kind of vision a leader needs to scale large mountains. Hillary's vision would not have come true if he had not creatively approached the challenge of climbing Everest. Many had faced the same obstacles before him and had turned back, but his ingenuity and innovation allowed him to go farther than anyone had ever gone. After Hillary proved it could be done, others followed. His accomplishment changed their paradigm. Hillary did not possess any special strength or skills; in fact, before he set out to tackle Mount Everest, he was employed as a beekeeper in New Zealand. He simply combined hard work with creativity. Not only had the mountain been climbed in his heart, but it had also been climbed in his head.

One of the greatest rewards of creativity is knowing that others will follow you to new areas of advancement. Roger Bannister had been told it was impossible to run the four-minute mile. Hundreds had attempted it before him, and no had succeeded. It was suggested that a human being was physiologically unable to run that fast for that long, but Roger Bannister did it. Interestingly, in the year after he broke the four-minute-mile barrier, 37 other runners did as well. The next year, over 300 runners ran the mile in under four minutes.[1] What some had said was impossible, Bannister accomplished, allowing others to accomplish it as well. We all have mountains and four-minute miles in front of us. The challenge of leadership is to conquer these challenges creatively by using a new paradigm. In doing this, we will inspire others to conquer their challenges as well.

What are the foundational principles to building a dynamic ministry? Do others succeed because they are smarter, more gifted, or simply get the breaks in life? Is it because they do not have any problems to contend with and everything seems to fall into place? Is it that they pray more than others? Are they just lucky? Or have they been able, through creativity, to break the paradigm around them? Like the men who followed Hillary and Bannister, we will follow in their footsteps doing tomorrow what could not be done today. How many remote regions of the world remain unevangelized because someone thought it was impossible to get there? How many people in the great cities of the world have not heard the gospel message because someone assumed the task was too great?

CREATIVITY FLOWS FROM CHRIST

A great truth of Scripture is the fact that Christ is the omnipotent creator of a hundred billion galaxies. Consequently, He is also the source of all creativity. Paul remarks, "He is the image of the invisible God, the firstborn of all creation. For by Him all things were created, both in the heavens and on earth, visible and invisible, whether thrones or dominions or rulers or authorities—all things have been created through Him and for Him" (Colossians 1:15-16). From His preexistent role as creator of heaven and earth to His humble life as the carpenter of Galilee, creativity was the mark of the Son of God. Because Christ is the sovereign creator of all, we would be foolish indeed to try to create anything in ministry without depending on Him. Jesus said of Himself, "I am the vine, you are the branches; he who abides in Me and I in him, he bears much fruit, for apart from Me you can do nothing" (John 15:5).

Practically, how do we submit our creativity to Christ? By submitting every thought to Him. Paul writes that we are to take "every thought captive to the obedience of Christ" (2 Corinthians 10:5). Only then can we have confidence that our creativity in ministry reflects "whatever is true, whatever is honorable, whatever is right, whatever is pure, whatever is lovely, whatever is of good repute, if there is any excellence and if anything worthy of praise" (Philippians 4:8).

Once we have surrendered our creativity to Christ, the effect is to stimulate our brains. Biblically, the mind and the brain are not the same thing. The mind is ethical in nature while the brain is physical. When we submit our creativity to Christ, we are being renewed in our minds.

Once the Holy Spirit controls our minds and consequently our creative processes, this unleashes the vast potential of our brains to accomplish more than we could possibly imagine.

Creativity Begins in the Mind

Most scientists believe that the human brain is the most complicated object that science has ever tried to understand. The whole brain contains nearly ten billion nerve cells. Because of the intricate complexity of the brain's circuitry, the number of possible interconnections between the cells of the brain is many orders of magnitude greater than the number of atoms in the entire universe. This is amazing! The vast elaborate circuitry of the human brain gives it a subtlety and speed that even a hundred supercomputers working in sync could never hope to match. Researchers believe the human brain is capable of reviewing up to 10,000 separate factors at once, giving new meaning to the question, "What are you thinking about?"

Did you know the average person has over 50,000 thoughts a day? For most people in a 16-hour day, that amounts to almost a thought a second. That means day in and day out, our minds are constantly whirring with impulses, notions, and urges of one sort or another in that intuitive process we call "thinking." We need to look closely at this statistic. How many thoughts of the average person are actually new thoughts each day? Naturally, we must have some repetition for memory's sake, but the essence of creativity is our ability to accommodate as many new thoughts as possible. The worst-case scenario would be having the same thought 50,000 times a day!

A great barrier to creativity is thinking today along the same lines as yesterday, the day before, five years before, and even a generation before.

A great barrier to creativity is thinking today along the same lines as yesterday, the day before, five years before, and even a generation before. The noncreative mind mulls over the same ideas and beliefs, fears, and worries every day. The very act of entertaining the same thoughts repeatedly limits our capacity for new and creative thoughts.

To break the paradigm that binds us, we must become creative. To become creative, we must first take control of our thoughts. We must leave behind old, worn-out thoughts and open our minds to new ideas, new opportunities, and a new vision. We must change the way we think about our lives, our ministries, our world, and ourselves. This is literally all we really need to do in order to completely revolutionize our lives and change the way we think. We must determine to create new avenues to express new thoughts.

Our Thoughts Influence Our Lives

One of the most important foundational principles to building an effective ministry is realizing that our thoughts influence our lives. Proverbs says, "As a man thinketh in his heart, so he is" (23:7 KJV). This is a simple and challenging concept. The thoughts we choose to occupy our consciousness will influence what we become. Rather than copying someone else's ministry, we should allow someone else's ministry to become a springboard and sounding board for new, innovative ideas that catapult us forward into twenty-first century ministry. Our thoughts are the most powerful forces shaping our lives. In fact, our thoughts are among the most powerful forces in the universe. We are where we are and what we are because of the thoughts that have dominated our minds. As for the future, our destiny is being shaped by our thoughts right at this moment. Therefore, it is very important that we allow the "right" thoughts to preoccupy our thinking. We know the vast majority of ministers do not achieve their full God-ordained ministry potential. It is like that the majority of ministers do not even question where their thoughts are taking them. This is why knowing that our thoughts influence our lives is such an important key to personal ministry effectiveness. We are to take "every thought captive to the obedience of Christ" (2 Corinthians 10:5).

Many people feel that once they have created something new, there is no need to maintain the creative process. The creativity needed to found Global Church Network did not end with the ministry's inception. For over forty years, Global Church Network has been on the forefront of ministry effectiveness. When I began the ministry, there began a creative process. We can creatively reach another generation of unbelievers by first creatively addressing the needs of the church.

Focusing Our Thoughts

Once we realize that our thoughts influence our lives, we also realize the importance of taking control of our thoughts. This critical breakthrough gives us the power to decide where our thoughts are going to take us. When Christ has full control of our minds, our thoughts will be centered on His goals. We begin a systematic program of thinking about the kind of person He most wants us to become and the life He most wants us to live. Within a short period, we begin to steer the life God has given us in the direction the Lord wants us to go.

The first step in taking control of our thoughts is doing a "mental download." For a period of seven days, write down everything you think about. At best, you can keep a running list of all the thoughts that cross your mind during the day. Make sure your list represents a good cross-section of the things in your consciousness. Include all the hopes, worries, expectations, burdens, people, places, memories, or daydreams—whatever occupies your mind even for a fleeting moment. By the time you finish, it should amount to a whole laundry list of subjects and a good inventory of the thoughts that are influencing your life.

The next step is to go back and take a critical look at what you have written. Ask yourself, "Where are my thoughts taking me? Are my thoughts taking me where I believe God wants me to go? What do these thoughts tell me about myself?" Once you have studied your thoughts, it is time to get your thinking on track.

Set aside your "mental download" list and begin a "mental upload." Make a new list of the kind of thoughts that will support where you believe God wants you to go with your life. Evaluate all of the main quadrants of your life and ministry. Read biographies of people you greatly admire, focusing not on what they do in the ministry but on who they are. Once you have their good qualities in mind, begin putting them into practice. In a surprisingly short period, the Holy Spirit will weave these admirable qualities into the fabric of your character. You can learn from others and use role models to accelerate your progress. Study key bible verses that will help you advance in these areas of life.

We believe that creativity makes the difference between succeeding and failing, between growing and shrinking, between sleepwalking and living. Too many churches are following the same ministry patterns and paradigms of fifty years ago. This is not to devalue what has worked in the past. However, we must be willing to let go of old approaches that are no longer effective in the changing environment.

Our Innovative Creativity

How do you approach the ministry to which God has called you? To be effective leaders, we need to strive for creativity. While others continue to think of the same excuses to justify ineffectiveness, the thoughts of leaders are fresh and innovative. We have taken control of our thoughts, and now our thoughts will help us to become the people God intends us to be.

The leaders of the synergistic church are not just successful in life; they are successful at the right things in life. They understand that it is not good enough just to get things done; they must get the right things done.

I have been privileged to minister at the Holy Convocation of Liberty University in Lynchburg, Virginia, to over 10,000 students and faculty. At the end of that chapel service, I stepped off the platform and was met by a student. The young man said to me, "Dr. Davis, thank you for sharing your heart today. I greatly appreciated your message; it really blessed me." He gave me a card and walked away. I thanked him and did not think much of it until later that morning when I read the 3"x5" card he gave me. Written in bold letters were words that have convicted me ever since: I am not afraid of succeeding in life; I am afraid of succeeding at the wrong things in life.

The more I thought about these words, the more I realized that all of us will be successful in life. The question is whether we are succeeding at the right things in life. The question all leaders must ask themselves is whether they are successful at the right things or the wrong things.

You can be successful at being lazy. Some people succeed at failure. You can even be successful at sin. The world is filled with successful sinners, but none of these are the right things to do.

The leaders of the synergistic church are not just successful in life; they are successful at the right things in life. They understand that it is not good enough just to get things done; they must get the right things done.

In traveling around the world, we have found that the greatest pastors are successful at doing the right things. Many times, we have met pastors and church leaders who were forced to leave their places of ministry because they did not achieve the results people expected of them. Oftentimes during the conversation, we have found they were confused. From their perspective, everything was going well and they even thought they had been successful. Sadly, these ministers were often succeeding at the wrong things in their ministry rather than the right things. They had focused on the wrong goals because they were looking through the wrong paradigm. The real challenge is to produce a cutting-edge product or service that is in demand. Creative people find a "niche" for themselves or their product that puts satisfies a demand.

THE SYNERGISTIC PROCESS IN THE LOCAL CHURCH

Thomas Edison, the inventor of the lightbulb, invented over 1,300 different devices and machines to make life better for us. During the journey of discovery that led to the creation of the first lightbulb, Edison tried over 2,000 different experiments before he achieved success. A young reporter asked him how it felt to fail so many times. With a smile, Edison replied, "Failure? I never failed once. I invented the lightbulb. It just happened to be a 2,000-step process." Edison knew that there is a process to being successful. There must be a step-by-step journey to lead people through the process of change and excellence. Leaders are not made overnight, and great churches are not grown in a day. Edison was not more creative than anyone else; he simply was not satisfied with failure and never gave up.

In today's world, anyone can make a product or provide a service. With the right amount of energy and hard work, we all can be productive. Bill Gates created an operating system for computers that enabled everyone who owned a computer to work together. McDonald's created a cheap, fast meal that enabled people to eat quickly. They both approached the market creatively and made their products and services special. Many people may copy them, but they blazed the trail.

New ideas are wonderful, and innovation is needed, but if there is no process for change or implementation, the ideas will never take root.

This does not mean that Microsoft and McDonald's were created overnight. It took years for them to become the organizations we see today. These were years of creatively incorporating their new thoughts into their processes. As we lead the church, we must understand our thinking process and the creation of the ministry God gives us. Ideas will never see the light of day if they are not integrated into the existing system through a natural process.

New ideas are wonderful, and innovation is needed, but if there is no process for change or implementation, the ideas will never take root. Many great ideas, new inventions, and valuable changes have been doomed to failure because of a flawed process. Change is inevitable, but the way in which we direct that change determines our effectiveness as leaders. Great leaders help people change because they want to, not because they must. They do this through the creative process of innovation.

I have identified the five stages of this synergistic process. We believe that if you implement this process into your leadership style, you will see maximum results. Each stage is vital to the synergistic success of the organization, the local church or a ministry. Each step is unique but intimately tied to the rest of the stages. They build one upon another. There is no standard amount of time that a leader will spend in each stage. In some organizations, it is important to spend a lot of time at certain stages. This is determined by the group and the leader. What is constant is the necessity to go through each stage. If the leader tries to introduce a new concept or a change in direction without going through the stages, the desired change will take longer to occur. People will not understand why or how they are to operate in the new environment.

At each stage of the journey, it is important to understand the needs and the reason the stage exists. Although change is necessary, most people resist it because they feel comfortable with the status quo. It is important to remember that people usually resist what they do not understand because they feel threatened. There will be people in your ministry who will initially be unable to see the vision God has given you. In fact, there will be people who will never embrace the vision or the process until after it is finished. There is comfort in remaining in the same place, but routine develops into a rut if a person is not careful.

As the Founder of Cutting Edge International and the Global Church Network (www.GCNW.tv), I have been privileged to travel over ten million miles worldwide. I have spent the equivalent of four years inside an airplane, nearly fifteen percent of my lifetime. I have been afforded the opportunity to preach the gospel in more than 1,500 hundred churches in America alone. While traveling, I have made it a practice to listen, to learn, to watch, and to write about outstanding pastors and churches. The leaders who have been the most successful are those who have understood this process and used it to their advantage. Whether it was launching a building program, planting a church, creating a new ministry, or leading their staff, the process takes place when people move from one way of doing things to another.

Stage One: Synergistic Purpose Determines Our Priorities

Any change or creative idea must have a definable purpose. There must be a sense of divine mission in the church before people will be motivated to participate in any ministry. Change for change's sake rarely accomplishes anything. Just as there must be direction before the departure of a plane, the church will never rise to its full potential without a clear, definable purpose. The established purpose of the church determines what the leaders see as their priorities. If I am in a church and their purpose is to evangelize the lost, most everything I see as a guest is centered on soul winning. They place a high priority on soul winning and outreach. If a church has a threefold purpose, the priorities of the church are multifaceted. The purpose of a church is reflected in what it views as important. When we try new ideas that are against our purpose, we waste time and energy chasing things that will not ultimately help us.

The leader's purpose is often reflected in a mission statement. The leaders should craft the statement through prayer and hard work. Most people assume they know their purpose, but many have never really thought it through. Without a clearly defined purpose, someone else's priorities will run the church.

Do you know what your purpose is in your ministry? In your church? Can you quickly and succinctly state your reason for being, your specific purpose, and the vital components of your life and ministry? If you have not come to terms with your own purpose, take out a pen and paper and write what you think your purpose is in life. Spend some time over the next few days determining what is important to you in life and ministry. Let your purpose in life determine your personal and professional priorities.

Imagine with me that a close friend from out of town comes to visit you. This friend who has never been to your home or your town calls you and asks how to get to your house. What is the first thing you will ask? Where they are calling from, of course. You cannot give directions without first establishing where they are. There are many pastors and church leaders who want to "get on the road" to the next destination, but they never check to see from where they are starting. When you go somewhere, it is necessary to leave one location in order to get to another. If you do not know where you are beginning your journey, you will never be sure of your final destination.

When I am asked why the Global Church Network exist? I answer succinctly, "The Global Church Network synergizes, mobilizes and finalizes the Great Commission." Over time we have been able to articulate our vision into nine words. All of our priorities, without exception. Help us to fulfill our purpose.

Stage Two: Synergistic Priorities Dictate Procedures

Once we have established what is most important to accomplish, we develop procedures to achieve those goals. We put plans and policies in place that make it possible to achieve the end we desire. Everything we do has a purpose. The manner in which we conduct our ministry reveals our priorities. For example, the ministry that does not see financial integrity as a priority will have sloppy procedures for spending and accounting for money. The church that sees the education of children as a priority will invest in strong Christian education and possibly a Christian school.

Whatever the procedure, it must be developed in light of the organization's priorities. There are many churches that have procedures in place that do not accomplish the achievement of their priorities or goals. In some cases, no one knows why the church operates as it does; it has always just done things that way. These churches are led by their procedures rather than by their priorities. How they do things is more important than what they do or why they do it. Procedure-driven churches care more about organization than they do about advancement. They have rules for every event, forms to be filled out in triplicate, and never run out of supplies. They rejoice in small victories, never realizing they are losing the war.

Our life and ministry do not simply come together. We have to create a magnet that draws the issues or ideas together.

When they allow the busyness of the church to interfere with the business of the church, they mix up the process. Eventually, people may begin to question why they do what they do. If they see that the procedure does not match their priorities, they will abandon the procedure—or worse, they will become loyal to the procedure rather than to the priorities of the church. This stifles creativity and hampers church growth.

In examining a church's procedures, it is easy to spot its priorities. Many churches talk about soul-winning, the lost, and evangelism; but they seldom give opportunities for people to be saved or equip believers for evangelism. Many churches talk about discipleship and spiritual growth but do not provide opportunities for their congregation to grow through teaching and learning. Many spiritual leaders talk about church growth and building a great church for God but come in late for work and give their golf game a higher priority. Our life and ministry do not simply come together. We have to create a magnet that draws the issues or ideas together. We communicate what is important to us by how we live our lives and how our ministries operate.

In making our procedures match our priorities, a simple five-step method can be used. Each step fits together to form the acrostic, GOALS.

G – Gather the facts. Before beginning a new enterprise, research the information. Find out what is important to the church staff, the board, and the laypeople. Spend time and energy to understand what is important to the people to whom you minister. Discover the benefits and drawbacks of establishing this new procedure. Does it match the priorities of the church? Is it the right thing to do?

O – Organize a plan. Great ideas must be organized. There is nothing more frustrating than to leave a staff meeting with great ideas and new, exciting ventures and then see them shelved or forgotten because no one took the time to organize how they would be implemented. Create a timeline of things to do in future meetings. Freedom to succeed is found in organization while slavery is found in chaos. Large projects and changes need to be broken down into small, manageable pieces. Establish due dates for tasks and assign responsibilities to individuals. By putting names and dates to tasks, you raise the level of accountability for progress and establish a way to measure advancement toward the final goal. A vision becomes a goal when you put a date to it. Dates provide a sense of chronological progress.

A – Act on it. After the research is done and the plan is organized, it is time to put the plan into action. The procedure will never become a reality unless it is purposefully put into place. Work slowly as you take this new idea or plan into the life of the ministry. Communicate to all involved what the purpose and expectations of the new procedure will be. Explain how it fits into the priorities of the church. Do not let it take anyone by surprise but let them know in advance how it will operate.

L – Look back and review. After the procedure has been put in place, study it to see how it is progressing. It has been said that life is lived forward and learned backward. In any new procedure for ministry, it is vitally important to plan review time. See how the process is going and how it can be improved. Ask a series of questions: Would I do it the same way again? Is there a more efficient way of doing it? Does it meet the need for which it was created? Have our priorities changed since it was created?

S – Set new goals. We cannot be content simply to bask in the glory of accomplishment. We must constantly be moving forward in planning and goal setting. Too many people rest on their laurels of success, never realizing how much farther they could go if they would set new goals. Accomplishment and success are only the foundations for future growth and dividend.

Stage Three: Synergistic Procedures Direct People

The most important component of any organization, church, or ministry is people. They are the reason we do what we do. People are why Christ came to the earth to give His life.

Leaders must keep people in mind throughout the entire process. People need to be led, not driven. We establish procedures that enable people to accomplish the work God has called them to do.

The effectiveness of leaders is determined by their ability to stay on the cutting edge of creativity and by their ability to implement their new ideas into existing structures.

If procedures do not serve the people, they do not need to be in place. Synergistic leaders know the difference between "using things" and "using people." People are not expendable commodities that exist for our personal achievement and advancement. Servant leaders understand that we exist for the benefit of the people. Leaders must find ways to make the policies and procedures of their ministry enable and assist people. They depend upon teamwork to accomplish the priorities of the organization. If the procedures do not serve the people, they should be abandoned, and new ones created.

How do leaders make sure that people are being served and better equipped in ministry? Leaders must communicate with those they lead. By immersing themselves into the culture of their church, leaders find out what people need and what procedures are working.

The closest group of people to the leader in a local church is the church staff. It is the staff the leader must understand and help first of all. Through creativity and planning, the church staff should become a team that effectively carries out tasks and accomplishes the overall mission of the church. The pastor serves as the primary motivator and facilitator for success. Leaders should encourage the men and women of the church to fulfill vital their vital, God-given roles in the local church. Church leaders cannot accomplish the Great Commission on their own; they must enlist and then equip all the members of the body of Christ to do the will of the Father.

Stage Four: Synergistic People Determine Our Programs

When it comes to pastoring a church, we must understand people and those people must come before programs. It is important to note that programs flow out of the needs of people and the purpose and priorities of the church; the church's purpose does not flow out of programs. Many pastors are looking for the "right thing" to do in ministry while they are missing what God is calling them to be in their community. There is nothing wrong with programs; they are vital to the health and growth of the church. However, they must never rise above people. When programs are more important than people, the church's priorities are out of sync. When Jesus walked the earth, He built relationships with people rather than establishing a formalized religion. In the local church, the five-year-old in the Christmas musical is more important than the success of the musical itself.

Stage Five: Synergistic Programs Deliver Our Product

Our product is a relevant, packaged gospel and mature Christians. This package may come in the many forms. It may be written, spoken, or crafted into dramatic presentations. Our goal is to creatively package the gospel and deliver it through up-to-date programs in the church. Programs achieve the desired result when they create synergy with the people of the church. Leaders do not look for the finished product of their work without first going through each stage of the process. Dictators demand results without process, managers demand process with no results, but leaders get results by honoring the process.

The effectiveness of leaders is determined by their ability to stay on the cutting edge of creativity and by their ability to implement their new ideas into existing structures. The same is true of the church. Without both the creative approach and the synergistic process, we will never experience sustained growth.

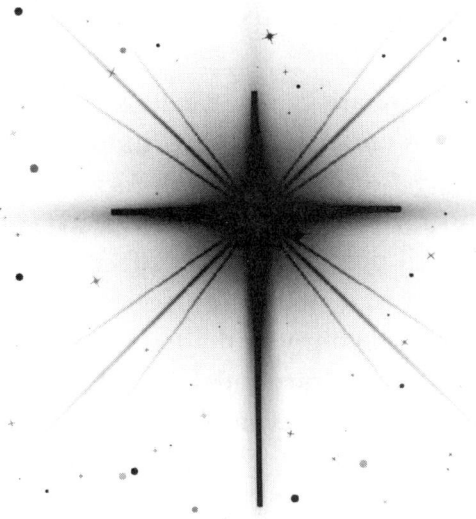

Conclusion

Jesus Christ: The Model of Synergistic Leadership

No one epitomizes synergistic leadership like Jesus Christ. The greatest leader who ever lived understood the eight principles we have discussed and incorporated them into His life. Over 2,000 years ago, the Son of God walked this earth and changed humanity. The goal of the synergistic church is not simply incorporating eight characteristics into what your church is doing. The goal is to be conformed to the image of Jesus Christ, allowing Him to live His life through us. In essence, we must become like Christ; and as we do, we will find that these eight principles are evident in our lives.

As we grow in our relationship with God and better understand His marvelous attributes, we develop a greater confidence in Him. We know we are called; we allow our character to be developed, and we demonstrate our commitment to Him. The roof is off in our relationship with Him. As a result, we are filled with compassion for those around us. We strive to cooperate with others to fulfill our mission, we effectively communicate the gospel, and we lead with Holy Spirit-inspired creativity. Christ operated in harmony with the Father in heaven and reached out to the world around Him. He has removed the barriers and walls in our lives and churches. As the head of the Church, He lived with no roof and no walls and is our model for life and ministry.

CONFIDENCE IN GOD

Jesus, of course, had an intimate relationship with the Father. His knowledge of the all-powerful and all-loving Father allowed Him to put His full faith and trust in the Father. He drew confidence knowing that God was in control. He lived His life in light of His understanding of God. He relied on the power of the Holy Spirit throughout His ministry. The Holy Spirit inaugurated His ministry (Luke 3:21) and directed where He went (Luke 4:1). Jesus was not just baptized with the Spirit, but He was also filled with the Spirit (Luke 3:21, 4:1). It was the Spirit of God upon Him who enabled Him to preach the good news and proclaim the year of the Lord's favor (Luke 4:18-19). He was empowered to accomplish His mission on the earth.

Many people are more dependent upon their own performance than on the power of the Holy Spirit. They equate activity and busyness with effective ministry. They are doing more and more and achieving less and less. Is it not amazing that technology has provided the Internet, email, faxes, television, radio, electricity, automobiles, sound systems, and many other means of communicating the gospel; but we have not yet reached our world for Jesus Christ? However, a small group of untrained and under-equipped disciples turned their world upside down, inside out, and right side up for Jesus Christ. Was this because they were empowered and guided by the Holy Spirit while we are motivated by our own programs? The Book of Acts could be summed up as follows: The Savior went up, the Spirit came down, the saints went out, and the sinners came in.

CALLING BY GOD

Jesus knew the God whom He served and what His own purpose was. He knew He was to glory in the Father and do His will. Jesus said, "I have come down from heaven, not to do My own will, but the will of Him who sent Me" (John 6:38). When Christ faced Calvary, He prayed that God's will would be done, not His (Luke 22:42).

Jesus knew He was sent to earth to "seek and to save that which was lost" (Luke 19:10). He understood His calling and knew He was to finish the race He was called to run. He was confident in who He was. He did not feel it necessary to copy others. When the Pharisees hurled accusations against Him and His disciples, He did not conform to their expectations. When they compared Him to John the Baptist, Jesus and His disciples did not replicate another's ministry or habits (Matthew 9:14-18).

Jesus understood that He was to serve those He had come to save. He was comfortable in being a servant even when all of Jerusalem wanted to crown Him king. Jesus knew that the deeper the service, the higher the significance. The night before He was betrayed, Jesus washed the feet of His closest followers. He knew that he had to reach for the towel first and the throne second. He understood He had been called to be the suffering Savior before He was to be the reigning king.

CHARACTER BEFORE GOD

Jesus Christ is the greatest example of consistent character the world has ever seen. He was obedient even to the point of death, and His character did not falter even in the greatest challenge of His life. Paul wrote:

Have this attitude in yourselves which was also in Christ Jesus, who, although He existed in the form of God, did not regard equality with God a thing to be grasped, but emptied Himself, taking the form of a bond-servant, and being made in the likeness of men. Being found in appearance as a man, He humbled Himself by becoming obedient to the point of death, even death on a cross (Philippians 2:5-8).

Jesus Christ is the greatest example of consistent character the world has ever seen. He was obedient even to the point of death, and His character did not falter even in the greatest challenge of His life.

Jesus, the only person to walk the earth who knew no sin, poured Himself out on our behalf (2 Corinthians 5:21). He humbled Himself to take upon Himself the nature of man so that He might save the world. He persevered even to the point of dying on the cross that we might have life. Throughout His life, He faced opportunities to forgo the Father's will. For forty days in the wilderness, Jesus resisted temptations so that His character could be developed (Luke 4). He modeled to His disciples and to us the importance of integrity and consistency. He went the second mile—He finished the race.

COMMITMENT TO GOD

In studying Scripture, we find no one else as consistent in demonstrating commitment to God as Jesus. Prayer, worship, and evangelism were top priorities and expressions of His commitments to His Father. It was His practice to pray to the Father often (Luke 5:16). He modeled and taught His disciples to pray while He was with them. He would pray in the early morning and late at night (Matthew 14:23; Mark 1:35; Luke 22:41). The greatest expression of Christ's commitment is found in the Lord's Prayer (Matthew 6:8-13). In teaching His disciples how to pray, Jesus revealed what was important in His life. He began by talking about His Father. The Father knows what we need before we ask; therefore, we should praise His holy name (Matthew 6:8-9).

Christ taught that we should pray for the Father's will (Matthew 6:10). He did not come with a personal agenda or list of needs; He came in humility. He prayed that God would give Him not extravagant wealth or riches but simply His daily bread—the amount sufficient to remain dependent upon God. Christ modeled prayer as something that was for every person every day.

Jesus Christ knew the awesome goal of His mission. He traveled all over Palestine, working to see His mission accomplished. He followed through even to the point of dying a humiliating, agonizing death on the cross. He also knew the necessity of training others to finish the task after He was gone; consequently, he spent more time with His disciples than He did with the multitudes. There was no "Plan B" for Jesus. He came and walked the earth, pouring Himself into His disciples. They were His only way for presenting the gospel to the world.

INTERDEPENDENT COOPERATION

Jesus also revealed the power of relationships. He knew that God's plan involved people reaching other people. From those who followed Him, He chose twelve to be His closest disciples. He modeled the principle of partnership. When the seventy and the twelve were sent out to minister, He sent them out two-by-two (Mark 6:7; Luke 10:1). He knew the power and accountability that resulted when leaders partner together for ministry, yet it was one of the twelve who ultimately betrayed Him. Judas was selected by Christ to be one of His closest servants. Although Jesus knew betrayal was coming, He did not avoid working with others. The danger of joining with Judas was overshadowed by the fruitfulness of joining with Peter, James, and John.

As a member of the Trinity, Jesus' entire existence and ministry were in harmony with the Father and the Holy Spirit. He is the ultimate example of the power of partnerships. This is seen in the relationship we each have with God. No one comes to the Father except through the Son, yet it is the Spirit who draws all men to the Son. It was the Father who sent the Son and the Son who glorified the Father.

IMPACTFUL COMMUNICATION

Jesus Christ was the greatest communicator in history. He proclaimed the truth of God to individual seekers (Nicodemus) and to the multitudes (the Sermon on the Mount). His words were simple and powerful. They brought people to repentance and life transformation. As a master communicator, He was able to disarm critics, inspire the hopeless, and convince the skeptics. He was anointed by God to preach the good news to all of Israel. Those who heard Him marveled at His ability to teach and preach (John 7:15). His message of hope and truth still rings in the hearts of those who read His words. Jesus' life and teaching modeled effective communication.

Jesus was a master teacher—every miracle He performed had a message and every sign had significance. Jesus never taught by accident; He taught purposefully. He answered questions and provided solutions to problems. If you are weary in mind, Jesus says, "Come to Me, all who are weary and heavy-laden, and I will give you rest" (Matthew 11:28). If you need basic worldly goods, "Seek first His kingdom and His righteousness, and all these things will be added to you" (Matthew 6:33). If you are worried about life, Jesus says, "Take courage, it is I; do not be afraid" (Matthew 14:27). If you want to be a witness to the lost, Jesus says, "You will receive power when the Holy Spirit has come upon you; and you shall be My witnesses" (Acts 1:8). If you are weak in body, Jesus says, "My grace is sufficient for you, for my power is made perfect in weakness" (2 Corinthians 12:9).

Jesus was a master teacher—every miracle He performed had a message and every sign had significance. Jesus never taught by accident; He taught purposefully.

When Jesus proclaimed His message, He engaged the minds of the listeners so that they might learn the truth and then engaged the hearts of the listeners so that they might put the truth into practice. Jesus was the logos (John 1:1), divine Word of God on earth. Words are the outward expression of the unseen thoughts of the mind. God's thoughts cannot be seen, but He revealed those thoughts through the life of Jesus. Jesus became the outward expression of the hidden thoughts of God. He took blind truths and thoughts and turned them into reality for His people.

INGENIOUS COMPASSION

Jesus was filled with compassion. It was love that motivated His very presence on the earth: "Christ loved us and gave himself up for us as a fragrant offering and sacrifice to God" (Ephesians 5:2 NIV). Jesus came to seek and save the lost. He died to draw people to Himself. Whether it was the woman at the well, the thief on the cross, Zacchaeus the tax collector, or Nicodemus the teacher, Jesus wanted to give people an abundant and eternal life. He preached the good news of the kingdom of God and brought hope and healing to the multitudes. The last words He spoke on the earth were to command His followers to go into the entire world and make disciples.

Jesus and His disciples approached Jerusalem in the final days before the crucifixion (Luke 19:41). Seeing the city in the distance, Jesus wept. He did not weep for Himself but for Jerusalem because they did not recognize the time of the Lord's coming and would soon be destroyed (Luke 19:44).

The passion He had for His people caused great joy when they came to know the truth and great sorrow when they rejected it. Jesus wept because they would not know Him. When was the last time we as leaders wept for the people in our community who do not know Christ? If we are passionate for souls like Jesus was, there will be rejoicing and there will be sorrow.

Jesus also cared for His friends and family. He kept in contact with loved ones such as Lazarus, Mary, and Martha. While on the cross dying for the sins of all mankind, His heart turned toward the care of His mother. He comforted her and asked John to take care of her after His death (John 19:26-27).

INNOVATIVE CREATIVITY

Jesus operated with a paradigm. He saw past the religious structures and human traditions of His day and brought a life-changing message to as many as would listen. He was creative in His approach to reaching people because the higher the predictability, the lower the communication. He preached, wrote words in the sand, cursed trees, performed miracles, turned over tables, and quieted a storm. He told parables and taught principles. He rode into Jerusalem on a colt and left carrying a cross. Jesus painted pictures for the creative side of the mind and preached principles for the cognitive side of the mind. In other words, Jesus engaged the whole person when He approached ministry.

Jesus lived His life in light of the process. He thought through challenges and prepared Himself and the disciples for the moment when their task would be at hand. He allowed them to prepare mentally for what would occur before the events of Passion Week. Jesus did not rush into ministry without first processing all the stages. He lived with the end in mind. He knew from the beginning of His ministry that the end would be the cross. His entire ministry can be understood in light of His preparing the disciples for the time when He would leave them.

Synergistic leadership requires that we put the person together first before we try to help save the world. We must become more like Christ if we are ever to "put the world back together."

The father of a young boy spent all day at work looking forward to watching a baseball game on television. After he came home, he settled into his recliner. He was just beginning to relax and catch up on his favorite team when his ten-year-old son came in. "Dad, can we go play catch?" the son asked. The father, intently watching the game, told him to wait a little while and they would go play. After a few minutes, the boy asked his father again, "Dad, can we go play catch?"

The father, reluctant to leave the comfort of his easy chair told the boy to wait. After several requests and several "wait a little whiles," the father decided he would distract his son. Seeing a magazine with a picture of the world on it, he tore off the back page and cut up the world into very small pieces. Many of the pieces looked just like the others. He poured the pieces on the floor and told his son that when he could put the world back together, they would go play catch. Settling back into his easy chair, the father assumed it would take hours for his son to "put the world back together." After 10 minutes, the boy ran to his father with the completed puzzle. The bewildered father asked how he had done the impossible task so quickly. "That's easy," the son replied, "On the back of the picture of the world was a picture of a man. All I had to do was get the man put together and the world came together."

Synergistic leadership requires that we put the person together first before we try to help save the world. We must become more like Christ if we are ever to "put the world back together."

We pray that God gives you the keys to unlock the puzzle of the future as we journey together, leading others by the power of the Holy Spirit.

We challenge you to dream big dreams and cast a vision that will last beyond your lifespan. It is far better to shoot for the stars and land on the moon than to shoot for the trees and hit the ground. How high are you aiming?

Jesus Christ was the greatest leader who ever walked the earth. In less than four years, He took twelve men of diverse backgrounds and abilities and turned them into world changers. In less than four years, He established a group of followers who would advance the kingdom of God until it swept the entire world. Through the power of the Holy Spirit and the blessing of the Father, the Son of God supernaturally lived His life and led His followers. He was and is the greatest example of a leader.

Ask yourself where you will be in twenty years. What will be your legacy? What kind of leadership will you give to those you are called to shepherd? We pray that God gives you the keys to unlock the puzzle of the future as we journey together, leading others by the power of the Holy Spirit.

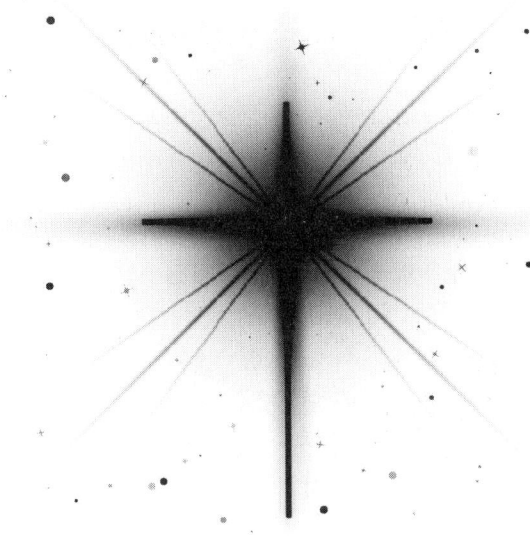

Appendix 1

Why and How the Great Commission Will Be Completed

In the summer of 2015, Dr. Leonard Sweet, renowned author, futurist, and leading evangelical, and Dr. James O. Davis, Founder of Cutting Edge International and Global Church Network were conversing on the phone regarding the future. During the phone conversation, Dr. Sweet mentioned to Dr. Davis that the 500th anniversary of Martin Luther nailing the 95 Theses on Castle Church door in Wittenberg, Germany, would take place in 2017. Then, Dr. Sweet asked Dr. Davis, "I wonder if anyone is going to do something about it."

Dr. Davis responded and said, "It seems like someone, or some organization needs to pause and celebrate the 500th anniversary. In that same conversation, Dr. Sweet also said to Dr.

Davis, after the 500 years celebration of Martin Luther nailing the 95 Theses on Castle Church door, will be the 2,000-year birthday of the Church.

In the year of 2014, the Holy Spirit began to flood Dr. Timothy Hill's mind regarding FINISH. At that time, Dr. Hill was serving as the World Missions Director for the Church of God. Today, he serves as the General Overseer of the Church of God worldwide. On an international flight into Romania, the Holy Spirit filled Dr. Hill's mind and heart with the six-step-acronym for FINISH: Find, Intercede, Network, Invest, Send and Harvest.

In the summer of July 2015, Dr. Davis flew to Berlin and then took a train to Wittenberg, Germany. Weeks earlier, he had reached out to the President of the Wittenberg Seminary, Dr. Hana Kasparick, who also managed Castle Church. After waiting for a little while on a beautiful summer morning, Dr. Davis met with Dr. Kasparick. During the meeting, he looked directly in her eyes and asked, "Would it be possible for us to have Castle Church on November 1, 2017, during the 500 years celebration?

Dr. Kasparick instantly grabbed her calendar and opened it up and said, "No one has booked November 1 yet." Dr. Davis response by saying, "Are you sure about this? Five hundred years does not slip up on us very quickly." She said, "I am the only one who keeps the calendar and nothing is booked on that day." He quickly responded, "Could we have it?" She said, "I do not see why you can't. Please give us a letter of your intent and ask for the specific date that you would like to have Castle Church and I will take it to the committee."

Six weeks later, Dr. Davis received a confirmation letter from her stating that the Global Church Network would have the opportunity to host the Wittenberg 2017 Congress in Castle Church on November 1st, 2017. The Global Church Network was the only Christian organization permitted to have an international event in Castle Church during the 500 years celebration of Martin Luther nailing the theses on Castle Church door. GCN began to synergize toward the 500-year celebration of Protestantism and at the same time, began to make plans for the 2,000-year birthday of the church.

During the close of the Wittenberg 2017 Congress, at the graveside of Martin Luther, Dr. Timothy Hill led the more than 600 attendees, from 12 world regions, in what is called the Finish Declaration. The prayer commitment to finish the Great Commission by the 2,000-year birthday of the church.

During the Wittenberg 2017 Congress, Dr. Davis articulated that the 2,000-year birthday of the Church would take place between AD 2030 and AD 2033. He carefully stated that different groups around the world would see the dates differently and that we would make plans for the Global Church Network to celebrate for a 4-year period of time, beginning in 2030 AD and continuing until 2033 AD.

We are living in an unprecedented time throughout the entire Body of Christ. We're living in a time when it is possible for the Global Church to complete the Great Commission in our lifetime. Generations have come and gone with the hope, ambition, and dream to finishing what the Lord commanded us to do nearly 2,000 years ago. It is important for us to understand why and how the Great Commission will be completed by the 2,000-year birthday of the Church.

WHY THE GREAT COMMISSION WILL BE COMPLETED

First, as relating to the reasons why the Great Commission will be completed the Church has enough **members**. Over the last 100 years, the Church has grown exponentially, compounding each and every year. Yes, there's been the rise of false religions, but Christianity has continued to grow each and every year. In the final analysis, there are only two kinds of religion: true and false.

In 1900, there were several hundred million Christians throughout the world. One hundred years later, the number is approaching 2.5 billion Christians. There are more Christians alive today than there's ever been before. We have enough members!

Secondly, the Church has enough **methods**. We have all kinds of methods in order to execute ministry today. We have accounting methods, financial methods, holistic methods, Bible study methods, leadership methods, training methods, children ministry methods, singing methods, youth ministry methods, elderly methods, preaching methods and countless more. We have methods by which we evangelize and how we disciple. We have methods upon methods. The church has enough methods!

Third, the Church has enough **models**. Even though methods and models are similar, models do help make the concepts more tangible. Over the centuries, the Church has produced untold number seminaries, Bible schools, local churches, universities, leadership centers and, orphanages. With emergence of the Internet, the Church is learning and applying online and on-ground models. There are more than 10,000 bible schools today!

Forth, the Church has enough **multiplication** in order to finish the great commission. The Church is growing faster today than it has ever grown before. In China there are 108 million Christians, with an average, 45,000 are coming to Christ every day. In India, there are more than 60 million Christians with 30,000-plus coming to Christ every day. It is estimated by 2035, that Africa will become the very first Christian continent. There are more than 400 million Christians in Africa, and the gospel is marching north throughout Africa. The reason there's so much persecution in the church in Northern Africa today is because the gospel is headed. Throughout Central and South America, in the last 75 years, more than 300,000 churches have been planted with tens of millions of people who have come to Christ. Think about what the Lord has done throughout the world. Yes, there

Appendix 1

are still hard places, and yes, there are places of spiritual decline, but the Church is multiplying faster than it has ever done before.

The Church has enough **money** to finish the Great Commission. No single organization in and by itself has enough money to complete it. However, the Church together has enough money to complete the Great Commission. It is time…in fact, it is past time to quit duplicating our efforts and spending money twice when it could be applied synergistically between different organizations to spend money once in order to finish the Great Commission. It is now imperative that every dollar be invested wisely to move us closer and closer to the finish line. The Church has enough money!

Sixth, the Church has enough **motivation** to finish the Great Commission. Twenty years ago, the Church did not have the willpower to overcome the obstacles and turn them into opportunities. However, today the mindset is gradually changing and there is enough motivation to get to the finish line. We're moving from ego and logo to we-go. We are moving from the mindset of what will it take for our organization to complete the Great Commission, to what will it take for the Church to complete it. The Lord gave the Co-Mission; not the Mission.

We're moving from silo missions to synergistic missions. In other words, in the past, we only invested into missionary projects that benefited our organization, but today, we believe it is possible to grow our organization and at the same time synergize with other organizations.

We're moving from name-branding to networking. Several years ago, I was invited to speak for a friend and his organization in San Francisco, California. As he was preparing to make the trip to go, James heard his friend say on the phone, "I'm very excited about our team learning more about networking, but I'm concerned about losing our brand." James responded and said, "Jesus Christ is the brand. It is not just about the name of our organization on the door, as it is about the name of Jesus Christ being preached and proclaimed throughout the earth." We are moving from name-branding to networking.

We're coming to understand that those who are not networking will eventually be not working. We're moving from consumers to contributors. In other words, instead of asking, what do we get out of it, we're asking what we can sow into it. We're moving from WIFM, what's in it for me, to WIFJ, what's in it for Jesus Christ.

The Church has enough **momentum** to get to the finish line. Not only does the church have enough motivation, but the church has enough momentum. Look how far we have come over the last 120 years. In 1900 AD, the church had evangelized 45.69% of the world. By the AD 2000, the church had evangelized 73.09%. However, with the growth of the population of the earth and the pace of the population growth of the earth, outpacing the growth of the church, even though the church will continue to evangelize over this century, by AD 2200, it is estimated at our current rate that 83.25% of the world will be evangelized.

With the previous paragraph in mind, even with the growth of the Church, approximately 2 billion people will still be unreached, the exact same number that's approximately unreached today. So, what is the answer? It is the synergistic model of building the Body of Christ together and speeding things up accordingly to cut that distance down by the 2,000-year birthday of the church. Population is going to continue to grow, and evangelization will continue to go. But if we're going to finish the great commission by the 2,000-year birthday of the Church, synergy is the only way this will be accomplished.

It is important for us to understand that we're living in an unparalleled time in the Body of Christ, and it is possible for us to complete the Great Commission. Why? Because we have enough members. We have enough methods. We have enough multiplication. We have enough money. We have enough motivation. We have enough momentum. And, with all these

Appendix 1

powerful forces synergized together, it is possible to finish the grandest race of our lifetime, the Great Commission.

HOW WILL THE GREAT COMMISSION BE COMPLETED?

Why is the doorway to wow. Without the correct why, the buy-in necessary, to get to wow and on to how cannot be achieved. A big enough why will produce a big enough how. So, with the why we will finish the Great Commission in mind, now let us focus on how we will finish the Great Commission. I believe that when the Holy Spirit downloaded into Dr. Timothy Hill, the acronym for FINISH, I believe at the same time, it became a roadmap for the Church of God in particular, as well as the body of Christ worldwide to get to the finish line.

Dr. Timothy Hill and Dr. James O. Davis have discussed at length what it will take to complete the Great Commission. Dr. Davis has committed to all he can through the Global Church Network to synergize the church leaders throughout the Body of Christ. The church leaders have the opportunity to help lead the rest of the body of Christ toward the finish line. We can either be part of the parade, or we can read about the parade that has marched down main street to the completion of the Great Commission.

Over the last five years, Dr. Davis has shared the FINISH acronym and the roadmap with key Christian leaders all over the world. It is simple, it is memorable, and it is transferable. It is easy to understand. It is easy to remember. It is easy to apply. It is so simple, it is profound. The late Dr. Adrian Rogers used to say, "Simplify, simplify, and simplify again, and people will call you profound."

The FINISH acronym are six strategic steps that will take the Body of Christ general, to the finish line.

First, we have to FIND the remaining unreached people groups. A lot of leaders like to shoot the arrow and then move the target accordingly, so it looks like they have shot the arrow correctly. But we are putting out our targets first and shooting our arrows second.

Even though there are over 6,000 unreached people groups left, we have chosen to focus on the hardest 3,000 unreached people groups. As a network, we decided before we went to Wittenberg 2017, that we would focus on the hardest 3,000. And the reason it is important for us to focus on the hardest groups it is because if the Church is ever going to finish the Great Commission, the Church has to get the hard ones done first. So, oftentimes the Church continues to pick the easy fruit rather than climbing the mountains where the hard fruit is.

For example, the Global Church Network is building, in partnership with every major denomination, the very first-ever Mount Everest Training Center in the high altitudes of Nepal. It is located just five minutes from the Hillary-Tenzing Airport at the elevation of the 8,500 feet. This state-of-the-art leadership center will be used to train church planters from every major denominational group to plant churches in the highest altitudes in the world.

For 2,000 years, villages have existed across the high altitudes of 15,000, 18,000, 21,000 feet, but there's never been a church planted there ever. The reason it's so hard is because there are no roads there. You can't take a car, a motorbike, a bike, or a helicopter to these villages. The only way the gospel can go there is that a man takes the gospel and plants a church there. The Mount Everest Training Center gives access of the finest training to leaders in the high altitudes that they've never heard before.

The hardest groups must be our focus in the next 8 to 10 years. Reaching the hardest 3,000 unreached people groups will guarantee the completion of the Great Commission.

Additionally, the Church in general and the local church in particular, must synergize their efforts together, for the hardest 3,000 Bible translations. There is a massive biblical translation paradigm that is taking place.

Appendix 1

In 2003, Dr. James O. Davis visited with Dr. Roy Peterson, then President of Wycliffe Bible translators in Orlando, Florida. While he was showing him the vision walk that was outside his office, he was articulating that the bible translation vision included a completion date of 2,250 AD. While this vision was being shared, James did not know how it could be done faster, but thought to himself, "There has to be better and faster way to complete this." He stated to Dr. Peterson, "At this rate, world population would have to die twice before everyone in the world had access to the Word of God."

With this in mind, the next year, while James was lifting his Chinese daughter, Olivia into the air overhead in a nearby park, the Holy Spirit said, "Look at who I have lifted up all over the world." With that admonition, Dr. Davis began flying worldwide to meet with a single key leader, who the Lord had lifted up and began tying relational knots worldwide.

Today, the mission field has become a mission force. We are moving from parenting to partnering. It is now possible for the Church worldwide to participate in Bible translations. By the year 2030 to 2033, nearly 3,500 more translations will be completed. And the focus is on the hardest, unreached people groups and the hardest Bible translations left to be done. It will put the church in a position of reaching out and completing the Great Commission. In the last 80 years, just over 700 Bible translations have been completed. However, in a fifteen-year period of time, another 3,000 plus translations will be finished!

Dr. Roland Vaughn former World Missions Director for the Church of God, developed the Missionary Arrowhead for unreached peoples. It is a masterpiece of strategic thinking. I have taken the arrowhead and I've tweaked it to represent a little different feel, but Dr. Vaughn perfectly thought this through.

What we need to do is seek the unreached. Jesus came to seek and to save. Our goal is to find in the unreached people groups one, two, three or handful of disciples. God has His people everywhere. There are Christians in every nation. I believe that God is the greatest manager of all time. We need to seek the unreached.

We need to get as close to where these men and women are. And how do we do this? We go to save the unreached. The neighbors know the neighborhood. If we do not know any specific Christians in an unreached group, we go to the next level, to the neighbors, because the neighbors know the neighborhood. Many years ago, when a missionary left his/her own country to go another nation, he did not necessarily need to ask, "Are there Christians there or other missionaries in the area?" However, today, when a missionary goes to another country, he/she must ask if Christians or other missionaries or there. We must not go to compete but to complete.

Next, if we do not know any neighbors, we synergize the national church in the nation. We synergize for the unreached, the national church, national leaders, Bible schools and missionaries in that nation that gets us closer to the neighbors that gets us closer to the neighborhood.

However, if we do not know or there does not exist a national church organization in it, we take the next step of sowing into the region, closest to the unreached people we are interested in reaching. We look at the region because those in the region would know some in the nation who would know some in the neighbors, among the neighbors who would know the neighborhood.

And if in some cases, if the first four approaches do not work, we go to leading pastors and we encourage them to adopt and send to work toward the specific unreached people group that God has laid upon their heart. What is our overall strategy? We seek, save, synergize, sow, and we send. Find the world's unreached people groups and we engage them.

Secondly, not only do we must find in order to get to the finish line, but we must INTERCEDE in order to get to the finish line. The Church is filled with prayer warriors. The Church is filled with intercessors. The Church is filled with men and

Appendix 1

women who believe in fasting and prayer. It is important that we build a prayer movement like this world has never seen before. In October of 2011, there were 7 billion people on this planet. In November of 2022, we crossed 8 billion.

By the time we get to 2030 and beyond, we will have 8.7 billion people in the world. The Global Church Network has proposed that we pray 8.7 billion hours for the 8.7 billion people that will be on this earth during our watch. We should motivate and challenge the Church worldwide to pray at least one hour for every person on the planet.

8.7 billion prayers hours can be achieved by:

- the personal level: a person commits to pray for 100 hours over a 10-year period of time. 100 hours over a 10-year period of time is only 10 hours per year.
- the partner level: pray with others in order to compound our hours. 500 hours is only 5 prayer partners over the next 10 years.
- the pastor level: 30 members equals 3,000 hours, 120 members,12,000 hours, 240 members equals 24,000 hours.

Dr. David Mohan, the Founder of New Life Assembly in Chennai, India, says, "If we are not praying we are not planting. We have to first break the stronghold of enemy in the town or city." New Life Assembly averages 45,000 each weekend.

NETWORK is the third step to completing the Great Commission. For far too long, we have tried to finish the Great Commission alone. For hundreds of years, various organizations have said, "We will finish the Great Commission ourselves." And with each attempt, the Great Commission has not been completed. We have to tie relational knots for national, regional, and global impact. In other words, we have to tie relational knots for our nations, for our regions, and for our world. Relationship currency properly invested becomes relationship capital and with relationship capital, we can complete the Great Commission. Relationship currency is the greatest currency in all of the world.

Many years ago, Dr. Davis was asked, "How do you expect to finish the Great Commission?" His answer was then and still is today, "We will finish our assignment by tying enough relational knots; no knots, no net, no net, no catch, no catch, no harvest, no harvest, no completed assignment. Without the tying of the knots, all we are, are little strings loosely laying on the sand of time. We cannot accomplish much until we learn to tie relational knots. Not only do we need to tie relational knots but transform our mental paradigms.

What is the hardest part about networking? Changing people's mindsets, transforming people's perspective." It is not you or me. It is us together. It is too late in the day to be arguing over the little things that do not matter. The Lord did not call us to defend our distinctives to the point of not being able to preach the gospel to all the world. The main thing is to keep the main thing the main thing. For far too long, we have more interested in obtaining missions credit in our denomination or fellowship, without asking or considering whether or not we were getting closer to the finish line.

It is imperative that we transform our old mental paradigms. The battle is between our ears. If we believe what the Scripture has said, then we are to love all the saints and pray for all the saints. We will have to enlarge our circumference of love large enough to finish the Great Commission. If we will commit to digging deeper and expanding wider, then we will be able to build high enough to network the Body of Christ together. The Church is poised in a position to build a circle of love like never before that will not grow the Body of Christ worldwide.

We must learn to network like never before. We need to synergize the best relationships. We need to systematize the best training. We need to strategize for the unreached and scripturalize for new Bible translations. The Global Hubs of Christianity

Appendix 1

is the prime example of leaders being able to synergize, systematize, strategize, and scripturalize. It is there where leaders from different streams of Christianity are equipped in the various countries to go to the finish line.

Recently, Dr. Peter Thomas, Africa Director for the Church of God, met with Dr. James O. Davis in Zambia, Africa. For four hours they synergized their efforts together, along with the key leaders representing 46 nations to finish the Great Commission. They are currently synergizing their efforts to place a hub in all 46 of these nations led by Church of God leaders so that the Church of God leaders can help tie relational knots in the Body of Christ that moves us closer to the best training and best strategies for fulfilling the Great Commission.

Next, we need to INVEST strategically in order to finish the Great Commission. We need to invest our time. We need to invest our time into relationships, into our thinking, into our strategies. We need to invest our talents. We all have a role in the goal. We all have a part in God's heart. God gave you a skill or a talent in order to help fulfill the Great Commission. We need to invest into our temples. We are the temple of the Holy Spirit. We need to take care of ourselves. We need to eat right. We need to exercise right. We need to learn to move from racing to pacing in order to finish the Great Commission.

We need to invest our treasure. Yes, we need to invest our money. We need to invest what God has placed in our hands in order to complete the Great Commission. We need to lead by example and encourage others to do likewise. The Church is going to need at least another billion dollars to complete the Great Commission. Dr. Timothy Hill recently made reference at the Church of God General Assembly, to the bank metaphor. He said a bank was established for church planting with $1 million, and another half a million was added to it. The Church needs a bank. We need a bank filled with resources, focused on fulfilling the Great Commission. The Church will need at least $1 billion worldwide to invest into training the young emerging generation to go further than we've ever gone before. If the Global Church was to invest $100 or $1000 into the training of 1 million young God-called leaders, the cost would be 100 million dollars and 1 billion dollars respectively.

On the heels of invest, we need to SEND. We need to send young, equipped leaders into the harvest field. There is no Christian organization who can say, "We have plenty of young men and women who are called into ministry coming up in our ranks. You can pass us by and give them to somebody else." There is no Christian denomination that can say, "We have plenty of young called ministers in the pipeline. You can pass us by." One of the greatest needs, if not the greatest need is a harvest of young men and women called into ministry like never before. Most preachers are called during their teenage years.

We not only need a harvest of young men and women called into full-time ministry, but they need to be equipped, empowered, and energized in order to take the gospel further than we have ever gone before. We call this the Million Ministers Mandate. The Church must look for and believe God for at least 1 million new young men and women called into the ministry in the next 10 years, who will carry the gospel to the hardest places on earth.

We need to inspire young called ministers, instruct online young called ministers, and involve young called ministers today. Every denomination should know what God is doing in their local churches, as well as in your youth camping ministry programs. Dr. Davis is encouraging all youth leaders to provide a list of names and email addresses, each quarter to their general superintendents, who have been called into ministry. We need at least 1 million new ministers in ten years.

We will need at least 250,000 church planters, 250,000 more pastors, 250,000 youth leaders, 150,000 evangelists, and 100,000 missionaries worldwide. The Church must create the learning on-ramps necessary for the emerging generation. While we celebrate the traditional models of equipping and training through

Appendix 1

our seminaries and Bible schools around the world, these models in and by themselves will not get us to the finish line. What got us here will not get us there. The traditional models that we have had in this current generation are too slow to get the men and women to the harvest field in time, with the advancement of population growth like never before.

In every global hub, our goal is to have at least 40% of the hub membership to be between 15 and 35 years of age. If we are going to finish the Great Commission, we need a huge army of Kingdom-minded and Christ-centered young leaders who are willing to go to the hardest places in the world with the Gospel.

It takes two wings to fly. You'll never get a one-wing bird off the ground. You'll never get a one-wing sermon off the ground. You have to have two wings to get a sermon off the ground. You must have style and substance. In this generation, we must have online and on-ground. We must create the on-ramps necessary for the young leaders to get on the highway where we are today. The Global Church Network created, what's called the Global Church Divinity School (www.GCDS.tv). We established preaching, teaching, healing, story, arts, Christ formation, and contextual semiotics as seven major ministry training tracks for the upcoming generation. The GCDS was not created to replace what other organizations my currently have but to offer further assistance in the training of 1 million ministers, from every major denomination and independent groups.

And if we are faithful to find, intercede, network, invest, send, we will bring in the HARVEST like the world has never seen before. The harvest requires both decision-making and disciple-making. We will have a revival like the world has never seen before. We will have a sweeping, weeping, reaping revival. We will have a harvest where the churches are full. We will have a harvest where new churches are being planted, where there's never been churches in 2,000 years since Jesus Christ came out of the grave. Our harvest will be measurable. We will see compounding growth. Our harvest will be motivational. People want to be involved in the harvest like never before. Our harvest will be memorable. People will write in their church history books what God did in the early 21st century.

WHAT DOES A FINISHED GREAT COMMISSION LOOK LIKE?

What does a completed Great Commission look like for us? When we have found, interceded, networked, invested, sent, and harvested, what kind of harvest will we be looking at by the 2000-year birthday of the Church?

First, we submit to you in this harvest, we will have a **church that is synergized and mobilized**, a church that is moving like it has never moved before.

Secondly, we will have a **hub in every nation**. We will have a place where synergy replaces silo mentalities, where the body of Christ can come together, and each and every nation to really focus on what it will take to finish the Great Commission in their nation, in their neighborhoods, in those unreached people groups.

Third, we'll have a **Bible in every language**. As the mission field becomes a mission force, as we move from parenting to partnering, we will have opportunity to provide a Bible in every language.

Fourth, we will have a **harvest of young, equipped leaders**. We will have more young men and young women answering the call of God and then equipped for the harvest field like never before.

Fifty, we will have a **church within walking distance**. Instead of planting a church down the street where another strong Bible-believing spirit-filled church is located, we will place churches where there are no churches. We will be more strategic and more relational than we've ever been before. And we will then have a completed Great Commission.

Appendix 1

You may say, "This is impossible." Well, the majority of the world, does not drive a car or take a bus to church on the weekend. I think about my friends in the underground church in the Middle East and my friends in the "upper-ground church" in the Himalayan Mountains. They must have a church within walking distance. The most efficient way to break the back of demonic oppression in an area, is to plant a Bible-based, Spirit-filled Church. There is a tidal wave of church planting engulfing this world. More than 10,000 churches are planted each week and more than 500,000 per year.

What does finish look like? For the lost it is found in these words, "Whoever was not found written in the Book of Life, was cast into the lake of fire (Rev. 20:15). For the saved, finish is The Marriage Supper of the Lamb. For the first time, the entire family of God, will gather together around the Lord's table. Until that day, may each of us keep the angels extra busy placing more chairs at the table (Rev. 20:7-11)!

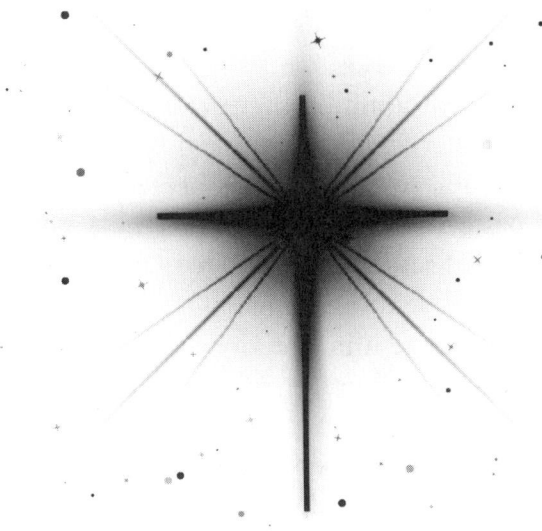

Appendix 2

Synergistic Global Missions

I grew up in a progressive home, where my parents lived full lives and taught their children to think broadly, work hard, and believe for the best. As a family we possessed a can-do attitude with a follow-through aptitude. I believe this background prepared me to be ready for open doors and to view the world from different viewpoints.

When I left home in January 1982 to attend Central Bible College in Springfield, Missouri, I had already made some smaller decisions of "this for that" as I thought through the options before me in the light of the bigger picture that the Lord was showing me. Upon getting to Central Bible College, I was confronted with various kinds of worldviews as well as with different levels of understanding of the Church. I remember a conversation with my roommate in which I shared that I planned to preach and minister during my time in Springfield.

"You won't be able to do that since there are already so many preachers and pastors in the area," he said.

"Oh yes, I will!" I responded.

"Why are so confident?"

"Since I am willing to minister anywhere," I said, "there will always be a place for me to preach and minister."

Herein lies one of the greatest leadership secrets: If we are willing to serve anywhere, there will always be a "where" for us to serve. This is the kind of outlook that is needed to see the unseen paradigms that are before us. I have discovered that most pastors genuinely believe that they are doing global missions and helping to fulfill the Great Commission in our generation. Yet, their traditional paradigm is not adequate to help them to see what they are not seeing and learn what they were not learning. It took me years before the unseen and unlearned became seen and learned. I must confess there is still so much more that I do not know!

In order for us to move from a traditional missions paradigm to a global one, we must first adjust our mindset. The old school was primarily based on *funding* and *training*. The new school is based on *networking* and *partnering*. In other words, we have to change our missions mindset from "parenting" to "partnering." This is not easy as to achieve as we might first think. As soon as we begin to adjust, we run into missional systems that have been in place for decades and are hardened against quick revision.

For example, if your church has worked from a traditional missions viewpoint for a long time, you no doubt support a number of missionaries who primarily train and teach the national church in some region of the world. Most likely the majority of these missionaries do not live on the edge of missional endeavors among the unreached/unengaged people groups of our generation.

Dr. James Hudson Taylor IV of OMF International (formerly the China Inland Mission and Overseas Missionary Fellowship)

Appendix 2

teaches the following steps for moving from "parents" to "partners." First, we have to build relationships. There are no shortcuts here. The deeper the relationship, the shorter the distance between the idea and its execution. Second, there has to be mutual ownership. People have to see themselves in the outcome in order for them to go on the long run. Third, effective communication is paramount. Verbal and non-verbal communication must be taken into account. Fourth, we have to leverage diversity and unity. The more we can harmonize, the more we can evangelize.

Oftentimes, leaders get these first four steps right, but they miss the fifth one: we have to put in place appropriate structures and best practices. If the structures are not right, others will be unable to get plugged in to various projects. Sixth, we need motivation for God's glory and the furtherance of His kingdom. We have to keep the main things the main things! I have included a graphic below so you can see what we now teach throughout the Global Church Network.

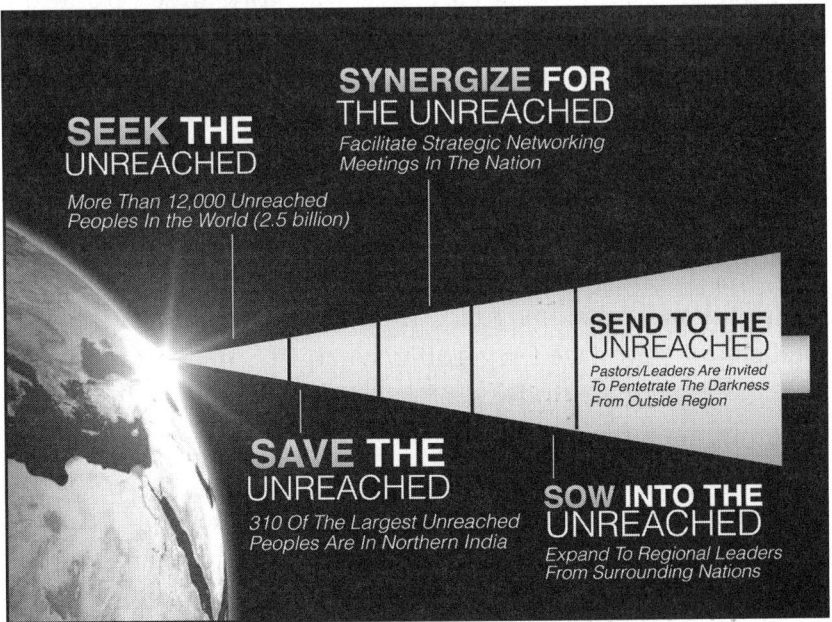

Once a local church or organization begins to make the mental shift from traditional to global missions, so many more options come into play to achieve the desire outcomes. I must confess I understood some parts of this shift, but the concept became clearer to me when Rev. Roland Vaughn, former World Missions Director for the Church of God, taught me this "Five-Point Arrowhead."

The five points of the missions arrowhead are:

- Seek the Unreached
- Save the Unreached
- Synergize for the Unreached
- Sow into the Unreached
- Send to the Unreached

This Five-Point Arrowhead depicts one of greatest shifts of missional understanding in our generation. It is my conviction that this networking paradigm will work anywhere in the world. We can see the significant differences between traditional and global missions by viewing them through the lens of the arrowhead.

TRADITIONAL MISSIONS

Here is the Five-Point Arrowhead from the perspective of traditional missions practice. Over the years, the hardest challenge I have faced regarding synergistic networking is the reshaping of the mindsets of leaders and organizations. For example, many leaders articulate their concern about loosing "their brand" through synergistic networking. However, we need to remind ourselves that Jesus is the brand, not the name of our ministry or organization. When it comes to finishing the Great Commission in the hardest places, we will need to synergize our thinking and efforts together; not duplicate our energies and spend money twice when we can spend it once.

Appendix 2

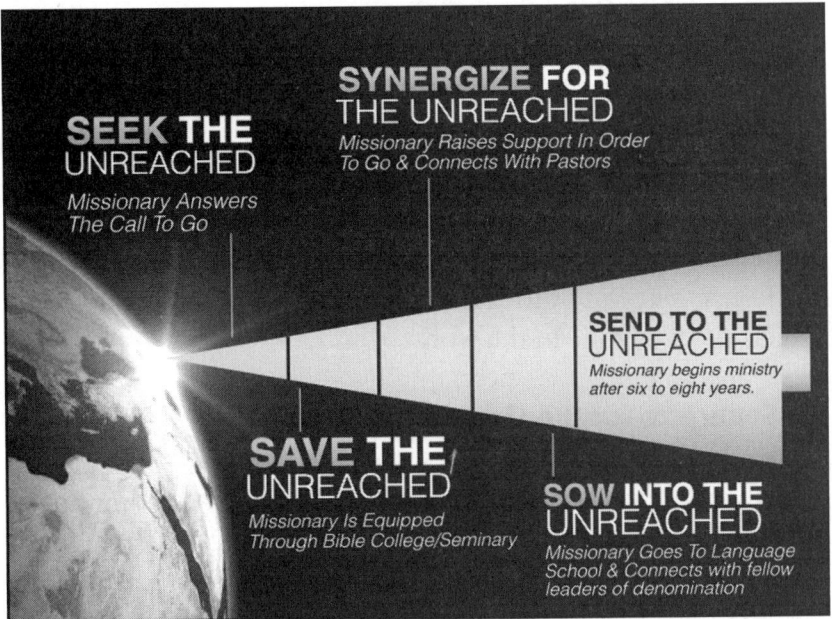

Be sure to carefully think through both paradigms (traditional and global) as you strive to move from one to the other. Keep in mind that the global paradigm becomes easier in time, as you get to know leaders outside of your silo in various regions of the world.

1. **Seek the Unreached: The missionary answers the call.**

Even though I have not officially served as a missionary in the traditional sense, I have served as a missionary in the global sense for decades. Our common understanding is that people, as individuals or couples, answer the call to be missionaries and connect with their denomination or organization. Oftentimes, this calling is first perceived in their youth and fulfilled in the years that follow. The call may be general or it may focus on a specific country or people group. At other times, the denomination or organization dictates where missionaries will fulfill our God-given calling.

2. Save the Unreached: The missionary is equipped.

For decades the Bible college/seminary approach has served the Church with exceptional results. Some missional organizations require up to eight years of training before their missionaries can land their feet in a particular world region. Again, while this model has served the Church well for a long time, it faces numerous challenges in the twenty-first century. For example, with the explosion of the Internet, online training is now at the fingertips of anyone in the world.

3. Synergize for the Unreached: The missionary seeks funding.

Once missionaries have gone through a certain amount of schooling, the next step, typically, is to begin to raise the funds necessary to actually go to the "called field." This is a grueling task. As they go to various churches and people, they share our vision and invite pastors and churches to partner in their effort to provide missions to a particular world region. Depending upon their fund-raising skill and how many people they know, this funding phase can take up to two years, and sometimes more.

4. Sow into the Unreached: The missionary learns the language.

Once missionaries actually get to the field, they have to learn the language and culture in order to do effective ministry. It is not that nothing is done during this phase; but the work is limited until the language is grasped enough for effectiveness. Regardless of whether the missions view is traditional or global, career missionaries do have to learn the language at some point, if they plan to stay in the area for any length of time.

5. Send to the Unreached: The missionary begins ministry.

Even though the missionaries have been in the field, they are only now really equipped for their assignment and able to begin multiplying ministry. How many years have elapsed since they first entered Bible college or seminary? Think about the answer for a moment. I'm not proposing that this traditional approach is evil; but this was adequate when the global church was young and not indigenous in so many regions like it is today. What has brought us this far will not by itself get us to the finish line.

GLOBAL MISSIONS

I realize that some people will have issues with the terms "traditional missions" and "global missions." In one sense, traditional missions has taken us to global missions. Yet, going forward, the traditional approach is *not* going to get us across the finish line of completing the Great Commission. Population growth alone compels us to find a more current, cutting-edge way to finish the assignment. In the next ten years, the population of the world will cross eight billion. Suliasi Kurulo of World Harvest Center in the Fiji Islands says it well: "Everything the Lord did not tell us to do, we have done; but, the very thing has told us to do, we have not done!" He commanded us to finish the Great Commission, and that's what we must do.

Even though reaching 9 billion people is just ten years away, we need to be already strategically planning how to reach 9 billion people in the next twenty years. Often, we give thought to how our organization can grow larger next year compared to past years, without giving long term thought to how our organization can add value to other organizations in order to reach untold millions with the gospel. Traditional missions helps us grow our own organization. Global missions helps us grow our organization and other organizations for the fulfillment of the Great Commission.

Let's envision the arrowhead again, this time through the global networking lens.

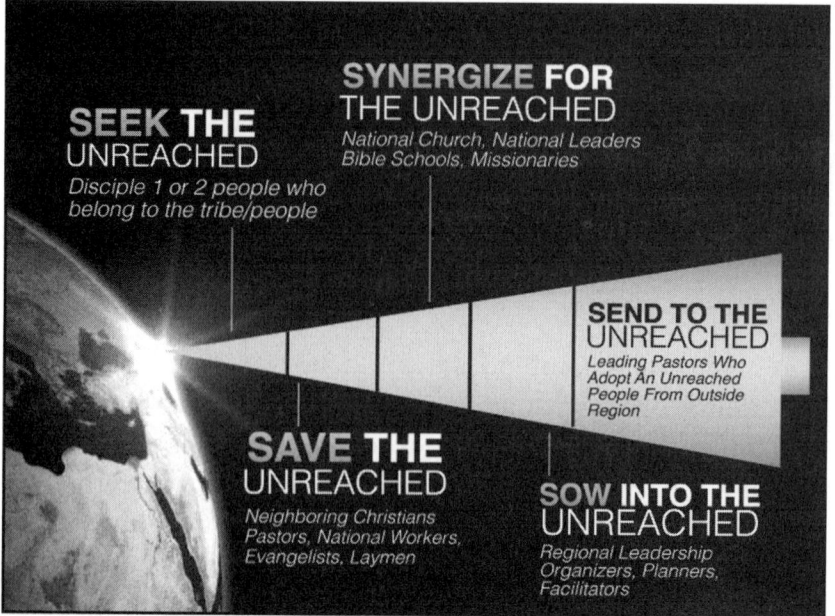

1. Seek the Unreached:

The missionary networks with one or two disciples who be-long to the unreached people group.

We are to begin with the target in mind and work our way from that point. As we've already noted, there are more than 16,000 people groups throughout the world. The Lausanne Covenant of 1974 introduced into missional thinking the concept of people groups, and the significance of that viewpoint has grown steadily over the years. The old question was, "How many nations are you in?" The better question is, "How many *ethnos* (ethnics or people groups) are you in?" This is far closer to the original mindset of the first "Great Commission" spoken by our risen Lord!

Of the world's 16,000 people groups, approximately 6,000 of these are unreached or unengaged people groups. (Unengaged means that not enough gospel penetration is taking place to make a significant difference.) Pastors and leaders who are targeting these people groups should begin by thinking through clearly where they want to start, and then build from there with the globe in mind.

We must be thoughtful and intentional, using all the resources God has made available, including other Christians. In the past, we used to simply answer the missionary call and go, without ever thinking about whether or not there were Christians already in the region. It used to be that there were so few Christians and denominations in these mission fields that it really didn't matter. That mindset can be summarized by Dr. Glen Burris, President of the Foursquare Church: "My old concept of unreached peoples was, if there was not a Foursquare church, they were unreached—no matter who else was there." Today, the Church has grown up enough to know that the Great Commission goal is better served when we take the time to ask, "Who else is there already?" If there are one or two disciples who are part of the people group, we can begin our work most effectively by networking with them.

2. Save the Unreached:

The missionary networks with Christians who live along the perimeter of the unreached people group.

Now we are getting somewhere! When we begin to realize that the Church has grown up, we can begin to move from parenting to partnering. Who else knows better how to get to the unreached people than their neighbors? I have witnessed the effectiveness of this approach time and time again in various world regions. In our Billion Soul networking summits, we ask, "How do we get from here to there? Who already lives in the region who will know what to do and how to do it?"

Of course, this model can be applied to the unreached in any area of the world. In my opinion, however, of all the dark places on the planet, Northern India is the darkest. This is where 310 of the largest unreached/unengaged people groups are found.

North of Delhi, between Nepal and Pakistan, more than 400 million live without adequate witness of the gospel. Yet, the old school of missions is still in session!

3. Synergize for the Unreached:

The missionary networks with the national leaders, Bible schools and other missionaries.

I realize that there are areas in the world where the Gospel has not penetrated. However, this does not stop us from networking with key leaders who are the closest to this region in order to build bridges in the area. In some nations, it is illegal to preach the Gospel; we *must* build networking bridges if we are ever going to finish the assignment in these regions.

In other areas, there are hundreds of unreached people groups, and every major organization is serving in some way. For example, India is filled with key leaders from various organizations. Each year key leaders hold a Finish Line Summit, where leaders from numerous denominations and organizations come together to connect with key Indian leaders who represent more than 125 unreached/unengaged people groups. Over the last five years, more than 120 of the unreached people groups have been adopted by key leaders. I cannot imagine a missionary going to India with the old mindset of working only with "my tribe" to finish the Great Commission!

4. Sow into the Unreached:

The missionary networks with others throughout the region.

Now, we broaden our minds and ministry to begin to connect with others, even those outside of the target nation, to discover who else is serving in that nation. I believe the global Church is located as it is throughout the earth because our Lord led tens of thousands of leaders throughout the decades, knowing that we would need to be able to network effectively to finish the assignment. In other words, the Gospel is where it is by God-given design. The Holy Spirit has placed various groups in various locations and has now called us to connect the dots. He has called us to network among ourselves to tell the rest of the world about Christ. It is amazing what we learn from other leaders when choose to begin seeking them out and then sowing into their lives.

5. Send to the Unreached:

The missionary networks with others outside the region.
As global-minded missionaries, we choose to network even beyond the region of our calling to drive the Gospel into the world's darkest places. Along with networking at the four levels highlighted above, we choose to think even more broadly and bring the global help needed to penetrate the darkness. In the past, we just invited pastors to come; today, we ask, "Who are the best people to come help us here, in addition to the local pastors who are assisting us?"

As we research and network to find others who have similar missional interests and burdens, we gain the knowledge that we need to make wise, concrete decisions. The same Holy Spirit who leads us to specific people groups will also direct our path to others who can come alongside us to work for the greater cause.

I am firmly convinced that this Five-Point Arrowhead is the right model for missions as we move forward in the decades ahead. Whether you serve as a pastor or a leader in an organization, these five steps will work effectively and powerfully for you, as you seek to serve the Lord and help fulfill the Great Commission in our lifetime.

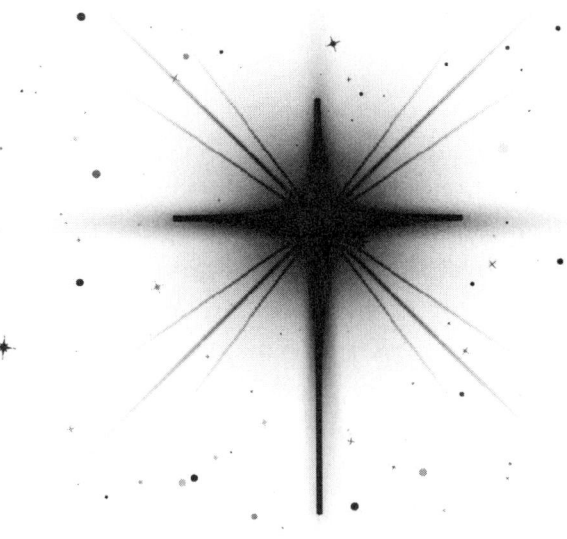

Appendix 3

Synergizing Across the Lines

Throughout this book I have stressed the importance of synergizing across the lines of denominations and organizations in order to fulfill the Great Commission. When this synergy is not achieved, it is typically because of doctrinal differences, narrow views of the Church, tight-fisted ownership of the local churches planted, and the lack of commitment to truly fulfilling the Great Commission in our lifetime—or any lifetime for that matter.

Yet, the stark reality is that everything the Lord did not command us to do, we have done. We have built great buildings, written powerful books and music, and the list goes on and on. Yet, the very thing He told us to do, we have not done! We were commanded to make disciples in every nation. Somehow we have to get to this bottom line of synergy if we are ever going to be able to say, "Job done!"

I have watched firsthand as key leaders have developed effective, synergistic ministries in every world region. Through synergistic networking over the last fifteen years, I have seen leaders in Northern India, for example, initiate and sustain a church planting movement across every major denominational line, resulting in 20,000 house churches! Alex has achieved this effectiveness by developing and following a seven-step model. This model is like a powerful wheel that can be rolled, when properly understood, in every region on earth. I have personally seen its success, and I recommend it to you for your prayerful consideration. In the graphic depiction below you will find a Synergistic Seven-Point Wheel.

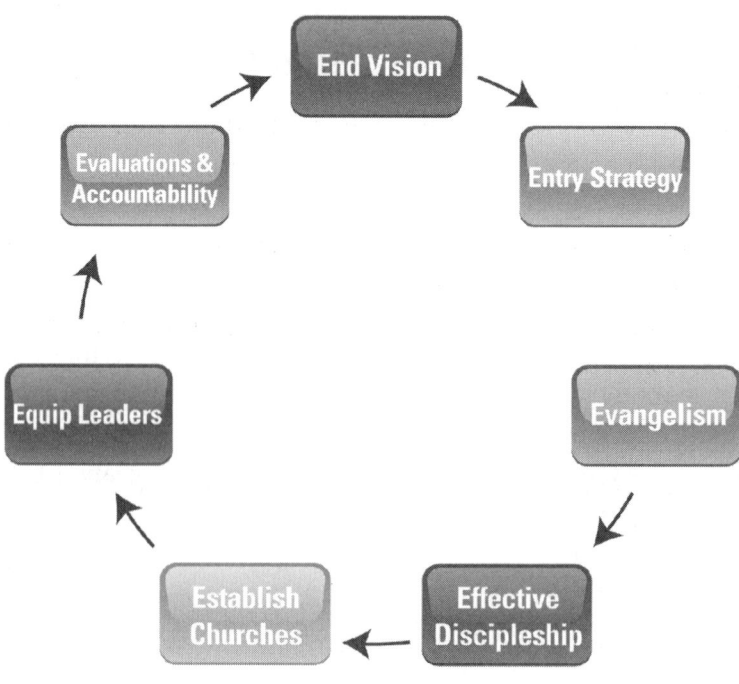

Appendix 3

Step One: End Vision

We are to begin with the end in mind. No target, no triumph! As we come to the realization that the weight of seven billion people is too much for any of us to shoulder alone, then we are compelled to network across as many lines as possible. Leaders serve in India, where the population grows by at least 60,000 per day! Can you imagine taking ownership of such multiplication and finding a way to get ahead of this population curve? It's mind-boggling! Keeping the end in mind forces every Bible-based leader to cry for help, lest the harvest is lost.

Step Two: Entry Strategy

When approaching a new unreached/unengaged field, we should think through the best way or ways to enter it. We need to synergize with fellow leaders, seeking their input and involvement as we go in. It is best to seek counsel and strategy from the beginning, rather than jumping in and then going back later to get approval or invite partnership. If you go too fast, you go alone. If you go progressively, you take others with you. There are several biblical steps we should consider:

- Create understanding and application of Jesus' model for entering new fields
- Compare and contrast contemporary strategies with Jesus' model
- Make personal application of Jesus' instructions for entry
- Apply simple, reproducible tools for entering the new field

The following graphic summarizes the four kinds of fields we will enter in our ministries.

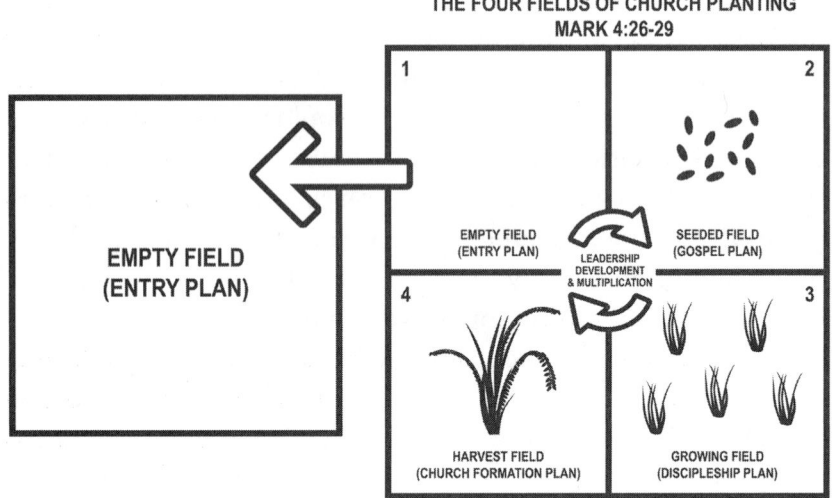

Step Three: Evangelism

The more we synergize, the more we can evangelize. The more we synergize, the more we can mobilize. Wouldn't be wonderful if we began with a plan in mind as to who was going to do what and when it was going to be done? I am not proposing that we "divide up the field" into portions among various denominational groups, who then keep to themselves. In the long run such an approach has been proven *not* to be sustainable. Yet, it *is* possible for various groups to serve together for the sake of evangelism and church planting. It takes effort, but the rewards are immeasurable!

Synergy is important not only on a denominational or organizational level, but also at the local church level. If the pastors in a particular area would take the time to sit down and strategize, they could address issues of money and assets and ownership. The key, again, is to keep the end in mind; we will give an account of stewardship during our time on the earth.

Step Four: Effective Discipleship

Today it seems that every major Christian organization has its own approach to discipleship. It is long overdue for key leaders to get together in a region or even around the world to discover the best practices for making disciples. Without effective discipleship, our efforts and energy will come to naught. What a waste of a life or ministry to serve the Lord in one generation, only to see it disappear in the next generation! History proves that after one or two or may three generations, the Church fails to continue to produce effective disciples.

Step Five: Establishing Churches

I love what Suliasi Kurulo does when it comes to establishing churches. After a person goes out to plant a church, and that church grows to a good number of members, then he or she is qualified to be ordained for ministry. Once there is lasting fruit, hands are laid upon the person to go out and plant more churches.

When crossing denominational lines, we need to have a common understanding of the following:

- What is a church?
- How do you form a church?
- What are the functions of a church?
- What are the offices of a church?
- What about headship and authority in the church?
- What are the signs of a healthy church?

A good, vigorous conversation with our networking partners about these questions is necessary at the beginning, so that there is no confusion later.

Step Six: Equipping Leaders

Once a church is planted, the goal of the church planter should be to train indigenous leaders from within the church. But, how can this goal be achieved across denominational or organizational lines?

Since we are working with Bible-based leaders, the best approach to reaching agreement and synergy is to use the biblical examples as much as possible. The mentorship of the Paul-and-Timothy model, for example, always works to get conversation and creativity going in the minds of leaders. It is critical that we have a true follow-up and follow-through plan with one another and with the local churches. Without this, we are wasting our time.

Step Seven: Evaluation

When we are transparent with our fellow leaders, trust is built and synergizing becomes easier over time. We need to be willing to admit, "There is a better way than what I am doing right now." When we evaluate our life and ministry through the measures of eternity, the treasures of the temporary, and the pleasures of soul-winning, we will have greater focus for the networking journey ahead.

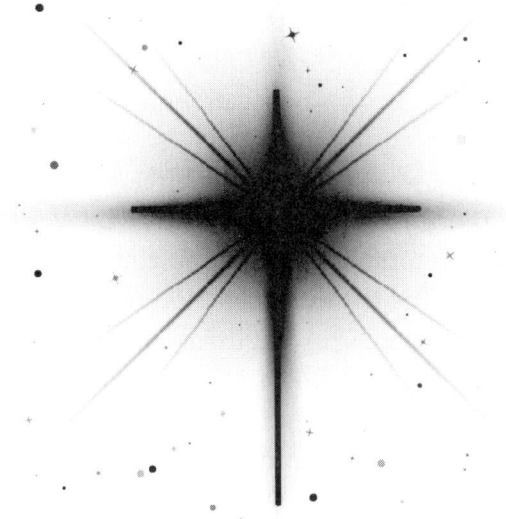

Appendix 4

The Global Church Network

More than 10 years ago, I was fortunate to visit Sir Edmund Hillary in his home. And as I was visiting with him, he is the first person to ever climb Mount Everest. If you've not heard of Mount Everest, it's the highest mountain in the world, more than 29,000 feet to the summit. He achieved it in 1953. And I was fortunate to be in his home in the remaining few months that he had before graduating for eternity, and I was conversing with him about this season of life. And I shared with Sir Edmund that I wanted every day to matter. I wanted to maximize this season of my life, and I wanted to be focused as a Christian leader. And he was 88 years young. And I asked him, "What do you recommend to help me to be as focused as I possibly can?" And he sat there for about a minute, there on his sofa, in his family room, in his home in Auckland, New Zealand. And then this is what he said:

"If you only do what others have already done, then you'll only feel what others have already felt. But if you would dare to do something that no one else has ever done, then you'll have a satisfaction that no one else has ever had. And when you're choosing your life's project, if there's no fear involved, you'll become bored with it and you won't even finish what you begin. But after you decided what it is you're going to do, start right now."

Think about what Sir Edmund said. If you only do what others have already done, then you'll only feel what others have already felt. What is the Christians' Mount Everest? I submit to you that it is the Great Commission. It is the mountain that we as Christians have claimed, climbed, and conquered. We know how big the mountain is. We know how tall the mountain is. We know where the reach people groups are. We know where the unreached people groups are. And I believe this can be the generation that hoist high the Christian flag on the roof of the world and declare that Jesus Christ is the king of the universe. I believe that this is our greatest moment. And then when we think about hoisting high the cross of Jesus Christ and putting it on the roof of the world, then how is that going to be done? Because the world is a big place and there are lots of many different streams of Christianity throughout the body of Christ.

The Global Church Network has celebrated 20 years of growth. And I'm grateful to be able to share with you that from the very beginning, it started with the uniqueness and the diversity of two men coming from two different streams of Christianity. And today, there are some 2,700 different denominations and more than 700,000 churches worldwide involved in different levels in the network. We often say that if you're not networking, you will eventually be not working. It's so important that we understand that the world has changed.

Now, I live in North America, in the United States, and here in North America we are thankful for the more than 50 million

Appendix 4

Christians that we have in the United States. Of course, I would love it that we had 100 million, but we have 50 million prospering Christians in America. That's about 3% to 4% of the Christian population in the world. That means 96% to 97% of the Christians do not live where I live. You say, well, what's the big deal about that? Well, it's not that big of a deal if you're not kingdom-minded and your goal is not to help fulfill the Great Commission. But if you are kingdom-minded and faith-filled and your goal is to help fulfill the Great Commission, then it matters where God has His people all around the world.

You see, the mission field has become a mission force. The Global Church is not looking for parents, but it's looking for partners. And the world has changed. And if we're going to finish the Great Commission in any generation, we're going to have to move past ego and logo and get to go. If we can get to go, we can make some progress. You know, if your movement is not moving, it's not a movement. It could be a monument. Oftentimes movements, if we're not careful, become the opposite of what they start out to be. That movement starts young and vibrant and full of faith and vision, but as it gets older, it slows down and oftentimes picks up a lot of stuff it doesn't need, and it becomes the opposite of what it started out to be. When we began to build the Global Church Network, we took it as a train on a track with many boxcars attached to it. And we believed that if we could just gradually build piece after piece of that train and have it on the vision of the rails going forward, that over time we could make progress.

I want to just briefly highlight some of the boxcars on this train, if you would, to help us to understand where we have come and where the network is going. I have four major overarching pieces for you. You'll find it very helpful to understand the big picture and understand how the parts fit together because we all have a role in the goal.

We all have a part in God's heart. It begins with the, what we call the **discovery phase.** Life is a discovery. As we move forward into areas where we've never been, we're going to meet people we never met, we're going to learn lessons that we have never learned. Life is filled with discovery, and as a network, we want to discover, we want to discover new partners and new fellowships and new streams of Christianity that maybe we've never known before. We've hosted summits all over the world and we're grateful for the men and women who have been involved in those conversations and in those discussions, as strategies have emerged out of these conversations. We believe that the network, the Global Church Network, is organic. We continue to sow the seed and we believe that God continues to increase it all around the world. We believe that relationship currency is the most valuable currency in the body of Christ today, and we believe that the kingdom of God rolls on the rails of relationship.

We thank God for discovery, but on the heels of discovery comes **development**. Once you learn something or encounter a new relationship or colleague, it's important that we develop it. So, we decided that we wanted to develop a curriculum, and develop courses. We wanted to cultivate our relationship currency, turn it into relationship capital so we could build phenomenal things in the kingdom of God together. Because you see, what got us here won't necessarily get us there. What has brought us this far in the body of Christ is not going to be the same that gets us all the way to the finish line. We have to understand that. As I have been privileged to travel in many different places around the world, I lost track many years ago of how many towns and cities that I've been to. I've been well over 140 countries. But as I've traveled, I've come to understand that God is raising up a new generation, and I celebrate it. This new generation is going to go further than my generation has gone. My generation went further than the previous generation. And the generation that God is raising up today is going to go further than my generation. I don't fear that, I celebrate it.

I love taking walks along by the beach. And when I do, I notice that there are constant waves in motion. But there's two waves that at some point have some tension, and that's the wave that's coming in and the wave that's going out. But 10 times out of 10, the wave that's coming in overcomes the wave that's going out. There is a generation that's graduating for eternity, but there is a new generation that's coming in. We call it the Million Ministers Mandate. I don't know of an organization anywhere in the body of Christ that can say, hey, we have enough young leaders, you can skip us by. God knows that we're living in a time when we need a massive influx of young men and women into the body of Christ who answer the ministerial call to go and help fulfill the Great Commission, to plant churches in areas where they've never been planted, or to reach into unreached peoples where it's never been before, or to be involved in Bible translation in their nation like it's never taken place before. We call it the Million Ministers Mandate. We are praying that in this generation, of one wave going out and the next wave going in, that we will see a huge influx of young men and women from every major stream of Christianity that will partner toward the finish line. And in the context of development, is also what we call the Global Church Divinity School.

As we continue the development, we also continue the **distribution.** It doesn't matter how good the content is if you can't get it to where it needs to go. I celebrate the reality that when we launched the Global Church Network more than 23 years ago, we also launched the online training at the same time. It wasn't an afterthought; it was a forethought; we have been involved in online training for over 23 years, and it's going to continue to grow. Today at the Global Church Divinity School, there's over 270 interactive, dynamic, incredible, courses taught by men and women all over the world. It's what we call the circumference of Christianity. It's no longer the West going to the Rest. It is the best around the world going to the rest of the world, and you can find this showcased in the Global Church Divinity School. We thank the Lord for this digital campus, and each of the buildings give honor to a key leader in the Global Church Network. These campuses or these buildings on the campus are interactive as well. However, most of the students will not take their courses by clicking on a building and diving into the courses, but rather they will come into what we call the Global Church Classroom, and the Global Church Classroom is made up of some amazing courses, again, by incredible men and women from every major world region.

In this Global Church Divinity School there are seven ministry tracks, and there are seven levels in each track. So, when you think about preaching, for example, it goes from novice to mentor, seven levels in preaching. When we think about teaching, there are seven levels from novice to mentor. It makes up 49 modules which is 196 courses. Once a leader has taken all those courses, they can go after the top layer, which is the Omega level or the Omega credential. Every hub is connected to the Global Church Divinity School. We want to bring the finest training credentials to the body of Christ today.

The Global Church Divinity School has what we call a Board of Governors made up of men and women from every major stream of Christianity to help bring compounding value and vision.

We're so grateful that the Lord has helped us to come this far. We're also building it into 25 major languages. We know that, of course, there are many more language than that, but we know that at 25 major languages, it will get us to 99% of the Christian leaders in the world. While your unique language in your country may not be included, it will be represented in the major languages. So, whether it be, like, for example, in Africa, there are four major languages there. Now there are additional languages, of course, in different countries. But when I think about Portuguese and Swahili and French and English, those are the four major languages in Africa. There are, of course, lots of other different languages, but we're focused on bringing the content, all the courses, in at least 25 major languages.

Appendix 4

If you have a language that you really believe that needs to be done in your nation, we would love for you to take all of the transcripts and translate all of those into your language, and then we will gladly upload those into the Global Church Divinity School. That would be a noteworthy project for you to put together a small team of leaders and over a year or two, translate all of those. We would be thrilled to upload those into the Global Church Divinity School. We have development, we have discovery.

Our fourth aspect of the Global Church Network we call **deployment,** which is the Global Hubs of Christianity. I'm so grateful for the growth of the hubs and we desire to make them better and better with each passing season. When we think about a hub, there are cities that are known as global hubs. There are airline companies that have hubs, there are computer companies that have hubs. When we think about the Global Hubs of Christianity, we believe that all these hubs are interconnected relationally, technologically, and strategically. Currently there are more than 100 such hubs, and the strategic goal is 800 hubs by 2030, one hub for every 10 million people on the earth.

We believe that every hub is multipliable, so we believe that we launch a hub in a key city, capital, that once the training is done, over a two-year period of time, our goal is at least 10% of the leaders that attend that hub will want to go start a hub in their city, community, town, or village. Again, they get the training just like everybody else in the larger cities. All hubs have several things in common. One, they *synergize the best relationships*. We want to invite the best people to come to the hub: kingdom-minded, faith-filled believers who are focused on fulfilling the Great Commission and synergizing the best relationships.

A hub is both online and on ground, bringing the best training. Each hub *systemizes the best training*. When pastors and leaders attend the hub in their area, for two years they will be taught by two trainers face-to-face and will have access to the same courses in the Global Church Divinity School (GCDS.tv).

Next, each hub *strategizes for unreached people groups.* For example, if your hub is in an area where we know that there are some particular people groups that have never heard the gospel, then we should adopt them and think of a strategy in order to achieve it. But go a step further, not only strategically for those unreached people groups within your reach, but what about other areas in the world? There have been hubs where they've adopted unreached people groups in other areas of the world. I'll give you an example. There's an incredible hub in Guyana that adopted Nepal, and what is going on in Nepal today is absolutely incredible.

In some cases, a hub scripturalizes new Bible translations. I'm extremely excited about this because, in order for God's word to get to all people, the church globally has to be equipped, enlightened, expanded in order to bring in Bible translation. And so, if we're working in an unreached people group and a particular hub is not too far away and they don't have God's word in their language, leaders have the opportunity to scripturalize, to translate God's Word.

I said earlier, the church is not looking for parents. The church is looking for partners. We believe that God has trainers all over the world, and our desire is that two trainers come to each hub based upon Luke 10, where Jesus sent them out two by two. These two trainers commit to two years. They want to pour in face-to-face in the hub and answer any questions that anybody may have in that hub.

The Global Church Network is in partnership with incredible ministries who specialize in Bible translations, and we'll be connecting these other key ministries with the hub leader or leaders of your hub, particularly if there are languages that need to be translated, so that these men and women don't just have a portion of the word of God, but they have the entirety of the word of God. Can you imagine when other men and women, maybe it's in your nation or in a nearby nation, gets their first copy of God's word and are able to read it in their own mother

Appendix 4

tongue, their own language? Can you imagine the celebration of that becoming a reality for them?

Included in the Global Hubs of Christianity, we have the Global Church Curriculum, online and on ground. It's not either or, it's both and. Every time the trainers come, they come for two days of intensive training.

If people do not have access to the Internet, then being involved in the hub is of paramount importance, because they are going to be taught face-to-face with incredible trainers. For those who do have internet access, they are able to listen to the original courses and watch them online and download the transcripts.

When a cohort of leaders complete all the training in the hub; there's a celebration or graduation. However, this is not end but just the beginning. Once leaders have completed the hub courses, they can go on to study the remaining courses in the Global Church Divinity School. Once they finish the first-level courses, all of the other courses in the Global Church Divinity School opens up to them. The number of courses that a leader is able to take throughout the entire GCDS, is like a Ph.D. program.

I'm often asked, well, can you get a degree through this? Well, you need to understand the world has changed. We're moving from the focus being on where we went to school to who taught us when we went to school. In the future, it's more important about who taught you than where you were taught. We don't offer the traditional degrees. We believe we offer something even better than that. We're offering eight prestigious credentials that are issued by the Board of Governors of the Global Church Divinity School, taught by men and women from all over the world, with more than 60% of all the teachers in the Global Church Divinity School have a Ph.D., or a doctorate to ministry. We want you to know that the men and women who are involved in the GCDS not only have their degrees, but they have their credentials. In other words, they're able to do what they say they can do.

We're working toward the fulfillment of the Great Commission in our lifetime. What does the fulfillment of the Great Commission look like? Well, I believe it's a church that is synergized and mobilized. I believe it's a hub in every nation, a Bible in every language, a harvest of young, equipped leaders, a church within walking distance, and then a completed Great Commission.

I want to encourage you, download the Global Church Network app on your smartphone, and you'll be able to stay current, what's happening. It's updated every week. I encourage you to be a part of the prayer movement. When you download the app, you will see the prayer emphasis that has taken place around the world.

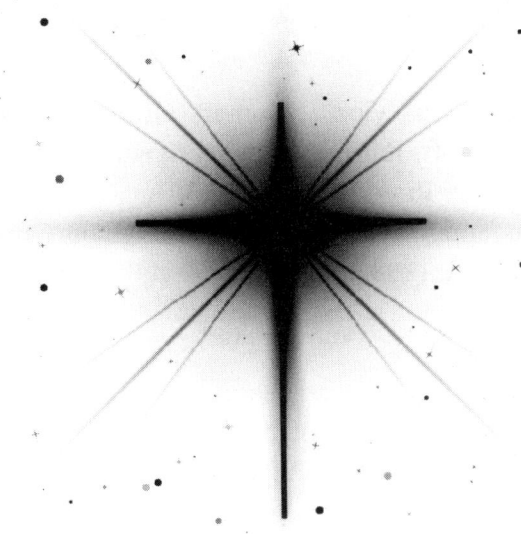

Recommended Reading

Following is a list of resources to assist you in moving beyond all the limitations you encounter in your life and ministry. We have divided the resources into the eight distinctives (Confidence, Calling, Character, etc.) to better help you focus on your needs in ministry, in addition to sources on networking and synergy. This list is only a sampling of the many resources available for building a synergistic church.

CONFIDENCE

Bright, Bill. GOD: Discover His Character. Orlando, FL: NewLife Publications, 1999.

Morgan, G. Campbell, and Charles Spurgeon. Understanding the Holy Spirit. Chattanooga, TN: AMG Publishers, 1995.

Niebuhr, H. Richard. Christ and the Culture. San Francisco: HarperCollins, 1986.

Packer, J. I. Knowing God. Downers Grove, IL: InterVarsity Press, 1973. Stott, John. Evangelical Truth. Downers Grove, IL: InterVarsity Press, 1999.

Trask, Thomas, and Wayde Goodall. The Blessing. Grand Rapids, MI: Zondervan, 1998.

CHARACTER

Anderson, Ray S. The Soul of Ministry: Forming Leaders for God's People. Louisville, KY: Westminster John Knox Press, 1997.

Malphurs, Aubrey. Value-Driven Leadership: Discovering and Developing Your Core Values for Ministry. Grand Rapids, MI: Baker Books, 1996.

Maxwell, John. Developing the Leader Within You. Nashville, TN: Thomas Nelson Publishers, 1993.

Failing Forward: Turn Mistakes Into Stepping Stones for Success. Nashville, TN: Thomas Nelson Publishers, 2000.

McIntosh, Gary, and Samuel Rima. Overcoming the Dark Side of Leadership. Grand Rapids, MI: Baker Books, 1997.

CALLING

Barna, George. The Power of Vision. Ventura, CA: Regal Books, 1992.

Buford, Bob. Half Time: Changing Your Game Plan from Success to Significance. Grand Rapids, MI: Zondervan, 1994.

Jones, Laurie Beth. The Path: Creating Your Mission Statement for Word and for Life. New York: Hyperion, 1996.

Novak, Michael. Business as a Calling: Work and the Examined Life. New York: The Free Press, 1996.

Stowell, Joseph. Shepherding the Church. Chicago, IL: Moody Press, 1997.

Gangel, Kenneth O. Team Leadership in Christian Ministry: Using Multiple Gifts to Build a Unified Vision. Chicago, IL: Moody Press, 1997.

Heenan, David, and Warren Bennis. Co-Leaders: The Power of Great Partnerships. New York: John Wiles & Sons, 1999.

Maxwell, John. Be a People Person: Effective Leadership Through Effective Relationships. Colorado Springs, CO: Victor Books, 1994.

Maxwell, John C., and Jim Dornan. Becoming a Person of Influence: How to Positively Impact the Lives of Others. Nashville, TN: Thomas Nelson, 1997.

COMMITMENT

Bright, Bill. Living Supernaturally in Christ. Orlando, FL: NewLife Publications, 2000.

Carson, D. A., gen ed. Telling the Truth: Evangelizing Postmoderns. Grand Rapids, MI: Zondervan, 2000.

Davis, James O. The Pastor's Best Friend: The New Testament Evangelist. Springfield, MO: Gospel Publishing House, 1997.

Guder, Darrell L., ed. Missional Church: A Vision for the Sending of the Church in North America. Grand Rapids, MI: Eerdmans, 1998.

Hybels, Bill, and Mark Mittelberg. Becoming a Contagious Christian. Grand Rapids, MI Zondervan, 1994.

Towns, Elmer. Fasting for Spiritual Breakthrough. Ventura, CA: Regal Books, 1996.

Warren, Rick. The Purpose Driven Church, Grand Rapids, MI: Zondervan, 1995.

Zschech, Darlene. Extravagant Worship. Castle Hill, Australia: Check Music, 2001.

COOPERATION

DePree, Max. Leading Without Power: Finding Hope in Serving Community. San Francisco, CA: Jossey-Bass, 1997.

COMMUNICATION

Arredondo, Lani. How to Present Like a Pro: Getting People to See Things Your Way. New York: McGraw-Hill, 1991.
Davis, James O. The Preacher's Summit. Springfield, MO: Cutting Edge Books, 2001.
Henderson, David W. Culture Shift: Communicating God's Truth to Our Changing World. Grand Rapids, MI: Baker Books, 1999.
Olford, Stephen. Anointed Expository Preaching. Nashville: Broadman and Holman, 1998.
Robinson, Haddon W. Making a Difference in Preaching. Grand Rapids, MI: Baker Book House, 1999.
Wiersbe, Warren. Preaching and Teaching with Imagination, Wheaton, IL: Victor Books, 1994.

COMPASSION

Barna, George. The Future of the American Family. Chicago, IL: Moody, 1993.
Bright, Bill. Five Steps to Sharing Your Faith: Leader's Guide and Study Guide. Orlando, FL: New Life Publications, 1996.
Hopler, Thom and Marcia. Reaching the World Next Door: How to Spread the Gospel in the Midst of Many Cultures. Rev. ed. Downers Grove, IL: InterVarsity Press, 1993.
Shawchuck, Norman, and Roger Heuser. Leading the Congregation: Caring for Yourself While Serving the People. Nashville, TN: Abingdon Press, 1993.

Sjögren, Steve. Conspiracy of Kindness: A Refreshing New Approach to Sharing the Love of Jesus With Others. Ann Arbor, MI: Vine Books, 1993.

CREATIVITY

Covey, Stephen. The Seven Habits of Highly Effective People. New York: Simon and Schuster, 1989.
Easum, William. Sacred Cow Makes Gourmet Burgers. Nashville, TN: Abingdon Press, 1994.
McClaren, Brian. The Church on the Other Side: Doing Ministry in the Post-Modern Matrix. Grand Rapids, MI: Zondervan, 2000.
Rainer, Thom S. High Expectations: The Remarkable Secret for Keeping People in Your Church. Nashville: Broadman and Holman Publishers, 1999.
Sweet, Leonard. Aqua Church: Essential Leadership Arts for Piloting Your Church in Today's Fluid Culture. Loveland, CO: Group Publishing, 1999.
Wilson, Len, and Leonard Sweet. The Wired Church: Making Media Ministry. Nashville, TN: Abingdon Press, 1999.

NETWORKING

Anne Baber, and Lynne Waymon. Make Your Contacts Count: Networking Know-How and Career Success. Seattle, WA: Amacon, 2001.
David Burkus. Friend of a Friend: Understanding the Hidden Networks That Can Transform Your Life and Your Career. New York, NY: Houghton Mifflin Harcourt Publishing, 2018.
Dale Carnegie. How To Win Friends and Influence People. New York, NY: Simon and Schuster, Inc, 1981.

Dale Carnegie. Make Yourself Unforgettable: How to Become the Person "Everyone Remembers and No One Can Resist. New York, NY: Simon and Schuster, 2011

Shelle Rose Charvet. Words That Change Minds: The 14 Patterns for Mastering the Language of Influence. Institute for Influence, 2019.

Nicholas Christakis, MD. PH.D. and James Fowler, PH.D. Connected: The Surprising Power of Our Social Networks and How They Shape Our Lives. Boston, MA: Little Brown Spark, 2011

Robert B. Cialdini, PH.D. Influence: The Psychology of Persuasion. New York, NY: Quill William Morrow, 1993.

Derek Coburn, and Chris Brogan. Networking is Not Working: Stop Collecting Business Cards and Start Making Meaningful Connections. Oakton, VA: Ideapress Publishing, 2014

David Ehrlichman. Impact Networks: Create Connection, Spark Collaboration, and Catalyze Systemic Change. Oakland, CA: Berrett-Koehler Publishers, Inc. 2021.

Keith Ferrazzi. Who's Got Your Back: The Breakthrough Program to Build Deep, Trusting Relationships That Create Success and Wont' Let You Fail. New York, NY. Crown Publishing Group, 2009.

Keith Ferrazzi, and Tahl Raz. Never Eat Alone, Expanded and Updated, And Other Secrets to Success, One Relationship at a Time. New York, NY: Crown Publishing Group, 2014

Seth Godin. Tribes: We Need You to Lead Us. Alberta, Canada: Portfolio, 2008.

Daniel Goleman. Social Intelligence: The New Science of Human Relationships. New York, NY: Bantam Books, 2006.

John Hall. Top of Mind. NY: McGraw Hill Education, 2017.

Scott Gerber and Ryan Paugh. Super Connector: Stop Networking and Start Building Business Relationships that Matter. New York, NY: Da Capo Press, 2018

Ronald Heifetz, Alexander Grashow, and Marty Linksy. The Practice of Adaptive Leadership: Tools and Tactics for

Recommended Reading

Changing Your Organization and the World. Boston, MA: Cambridge Leadership Associates, 2009.

J. Kelly Hoey. Build Your Dream Network: Forging Powerful Relationships in a Hyper-connected World. New York, NY: Penguin Random House, 2018.

Timothy Keller and John Inazu. Uncommon Ground: Living Faithfully in a World of Difference. Nashville, TN: Nelson Books, 2020.

Michelle Tillis Lederman. The 11 Laws of Likability: Because People Do Business With People They Like. New York, NY: HarperCollins Leadership, 2011.

Harvey Macay. Dig Your Well Before You're Thirsty. New York, NY: Random House, 1999.

Susan McPherson. The Lost Art of Connecting: The Gather, Ask, Do Method for Meaningful Business Relationships. New York, NY: McGraw Hill Publishing, 2021.

Michael Urtuzuastegui Melcher. Your Invisible Network: How to Create, Maintain, and Leverage the Relationships that Will Transform Your Career. Dallas, TX: BenBella Books, Inc. 2023.

Ivan Misner, Ph.D., David Alexander, and Brian Hilliard. Networking Like a Pro: Turning Contacts into Connection. Canada: Entrepreneur Press, 2009.

Germaine Moody. The 40 Laws of Networking: Keys for creating global Influence, Wealth, and Power. Become Endless Publishing, 2021.

Peter Plastrik, Madeline Taylor, and John Cleveland. Connecting to Change The World: Harnessing the Power of Networks for Social Impact. Washington, DC: Peter Plastrik, 2014

Reshma Sanjani. Brave, Not Perfect: Fear Less, Fail More, and Live Bolder. New York, NY: Currency, 2019.

David John Seel, Jr. Network Power: The Science of Making a Difference. Almanor, CA: Withorn Press, 2021.

Bryan D Sims. Leading Together: The Holy Possibility of Harmony and Synergy in the Face of Change. Cody, Wyoming: 100 Movements Publishing, 2022.

A.W. Tozer. Lead Like Christ: Reflecting the Qualities and Character of Christ in Your Ministry. Minneapolis, Minnesota: Bethany House Publishing, 2021

Margaret J. Wheatley. Leadership and the New Science: Discovering Order in a Chaotic World. San Francisco, CA: Berrett-Koehler Publishers, 2006.

Karen Wickre. Taking the Work Out of Networking: An Introvert's Guide to Making Connections That Count. New York, NY: Gallery Books, 2019

Devora Zack. Networking for People Who Hate Networking: A Field Guide for Introverts, The Overwhelmed, and The Underconnected. San Francisco, CA: Berrett-Koehler Publishers, 2010.

Jamil Zaki, The War For Kindness: Building Empathy in a Fractured World. New York, NY: Crown Publishing, 2019.

About The Author

For over forty years, **Dr. James O Davis**, the founder of Cutting Edge International and Global Church Network has travelled, trained, and taught millions of Christian leaders in more than 140 nations. Through his strategic, visionary, leadership, he has synergized over 2,700 denominations and 700,000 local churches to build a premier community of pastors worldwide to help plant five million new churches for a billion-soul harvest and to mobilize the whole body of Christ toward the fulfillment of the Great Commission by the 2,000th birthday of the Church. The Global Church Network (GCNW.tv) is the largest pastor's network in the world.

Christian leaders recognize Dr. Davis to be one of the leading networkers in the Christian world. More than 80,000 pastors and leaders have attended his biannual Pastor's conference and leadership summits across the United States and in all major world regions.

In addition to starting, Cutting Edge International and Global Church Network, he launched the National Evangelist office at the Assemblies of God World Headquarters, Billion Soul Network, Global Church Divinity School, Billion Soul Publishing, The Global Hubs of Christianity, The Synergize Pastors and Leaders Conference, The Great Commission Prayer Summit, Finish 2030-33, The Million Ministers Mandate, and Top One Percent Coaching. Such prolific work and impact have named Dr. Davis as one of the *top ten Christian influencers in the world.*

In 2000, he served on the Executive Task Force for Amsterdam 2000, hosted by the late Dr. Billy Graham. More than 11,500 leaders from 217 nations, provinces and territories convened toward the fulfillment of the Great Commission.

In October 2017, Dr. Davis spearheaded and hosted *The Wittenberg 2017 Congress* in Berlin, Germany. The Wittenberg 2017 Congress celebrated the 500th anniversary of Martin Luther's nailing his 95 Theses on Castle Church door in Wittenberg, Germany. This historic congress brought together more than 650 influential leaders from more than 80 different denominations and every world region.

Dr. Davis served 12 years leading 1,500 evangelists and training thousands of students for full-time evangelism as the National Evangelists' Representative at the National Office of the Assemblies of God. Ministering more than 45 weeks per year for 40 years, Dr. Davis has now traveled over 10 million miles to minister face-to-face to millions of people in more than 140 nations.

Dr. Davis earned a Doctorate of Ministry at Trinity Evangelical Divinity School, two Masters Degrees from Assemblies of God Theological Seminary, and a Bachelor's Degree in Bible at Central Bible College.

As an author, Christ has challenged him to move from production to reproduction, creating material worthy of fruitful

About The Author

propagation. While traveling and speaking, he has written 25 books, averaging 2-3 books per year.

He is one of the most sought-after speakers in the Church today, and is known for his keen Biblical insights, memorable statements, and contemporary wisdom.

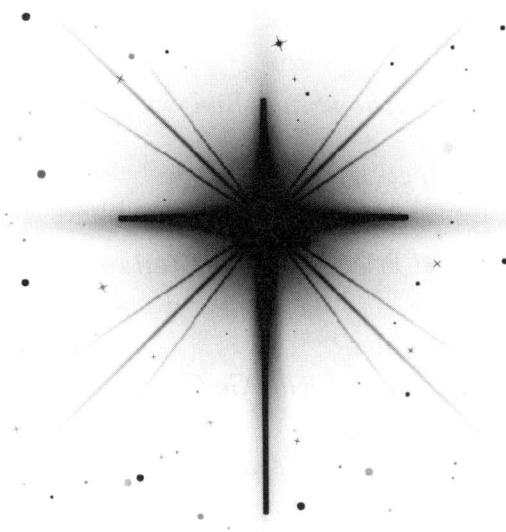

Dr. James O. Davis
Books and Resources
www.JamesODavis.com

- *We Are The Church: The Untold Story of God's Global Awakening* (coauthored with Dr. Leonard Sweet)
- *Living Life From A Heavenly Edge*
- *The Faith Book: The Master Key To A Grand Life of Faith*
- *Unhindered! Power Principles For The Extraordinary Christian Life*
- *The Forgotten Baptism: Your Visionary Path To Success* (coauthored with Dr. Kenneth Ulmer)
- *How to Make Your Net Work: Tying Relational Knots for Global Impact*
- *Scaling Your Everest: Lessons from Sir Edmund Hillary*
- *Gutenberg to Google: The Twenty Indispensable Laws of Communication*

- *The Great Commission Study Bible* (coauthored with Dr. Ben Lerner)
- *The Billion Soul Story*
- *12 Big Ideas*
- *The Pastor's Best Friend: The New Testament Evangelist*
- *Living Like Jesus*
- *The Preacher's Summit*
- *What to Do When the Lights Go Out*
- *It's a Miraculous Life!*
- *Signposts on the Road to Armageddon*
- *Beyond All Limits: The Synergistic Church for a Planet in Crisis* (coauthored with Dr. Bill Bright)
- *Winning Qualities Of High Impact Leaders*
- *The Adrian Rogers Legacy Collection*
- *The Ed Cole Legacy Collection*
- *The Elmer Towns Legacy Collection*
- *The Stephen Olford Preaching Collection*

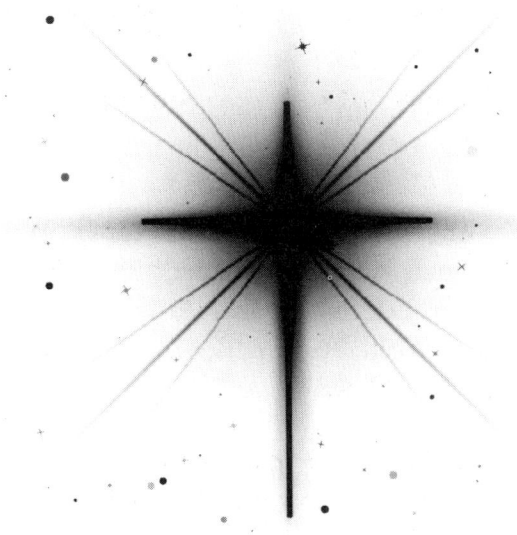

Endnotes

CHAPTER 1

[1] This figure is based upon statistics gleaned from www.google.com on October 23, 2001.

[2] The Barna Research Group, "More Americans Seeking Net Based Faith Experiences," May 21, 2001, www.barna.org.

[3] Shiloh Place Ministries, http://shilohplace.org/crisisin.htm.

[4] Hyrum Smith, The Ten Natural Laws of Successful Time and Life Management, New York: Warner Books, 1994, pp. 48-50.

[5] The Barna Research Group, "Annual Study Reports America Is Stagnant," March 5, 2001, www.barna.org

CHAPTER 3

[1] The Oxford English Dictionary, 2d ed., vol. XVII, J. A. Simpson and E.S.C. Weiner, eds., Oxford: Clarendon Press, 1989, p. 480.

² Stephen Covey, Seven Habits of Highly effective People, New York: Simon and Schuster, 1989, p. 263.

³ Ibid.

⁴ John Maxwell, Developing the Leader Within You, Nashville, TN: Thomas Nelson Publishers, 1993, p. x.

⁵ George Gilder, Telecosm: How Infinite Bandwidth Will Revolutionize Our World, New York: The Free Press, 2000, p. 265.

⁶ Laurie Beth Jones, The Path: Creating Your Mission Statement for Word and for Life, New York: Hyperion, 1996, p. x.

CHAPTER 5

¹ J. I. Packer, Knowing God, Downers Grove, IL: InterVarsity Press, 1973, p. 6.

² Stephen Olford, Manna in the Morning, Memphis, TN: Olford Ministries, n.d., p. 10.

³ Millard Erikson, Christian Theology, Grand Rapids, MI: Baker Book House, 1985, p. 846.

⁴ John Stott, Evangelical Truth, Downers Grove, IL: InterVarsity Press, 1999, p. 87.

⁵ G. Campbell Morgan and Charles Spurgeon, Understanding the Holy Spirit, Chattanooga, TN: AMG Publishers, 1995, p. 136.

⁶ Lyle W. Dorsett, "Ministry Maverick," Moody Magazine Online, Chicago, IL: Moody Bible Institute, 2000, www.moody-press.org/ MOODYMAG/maverick.htm.

⁷ Bill Bright, Living Supernaturally in Christ, Orlando, FL: New Life Publications, 2000, p. 156.

CHAPTER 6

¹ Bob Buford, Half Time: Changing Your Game Plan from Success to Significance, Grand Rapids, MI: Zondervan, 1994, p. 20.

² Stephen Covey, The Seven Habits of Highly Effective People, New York: Simon and Schuster, 1989, p. 108.

Endnotes

³ Michael Novak, Business as a Calling: Work and the Examined Life, New York: The Free Press, 1996, p. 34.

⁴ Laurie Beth Jones, The Path: Creating Your Mission Statement for Word and for Life, New York: Hyperion, 1996, p. 44.

⁵ Novak, p. 35.

⁶ Jones, p. 49.

⁷ Buford, p. 23.

⁸ William Bridges, Creating You & Co.: Learn to Think Like the CEO of Your Own Career, Reading, MA: Addison Wesley Publishing, 1997, p. 38.

⁹ Ibid., p. 39.

¹⁰ Statistics supplied by www.everestnews.com as of June 1, 2001. This number is an estimate.

¹¹ Jones, p. xviii.

¹² Leonard Sweet, Aqua Church, Loveland, CO: Group, 1999, p. 130.

¹³ George Barna, The Power of Vision, Ventura, CA: Regal Books, 1992, p. 12.

¹⁴ Novak, p. 35.

CHAPTER 7

¹ Gary McIntosh and Samuel Rima, Overcoming the Dark Side of Leadership, Grand Rapids, MI: Baker Books, 1997, p. 41.

² The Pastor's Story File, May 1993.

³ Ibid.

⁴ Reiner Scnippers, "equipping" in New International Dictionary of New Testament Theology, Vol. 3, Colin Brown, ed., Grand Rapids, MI: Eerdmans, 1986, p. 349.

⁵ J. Armitage Robinson, Commentary on Ephesians, Grand Rapids, MI: Kregel, 1979, p. 182.

⁶ Tubingen Michel, "oikos," in Theological Dictionary of the New Testament, volume 5, Kittel Gerhared, ed., Grand Rapids, MI: Eerdmans, 1967, p. 119-159.

⁷ A. Skevington Wood, Ephesians Volume 11, Expositor's Bible Commentary, Grand Rapids, MI: Zondervan, 1981, p. 59.

⁸ Joseph Stowell, Shepherding the Church, Chicago, IL: Moody Press, 1997, p. 254.

⁹ Michael Richman, "Scientist George Washington Carver," Investors Business Daily, May 14, 2001, p. 4A.

¹⁰ Max DePree, Leading Without Power, San Francisco, CA: Jossey-Bass, 1997, p. 163.

¹¹ John Maxwell, The 21 Irrefutable Laws of Leadership, Nashville, TN: Thomas Nelson, 1998, p. 134.

¹² Ibid., p. 221.

CHAPTER 8

¹ Brian Mansfield, "Singing the Praises of Strong Sales," USA Today, October 19, 2001, Sec. E, p. 2.

² Darlene Zsechech, Extravagant Worship, Castle Hill, Australia: Check Music, 2001, p. 6.

³ Ibid., p. 11.

⁴ Helen Lemmel, "Turn Your Eyes Upon Jesus," Singspiration Music, Nashville, TN: The Benson Group, 1922.

⁵ Leonard Ravenhill, Why Revival Tarries, Minneapolis, MN: Bethany House, 1979, p. 23.

⁶ Stephen Olford, Manna in the Morning, Memphis, TN: Olford Ministries, no date, p. 2.

⁷ Bill Bright, The Coming Revival, Orlando, FL: NewLife Publications, 1995, pp. 92-93.

⁸ Elmer Towns, Fasting for Spiritual Breakthrough, Ventura, CA: Regal Books, 1996, pp. 17-18.

⁹ Dutch Sheets, "Fasting With Your Church for Goals," in Fasting Can Change Your Life, Jerry Falwell and Elmer Towns, eds., Ventura, CA: Regal Books, 1998, pp. 171-176.

¹⁰ Walter Elwell, Evangelical Dictionary of Theology, Grand Rapids, MI: Baker, 1984, pp. 382-383.

¹¹ C. E. Autry, The Theology of Evangelism, Grand Rapids, MI: Zondervan, 1954, p. 32.

[12] David Barrett, "Dawn Report: State of Christianity 2001 #7," www.jesus.org.uk/dawn/2001/dawn07.html.

[13] Patrick Johnstone, "The State of World Evangelism: How Are We Doing? Are We Making Progress?" www.missionfrontiers.com/ newslinks/statewe.htm.

CHAPTER 9

[1] Karl Taro Greenfeld, "Blind to Failure," Time Magazine, June 18, 2001, pp. 52-63.

[2] David Heenan and Warren Bennis, Co-Leaders: The Power of Great Partnerships, New York: John Wiley & Sons, 1999, p. 8.

[3] Randy Jumper, "Reconciliation in the Twenty-First Century: Postmodern Bridge Building," sermon delivered June 8, 2001, Springfield, MO.

[4] Stephen Covey, The Seven Habits of Highly Effective People, New York: Simon and Schuster, 1989, p. 239.

[5] Leonard Sweet, Aqua Church: Essential Leadership Arts for Piloting Your Church in Today's Fluid Culture, Loveland, CO: Group Publishing, 1999, p. 192.

[6] Heenan and Bennis, p. 279.

[7] Blaine Lee, The Power Principle: Influence With Honor, New York: Simon and Schuster, 1997, p. 111.

[8] William Easum, Sacred Cow Makes Gourmet Burgers, Nashville, TN: Abingdon, 1994, p. 110.

CHAPTER 10

[1] John D. Beckett, Loving Monday: Succeeding in Business Without Selling Your Soul, Downers Grove, IL: InterVarsity Press, 1998, p. 142.

[2] D. Martyn Lloyd-Jones, Preaching and Preachers, Grand Rapids: Zondervan, 1971, p. 26.

[3] Ralph Lewis, Learning to Preach Like Jesus, Westchester: Crossway Books, 1989, p. 86.

[4] Howard Hendricks, Teaching to Change Lives, Portland, OR: Multnomah, 1987, p. 98.

[5] Joseph Stowell, Shepherding the Church, Chicago: Moody, 1994, p. 276.

[6] These books can be purchased through Cutting Edge International, Cutting Edge International, P. O. Box 411605, Rockledge, FL 32941, www.jamesodavis.com.

[7] Stephen Olford, Anointed Expository Preaching, Nashville: Broadman and Holman, 1998, p. 309.

[8] Haddon W. Robinson, Biblical Preaching: The Development and Delivery of Expository Messages, Grand Rapids, MI: Baker Book House, 1980, p. 20.

[9] William Quayle, The Pastor-Preacher, New York: Easton and Mains, 1910, p. 261.

[10] John MacArthur, The MacArthur New Testament Commentary: Ephesians, Chicago, IL: Moody, 1986, pp. 102-103.

[11] David Larsen, The Anatomy of Preaching, Grand Rapids, MI: Baker Book House, 1989, p. 25.

[12] See Walter Kaiser's excellent book on this process: Towards an Exegetical Theology.

[13] Haddon W. Robinson, Making a Difference in Preaching, Grand Rapids, MI: Baker Book House, 1999, p. 76.

[14] Thomas Troeger, Imagining a Sermon, Nashville, TN: Abingdon Press, 1990, p. 120.

[15] Warren Wiersbe, Preaching and Teaching with Imagination, Wheaton, IL: Victor Books, 1994, p. 297.

[16] Rick Warren, The Purpose Driven Church, Grand Rapids, MI: Zondervan, 1995, p. 228.

[17] Robinson, Biblical Preaching, pp. 160-165.

[18] Lani Arredondo, How to Present Like a Pro: Getting People to See Things Your Way, New York: McGraw-Hill, 1991, p. 36.

[19] Ron Hoff, I Can See You Naked, Kansas City: Andrews and McMeel, 1992, p. 30.

[20] James O. Davis, "The Paradigm of Preaching," The Preacher's Summit, Springfield, MO: Cutting Edge Books, 2001, p. 35.

²¹ Charles Brown, The Art of Preaching, New York: Macmillan, 1922, p. 15.

²² Arredondo, p. 65.

²³ Ibid., p. 70.

²⁴ Alan Street, The Effective Invitation, Old Tappan, NJ: Revell, 1984, p. 37.

²⁵ Lloyd Perry, Biblical Preaching for Today's World, Chicago: Moody, 1973, p. 113.

²⁶ Nancy Gibbs, "How Much Does the Preaching Matter?" Time, 158:11, September 17, 2001, p. 55.

CHAPTER 11

¹ John Maxwell, The 21 Most Powerful Minutes in a Leader's Day, Nashville, TN: Thomas Nelson Publishers, 2000, p. 29.

² George Barna, The Future of the American Family, Chicago, IL: Moody, 1993, p. 173.

³ Ibid., p. 185.

⁴ Brian McClaren, The Church on the Other Side: Doing Ministry in the Postmodern Matrix, Grand Rapids, MI: Zondervan, 1998, p. 27

⁵ Darrell L. Guder, Missional Church: A Vision for the Sending of the Church in North America, Grand Rapids: Eerdmans, 1998, p. 4.

⁶ Eddie Gibs, ChurchNext: Quantum Changes in How We Do Ministry, Downers Grove, IL: InterVarsity Press, p. 51.

⁷ Rick Warren, The Purpose Driven Church, Grand Rapids, MI: Zondervan, 1995, p. 156-157.

⁸ Joseph Stowell, Shepherding the Church, Chicago, IL: Moody Press, 1997, p. 45.

⁹ World Development Review cited Living Like Jesus, Ken Horn and James Davis eds., Springfield, MO: Onward Books, p. 263.

CHAPTER 12

[1] Harvey Mackay, Swim With Sharks Without Being Eaten Alive, New York: Fawcett Columbine, 1988, pp. 79-80.

PARTNER WITH US!

"The Global Church is moving from parenting to partnering like never before. Our Lord has raised up this ministry to help us to synergize, mobilize, in order to finalize the Great Commission. Yet we realize that no organization can accomplish this alone. Every monthly partnership empowers us to plant churches and develop leaders in every nation. I invite you to join us in the global effort."

James O. Davis
Founder / Cutting Edge International
Founder / Global Church Network

JamesODavis.com

PARTNER WITH US!

INVESTMENT LEVELS OVER 5 YEARS

WINNERS CIRCLE
$5,000 - $19,999

LEADERS CIRCLE
$20,000 - $44,999

NETWORKERS CIRCLE
$45,000 - $69,999

PRESIDENTS CIRCLE
$70,000 - $99,999

FOUNDERS CIRCLE
$100,000+

JamesODavis.com

The Global Church Network is the premier community pastors and Christian leaders from 2,700 denominations and 700,000 plus local churches. GCN brings the finest teaching though the Global Church Divinity School (GCDS.tv) and faith-filled training through its Global Hubs of Christianity. GCN synergizes Christian leaders and mobilizes the Body of Christ to finalize the Great Commission!

GCNW.tv

DOWNLOAD THE GLOBAL **CHURCH** NETWORK APP TODAY!

Register for events, access resources, manage giving options, and connect with our team.

GLOBAL CHURCH DIVINITY SCHOOL®
PART OF THE GLOBAL CHURCH NETWORK®

IN THE FUTURE, WHO YOU STUDIED WITH IS MORE IMPORTANT THAN WHERE YOU STUDIED.

THE BEST GLOBAL CHURCH CLASSROOM IN THE WORLD!
190 World Class Faculty

GCDS.TV

GLOBAL CHURCH DIVINITY SCHOOL®

PART OF THE GLOBAL CHURCH NETWORK®

250+ Interactive Training Courses

5 Membership Levels

ONLY
$82 per month

Sign Up Today!

GCDS.TV